T0386114

EARLY GREEK PHILOSOPHY

I

LCL 524

EARLY GREEK PHILOSOPHY

VOLUME I

INTRODUCTORY AND
REFERENCE MATERIALS

EDITED AND TRANSLATED BY
ANDRÉ LAKS AND GLENN W. MOST

IN COLLABORATION WITH
GÉRARD JOURNÉE

AND ASSISTED BY
LEOPOLDO IRIBARREN
AND DAVID LÉVYSTONE

HARVARD UNIVERSITY PRESS
CAMBRIDGE, MASSACHUSETTS
LONDON, ENGLAND
2016

First published 2016

LOEB CLASSICAL LIBRARY® is a registered trademark
of the President and Fellows of Harvard College

Library of Congress Control Number 2015957358
CIP data available from the Library of Congress

ISBN 978-0-674-99654-0

*Composed in ZephGreek and ZephText by
Technologies 'N Typography, Merrimac, Massachusetts.
Printed on acid-free paper and bound by
The Maple-Vail Book Manufacturing Group*

CONTENTS

CONSPECTUS OF THE VOLUMES IN THIS EDITION   2

PREFACE   5

NOTE ON EDITORIAL PRINCIPLES AND
TRANSLATIONS   19

ABBREVIATIONS   31

GENERAL BIBLIOGRAPHY   79

CONCORDANCES

     a. Diels-Kranz > Laks-Most   89

     b. Laks-Most > Diels-Kranz et al.   123

INDEXES OF NAMES

     a. Early Greek Philosophers   193

     b. Other Persons   199

GLOSSARY   219

INTRODUCTORY MATERIALS

CONSPECTUS OF THE VOLUMES IN THIS EDITION

Volume 1 (LCL 524): Early Greek Philosophy I. Introductory and Reference Materials

   Conspectus of the Volumes in This Edition. Preface. Note on Editorial Principles and Translations. Abbreviations. General Bibliography. Concordances. Indexes of Names. Glossary.

Volume 2 (LCL 525): Early Greek Philosophy II. Beginnings and Early Ionian Thinkers, Part 1

   Preliminaries: Doxography and Successions. Background: Cosmological Speculations; Reflections on Gods and Men. Early Ionian Thinkers, Part 1: Pherecydes; Thales; Anaximander; Anaximenes.

Volume 3 (LCL 526): Early Greek Philosophy III. Early Ionian Thinkers, Part 2

   Xenophanes. Heraclitus.

Volume 4 (LCL 527): Early Greek Philosophy IV. Western Greek Thinkers, Part 1

   Pythagoras and the Pythagorean School.

CONSPECTUS

Volume 5 (LCL 528): Early Greek Philosophy V. Western Greek Thinkers, Part 2

The Eleatics: Parmenides; Zeno; Melissus. Empedocles. Philosophy and Medicine: Alcmaeon; Hippo.

Volume 6 (LCL 529): Early Greek Philosophy VI. Later Ionian and Athenian Thinkers, Part 1

Anaxagoras. Archelaus. Diogenes of Apollonia. Early Greek Medicine. The Derveni Papyrus.

Volume 7 (LCL 530): Early Greek Philosophy VII. Later Ionian and Athenian Thinkers, Part 2

Atomists (Leucippus, Democritus).

Volume 8 (LCL 531): Early Greek Philosophy VIII. Sophists, Part 1

Protagoras. Gorgias. Socrates. Prodicus. Thrasymachus. Hippias.

Volume 9 (LCL 532): Early Greek Philosophy IX. Sophists, Part 2

Antiphon. Lycophron. Xeniades. The Anonymous of Iamblichus. *Pairs of Arguments (Dissoi Logoi)*. 'Sophists' and 'Sophistic': Collective Representations and General Characterizations. Appendix: Philosophy and Philosophers in Greek Comedy and Tragedy.

PREFACE

While we hope that the present edition will be useful to specialists, its primary intention is to present to the larger public the information we possess concerning early Greek philosophy. We have explicitly addressed problems of interpretation only to a small extent. There are few notes, and they are limited to factual information or indispensable clarifications. Our own understanding of the texts and problems is presented most often implicitly, not only in our translations but also by the way we have selected, configured, put into sequence, and introduced the texts with section titles. In the case of certain questions that are particularly controversial (for example, whether there was one poem of Empedocles or two, or one Antiphon or more), we have done our very best, without concealing our own position, to present the data openly and fairly. Our detailed justifications may well be supplied in later publications. As a general rule, the introduction to each of the chapters restricts itself to briefly situating, in temporal and doctrinal terms, the author or corpus in question, to indicating the fundamental editions or studies in which readers will be able to find more information, and to reproducing, last but not least, the complete outline of the titles and subtitles of that chapter, as a guide to reading it. In certain cases, the difficulties connected with the translation of an

author (Parmenides, chap. 19) or with the specificity of the
material (the Derveni Papyrus, chap. 30) have necessi-
tated somewhat fuller explanations; moreover, we have
added to the specific introductions for each individual
chapter one general introduction each to two groups of
chapters whose conception poses particular problems (Pythagoreans, chaps. 10–18; 'Sophists,' chaps. 31–42).

The term 'Presocratics' is often used for the authors
collected here. We have not prohibited ourselves from
using this term when refusal to have recourse to it would
have been artificial; but we avoid it as far as possible because of its undesirable connotations. To begin with, from
a simple chronological viewpoint, Socrates is contemporary with a good number of 'Presocratics,' and indeed he
is even earlier than some; it should be noted in this con-
nection that the collection of reference for Presocratic
thought, the *Fragmente der Vorsokratiker* of H. Diels and
W. Kranz, includes numerous texts of authors later than
Socrates, for example in the chapters on the Pythagoreans
or the Atomists. What is more, the indisputable shock that
Socrates represents for the history of philosophy does not
authorize us to apply the same negative identity—the ones
who did not know Socrates—to all those thinkers who did
not experience him or did not recognize themselves in
him. Indeed, in contrast to the custom followed by the
existing collections, we have devoted a chapter to Socrates
(chap. 33), taking him as what he was in his contempo-
raries' eyes: one 'sophist' among others. This latter term
too we have tried to avoid using without precautions, for
its connotations are no less problematic than those of
'Presocratic' (see the general introduction on the so-called
'Sophists'). Thus our collection takes as its object more the

Preplatonic philosophers than the Presocratic ones, following a line of demarcation that was usually Nietszche's too, and that corresponds essentially (though this line too is fluid) to the difference between those authors who are transmitted in the form of fragments and the first philosophical authors for whom a corpus of writings has largely or completely survived.

Each of our chapters is dedicated either to an author or to a corpus of texts. Those that are dedicated to authors—the majority—comprise three sections, with each entry in a section being identified by a number preceded by a letter valid for all the entries in that section:

P, for the information, not only reliable but also imaginary, regarding the philosopher as a person (= P) and his life, character, and sayings;

D, for his doctrine (= D), whether what is involved are the verbal fragments of his written work (printed in **boldface**) or the testimonia of his thought;

R, for the history of the reception (= R) of his doctrine in antiquity.

The distribution we have adopted has the effect of separating the biographical reception, which is found in **P,** from the reception of the doctrine, which figures in **R.** The undeniable formal inconsistency that results is, we believe, outweighed by greater intelligibility. Some of the 'author' chapters do not include a **P** section, when nothing is known about the author's person or when he is anonymous, or an **R** section, when the author's doctrine has left no trace in later literature. The chapter dedicated to the Derveni Papyrus, whose status is exceptional in every regard, follows its own logic, dictated by the nature of the

7

transmission. For the **R** sections, finally, we have, where possible, taken as a limit *ad quem* a collection of sayings attributed to various Greek philosophers available only in a Syriac version, or an anonymous alchemical text, *The Assembly of Philosophers,* which survives mostly in the form of the Latin translation of an Arabic original that dated probably to the tenth century AD. Our intention in so doing was at least to evoke the survival of early Greek philosophy within the non-European traditions—a complex and still inadequately explored territory, whose treatment would require another approach and different competences from our own.

The chapters dedicated to corpora are conceived thematically. By introducing these chapters we have provided room for what could be called the pre-philosophical representations of the world and of human beings, especially in Homer and Hesiod, but also in other texts of the Archaic period (chaps. 2 and 3); for early Greek medicine, especially the Hippocratic corpus, whose relations with the contemporary discipline of philosophy are particularly close (chap. 29); for the notions of 'sophist' and 'sophistic' (chap. 42); and for the treatment of philosophers and their philosophies in dramatic authors, both tragic and comic (chap. 43). Our very first chapter, by virtue of its methodological perspective, is situated at a different level from the others: it is designed to present readers with various aspects of ancient 'doxography,' a genre dedicated to assigning and summarizing philosophers' opinions. Its beginnings go back to the Preplatonic period but it was Aristotle who elevated it to philosophical dignity and centrality. 'Doxography' is one of the most important sources of information for our knowledge of early Greek philosophy, and in this regard it is invoked very frequently, especially under the name of Aëtius, throughout this whole collection. The texts collected in these thematic chapters are numbered together with the letter **T** (= text), as is also the case—for reasons specified in the introduction to chapters 10 to 18—in one of the sections of the chapters dedicated to Pythagoras (chap. 10 b).

Even if a number of features of this collection make it a work intended for general consultation, we hope that the community of specialists will find it useful too on account of our editorial choices, including our decision to reproduce (thanks to the help generously provided by a number of scholars) in their original languages those entries that are transmitted in Syriac, Arabic, Hebrew, and Armenian—as far as we know, a first for a collection of this type. In deciding which of the texts, extant in these languages, that are related to early Greek philosophy to include, we decided to limit ourselves to translations of Greek writings that have been lost in that language (e.g. Philo in Armenian translation, Galen and Nicolaus of Damascus in Arabic, Themistius in Hebrew) and to omit translations of Greek texts that survive in the original and other writings that represent more or less free adaptations or elaborations of Greek sources or recognizable errors.

For the chapters dedicated to authors, we have principally worked on the basis of the collection of H. Diels and W. Kranz (in general abbreviated DK, but D.-K. in the critical apparatuses), to which reference is made systematically in terms of the canonical numbering and by means of the concordances in this volume. But our edition differs from theirs in various fundamental aspects. On the one hand, we have omitted a certain number of chapters, most often short ones, dedicated to authors (1) who are minor or about whom we know almost nothing (Idaeus, Cleidemus), or (2) who, however important they might have been, do not seem to present an authentically philosophical profile (for example, Theagenes, Oenopides, Damon, Menestor, Critias, Ion of Chios), or else (3) whom we have integrated in one way or another into the **R** section of one of the chapters (for example, Metrodorus of Lampsacus is linked with Anaxagoras; the Democriteans Metrodorus of Chios, Nausiphanes, and Diotimus of Tyre are included in the chapter on the Atomists); nor have we accorded the same breadth of treatment to the Orphic material as DK did, and, without neglecting it, we have treated it differently. Thus, compared with the last edition of DK (1951/52), which includes ninety chapters, the present collection counts only forty-three. On the other hand, in a number of aspects our edition covers a terrain more vast than that of DK; first, because texts that are not included there figure now in our **P** and **D** sections, either because they were published in monographic editions and other studies later than DK, or because they were discovered more recently, for example the Strasbourg Papyrus, containing fragments of Empedocles, or the Derveni Papyrus; but also, and above all, because our **R** section, specifically dedicated to the history of reception, includes numerous texts that Diels and Kranz certainly knew but that they excluded because of their avowed project, namely the reconstruction, on the basis of fragments and testimonia, of the original doctrines of the earliest Greek philosophers. To this project of theirs, to which we remain loyal, we have decided to add a systematic, though not exhaustive, presentation of the ways in which these authors were appreciated, read, and interpreted, starting from their own times and continuing until the end of Antiquity. Thus our three sections **P, D,** and **R** do not correspond to the three sections of DK, in which the principal division rests upon a formal distinction between testimonia (A) and verbal citations (B), and the C sections, which bear very different titles (Echoes, Imitations, Forgeries, etc.), seem to be conceived in a rather inconsistent way, and function at most as appendices to the two principal sections A and B. In all the cases in which a text of ours does not figure in DK, we indicate this by means of the sign (≠ DK) on the side of the translation, while on the facing page the entry includes a reference, as the case may be, to a later edition of the author in question.

Like DK, we have included, as far as at all possible, the entirety of the fragments of the original works that are known via citation or direct transmission; the only complete texts that have survived are two speeches of Gorgias, his defenses of Helen and of Palamedes; so too Antiphon's *Tetralogies,* on the premise that the sophist and the orator are one and the same person (however, given that these are easily accessible, we do not include them here). By contrast, the testimonia on the doctrine in the **D** sections and the critical reactions, interpretations, and appropriations in the **R** sections have been selected with an eye toward their intrinsic interest or representativeness. In particular, we have eliminated doublets and insignificant parallels, for which the references have not been supplied either (thus, to give only one example among many, in the case of Parmenides **D22** the reader will not find out from our edition that the information found in Diogenes Laertius 9.23 is also found at 8.14): readers who might desire more complete information will need to seek it elsewhere.

The tripartition **P, D, R,** which is as it were the skeleton of this edition, and our deliberate choice to present the texts thematically, have led us sometimes to abridge the texts of our secondary sources (fortunately, the question poses itself much more rarely in the case of the verbal fragments) as a function of the kind of information they supply, in order either to distribute portions of them between the **D** and **R** sections, or, within the same section, to extract those parts of them that correspond to a given subject. To be sure, this procedure sacrifices the logic of the source considered, for example Aristotle or Diogenes Laertius. But we have found that this mode of presentation, practiced only relatively seldom, in fact makes it much easier to understand the data. It might have been expected that the distinction between **D** and **R** would often turn out to be impossible in practice because it would attempt to transform infinite shades of gray into too sharp a contrast between black and white: clearly this impression is not totally false in a certain number of cases, and we have had to make decisions, from case to case, that others might have made differently (for example: does not Parmenides **R35** in fact belong under **D**?); but we ourselves were surprised to see how often it turned out to be easy to distinguish unambiguously between information on the one hand and interpretation and criticism on the other: and the advantages of this kind of presentation seemed to us greatly to outweigh the disadvantages, however real these latter might be. In particular, this mode of presentation makes it possible to trace the contours of the large-scale currents of ancient interpretation of these archaic authors (for example, the Stoic reading of Heraclitus, the Neoplatonic reading of Empedocles), which often continue to determine modern readings, and also to sketch the outline, for each author or group of authors, of

the ways in which different philosophers and philosophical schools read, discussed, and exploited them over the
course of more than ten centuries. In a large number of
cases, we have indicated, within the texts we have abridged,
the places where the interested reader will be able to find
the section of text that has been omitted if it is found
elsewhere within the same chapter or in another chapter
of the collection (see our "Note on Editorial Principles
and Translations"). Of course, the reader will always be
able to refer, by consulting the relevant editions and translations, to the full text of all the sources we have utilized.

We have established all the original texts on the basis
of the edition of reference of the original author or of the
later one who cites the text reproduced; our edition is thus
not critical in the technical sense of the term (the Derveni
Papyrus represents a separate case in this regard, because
of the generous assistance provided by Valeria Piano: see
the introduction to chap. 30). To say that the texts have
been established on the basis of these editions, which are
listed in this volume, does not mean that we necessarily
reproduce their text (though this is often the case), nor
that our critical apparatus is based exclusively upon them:
we have followed these editions for the essential information concerning the manuscript readings; but we have
chosen freely, on the basis of our own judgment, among
these readings and the conjectures proposed by scholars;
likewise, we have taken account of information or conjectures proposed in other works (for example, monographic
editions or specialized articles on the manuscript tradition
of this or that text); and, in certain cases, we ourselves have
made what we believe are new suggestions. In any case,
the reference to DK reproduced in the lemma of each
entry does not signify that we have adopted its text or

extent: in fact, we use the signs > and < to indicate those cases in which the portion of text reproduced here is larger or smaller than the one that figures in DK.

The critical apparatus has been deliberately simplified. We have indicated only those readings and corrections that, for one reason or another, we have judged to be philosophically significant or interesting in one regard or another; mere orthographic variations, iotacisms, manifest errors and evident normalizations, omissions and readings with no effect on the meaning (such as inversions or variations between certain particles) have not been indicated. Likewise, we have eliminated the data that are of interest only for the history of transmission, and we have not homogenized the dialect of those texts composed in Ionic (for example in the Hippocratic corpus or the fragments of Democritus) or in Doric (especially in the Pythagorean corpus, but also in the *Pairs of Arguments*). For all these aspects of the text, the interested reader will have to refer to the edition of reference. This is particularly the case in the thematic chapters 2, 3, and 43, where the only indications in the critical apparatus signal some divergences with regard to the critical editions of reference, while the text presented there is usually maintained as such within the framework of the present collection—without prejudging what we ourselves would do if our objective had been to edit Aeschylus or Aristophanes.

Our own tendency as editors has been to conserve, when this was possible, the transmitted readings and to accept various degrees of roughness and heterogeneity rather than to seek simplification and normalization by recurring to conjecture. We indicate a certain number of

conjectures, of which many are due to Diels (because of
the historical importance of his work), in order to alert
the reader to the existence of potential difficulties and
of other strategies for resolving them than the ones to
which we have given the preference. After hesitating for
a long time, we have decided not to indicate precisely the
exact reference to the text in which Diels made his suggestions—this can be one or the other edition of his collection (1903, 1906, 1912, and 1922), then of DK, or the
Doxographi Graeci, his separate edition of the poem of
Parmenides, or numerous articles and contributions to the
works of other scholars. Such precise references would
have been of interest for understanding the history of his
scholarship on these texts, but they would have complicated further a critical apparatus that we have preferred
to simplify.

Many people have helped us in different ways in the
course of our preparation of this edition. Our greatest debt
is to Gérard Journée (Centre Léon Robin, Paris), who,
during the whole long course of our work, made available
to us his remarkable competence with regard to the transmission and edition of ancient texts, including his familiar-
ity with doxography, astronomy, and chronography, and
who furnished the electronic version of the great majority
of the Greek and Latin texts edited here; and to Leopoldo
Iribarren (Centre Léon Robin, Paris/University of Leiden), whose careful reading and rereading made it possible gradually to define and follow the rules of formal presentation adopted here and who devoted much time to
verifications and checks of all kinds, including transla-

tions. But many others have also assisted this edition in various ways.

Given the limitations of our own competence, it would not have been possible for us to provide the texts in languages other than Greek and Latin without the generous and expert help of other people. For the texts in Arabic, Cristina d'Ancona (Pisa), Germana Chemi (Pisa), and Peter E. Pormann (Manchester) have provided us with their guidance and have supplied us with electronic versions and translations of the relevant texts; Henri Hugonnard-Roche (CNRS, Paris) did the same for Syriac, Alessandro Orengo (Pisa) and Irene Tinti (Pisa) for Armenian, and Elisa Coda (Pisa) for Hebrew. Peter E. Pormann also checked the Syriac and Hebrew texts and translations.

Numerous colleagues and friends have read versions of the various chapters or of groups of chapters in different stages of their development and have given us their criticisms and suggestions, thereby improving them in many ways. We cannot thank them enough for their interest and generosity:

- for Background: Pierre Judet de la Combe (EHESS, Paris)
- for Thales: Andreas Schwab (Heidelberg)
- for Xenophanes: Alexander Mourelatos (Austin)
- for Pythagoras and the Pythagoreans: Constantin Macris (CNRS, Paris), and, for the mathematical and musical texts in these and other chapters, Alison Laywine (McGill University) and Monica Ugaglia (Pisa)
- for Melissus: Mathilde Brémond (Paris/Munich)

PREFACE

- for Empedocles: Jean-Claude Picot (Paris), who also offered generously to read a large number of other chapters in their penultimate version
- for Archelaus: Gabor Betegh (Cambridge)
- for the Atomists: Walter Leszl (Pisa) and Francesco Ademollo (Florence)
- for early Greek medicine: Paul Demont (Paris-Sorbonne) and Orly Lewis (Berlin)
- for Alcmaeon: Stavros Kouloumentas (Berlin)
- for the Derveni Papyrus: Valeria Piano (Pisa), Maria Serena Funghi (Pisa), and Richard Janko (University of Michigan)
- for all the chapters on the 'sophists': David Lévystone (Seoul)
- for Gorgias: the members of the 2014–15 research seminar in Greek philology at the Scuola Normale Superiore di Pisa
- for Socrates: Ineke Sluiter (Leiden) and Maria-Michela Sassi (Pisa)
- for the chapter on philosophy and philosophers in tragedy and comedy: Christine Mauduit (ENS, Paris), Olimpia Impero (Bari), Josh Billings (Princeton), and Pierre Judet de la Combe (EHESS, Paris)
- for a number of chapters in their initial versions: the members of the research group 'Philosophie présocratique' of the Centre Léon Robin, which from 2007 to 2010 benefited from the support of the ANR 'Présocratiques grecs/Présocratiques latins'

Among the people we have consulted on particular points, we would like to mention Suzanne Amigues (Montpellier), Teddy Fassberg (Princeton), Silvia Fazzo (Uni-

17

versity of Calabria), Andrew Ford (Princeton), Xavier Gheerbrandt (Lille), Jaap Mansfeld (Utrecht), Christoph Markschies (Berlin), Stephen Menn (McGill University), Oliver Primavesi (Munich), Marwan Rashed (Paris-Sorbonne), David Runia (Melbourne), Barbara Sattler (St. Andrews), and David Sedley (Cambridge). Finally, the production of this Loeb edition posed a variety of difficult challenges. We wish to thank a number of colleagues and friends who provided precious assistance with the onerous task of proofreading, in particular Luca Ruggeri (Pisa), and Jeffrey Henderson, Cheryl Lincoln, and especially Michael B. Sullivan of the Loeb Series for their understanding and help with an extremely complex editorial process.

We are grateful to all these scholars and friends, and to many others we do not name here, for their spontaneous, time-consuming, and generous help. The sense of being part of a large and benevolent community of scholars has made our work even more gratifying. Of course, it is the two coeditors who have had to take the final decisions.

This edition is the result of an intense and friendly collaboration between the two of us over the course of a number of years. There is not a single word in it for which we do not fully share the responsibility.

ANDRÉ LAKS
Mexico City
May 2016

GLENN W. MOST
Florence
May 2016

NOTE ON EDITORIAL
PRINCIPLES AND
TRANSLATIONS

GENERAL PRINCIPLES OF
PRESENTATION

We avoid repeating identical metatextual indications on
the two facing pages, except for the section titles and the
canonical numbering of the entry to be found in Hermann
Diels and Walther Kranz's edition (DK) and other kinds
of indications that make sense on both pages. If the passage in question is found in DK, the DK reference is given
on both facing pages, with < or else > to indicate cases in
which we provide less or else more than is to be found in
DK; if the passage in question is not found in DK but is
found in another critical edition indicated in the bibliography to that chapter, on the left page is given the reference to that other edition, while on the right page we write
(≠ DK), to indicate its absence in DK; if the passage in
question is found neither in DK nor in any other critical
edition, we write (≠ DK) on both pages. On the left page,
together with the texts in the original languages, will be
found, in the lemma, the exact reference (in abridged
form) to the source of the text reproduced and, in the text,
an indication of passages omitted here and of those sup-

plied elsewhere; references to other texts that explain the meaning of a given text are provided in the translation, on the right page. By simply comparing the indications omitted on the translation side with those that are furnished on the facing page, readers will be able to complete the information supplied even if they do not know the original languages.

All editorial interventions within the texts (the numbering of paragraphs, explanations, internal references, references to existing collections of fragments, and any other references) appear between square brackets [ ], except for the transcription of Greek terms in the translation, which are placed between parentheses ( ). Three dots surrounded by brackets [. . .] indicate that we have omitted some transmitted material; three dots without brackets . . . indicate that the transmitted text is incomplete.

In the passages that we have abridged, an element (subject, verb) must sometimes be supplied if a sentence is to be intelligible. In general, this element is not reproduced in the text in the original language; the supplement necessary for understanding appears in the translation, introduced by [i.e.] or [scil.].

In our presentation of the Greek text of dactylic hexameters that are transmitted or cited incompletely, by convention we have always indicated missing feet as – ∪ ∪, even where – – would be possible.

Citations deriving from the original work of the early Greek philosophers, and also a certain number of terms or expressions that appear in the testimonia and that we consider there to be good reason to attribute directly to the original work (i.e. exact verbal citations rather than paraphrases or reports) are printed in **boldface**; readers should bear in mind that in the latter case the decision is

often difficult or uncertain and that other editors have
been more, or less, restrictive than we are. For evident
reasons of appearance, texts that have reached us, *in ex-
tenso* or in their entirety, by direct transmission via medi-
eval manuscripts (Gorgias' speeches on Helen and Palamedes; *Pairs of Arguments*) are not set in boldface.

In some chapters, roman and italic type is reversed in
a certain number of texts, in order to indicate that they are
of uncertain attribution. In particular, this is the case for
a large number of maxims attributed to Democritus and to
Antiphon; but see also the chapters on Xenophanes, Philolaus, and Archytas, and the fragments of Ps.-Epicharmus
in the chapter on dramatic texts.

CROSS-REFERENCES

There are two kinds of cross-references:

1. "Content references": these involve the thematic
relation established between two passages. They are introduced into the translation (not into the original text) in
order to explain an allusion, to provide relevant information found elsewhere in our collection, or to indicate that
a text cited or referred to by an author is found somewhere
else in our collection. For example, in the following passage from Plato's *Cratylus* (our **DOX. T3**): "Heraclitus
says something like this: that all things flow and nothing
remains; and comparing the things that are to the flowing
of a river, he says that you could not step twice into the
same river [cf. **HER. D65c**]," the reference is made by
[cf.] because it refers to a different text. But when the
reference indicates that one passage appears in identical
form in another place (this happens especially in the case
of citations), the reference to the entry in question is gen-

erally preceded by an equal sign [=], as for example in the following passage from Plato's *Theaetetus* (our **DOX. T2**): "[. . .] Homer [. . .], who when he says

> Ocean, the origin of the gods, and mother Tethys
> [= **COSM. T10a**]

is stating that all things are born from flux and movement." Evidently, these two possibilities also apply to references made to texts that are found in the same chapter as are the texts from which reference is made. In these latter cases, the abbreviation of the title of the chapter is omitted. As indicated above, this type of reference appears only in the translations.

2. "Text references": these concern parts of a sentence or passage that, because of the different kinds of abridgment we have performed on the texts (see "Preface"), are found in a different place in the chapter in question or in a different chapter. These references allow the reader to reconstruct, sometimes exactly, sometimes approximately, the entirety of the text before abridgment. For example, in this extract from Aristotle's *Metaphysics* (in **THAL. D3**), "τὸ μέντοι πλῆθος καὶ τὸ εἶδος τῆς τοιαύτης ἀρχῆς οὐ τὸ αὐτὸ πάντες λέγουσιν, ἀλλὰ Θαλῆς μὲν [. . . = **R9**] ὕδωρ φησὶν εἶναι (διὸ καὶ τὴν γῆν ἐφ᾽ ὕδατος ἀπεφήνατο εἶναι) [. . . = **R32a**]," the reader is informed in this way that this phrase is derived from a longer passage of which the omitted portions can be found in **R9** and **R32a** of the same chapter. As indicated above, this kind of reference appears only on the page of the texts in the original languages.

EDITORIAL NOTE

CRITICAL APPARATUS

For prose texts, the indications of the critical apparatus are usually keyed to superscript numbers in the Greek text; for poetic texts, inscriptions, or papyri the number in the apparatus refers instead to the line number.

We do not give a list of the manuscripts used; the interested reader will have to refer to the edition of reference.

As often as possible we have replaced the symbols used in the editions of reference to designate manuscripts with "mss." or "ms." As the case may be, these abbreviations may refer only to the archetype, to subarchetypes, or to the principal manuscripts. For all these indications and their interpretation, we have naturally depended upon the editions of reference of which a list is supplied in this volume. We have not been able to solve all the problems (the Teubner edition of Censorinus is particularly difficult to decipher). Hence our apparatuses have essentially an indicative value.

With regard to the emendations we have included, we have done our best to identify the earliest scholar to have suggested a reading (that was not always possible), leaving to the reader the task of verifying whether or not it was adopted by later editors, and in particular in DK. We indicate by "nos" a conjecture that, as far as we know, we are the first to propose.

DK is indicated as D.-K. in the critical apparatuses in order to avoid confusion with letters designating manuscripts.

LEMMATA

In the chapters for which DK does not distinguish between A (testimonia) and B (fragments)—this is in particular the case for a number of chapters relating to the Pythagoreans—we indicate the number of the chapter in DK followed by the number there, separated by a period: 18.3 or 58A.25 (where the A refers to a different division than that found in most of the chapters, of the type 31 A72).

The name of the editor is usually not reproduced in the lemma; the edition used is indicated in the list of the editions of reference in this volume. However, mentioning it is sometimes necessary in order to facilitate certain identifications, notably when the edition of reference is published in an article in a scholarly journal. Moreover, the pagination indicated can sometimes refer to a canonical edition that is older than the edition of reference. For example, Proclus' commentary on Plato's *Parmenides* is cited from the edition by C. Steel, but the pagination indicated is that of the edition by Cousin, which Steel's edition also reproduces.

The lemmata of Aëtius are a special case, since this is a text that has been reconstructed on the basis of a number of different versions (we have provided a visual representation in **DOX. T17**). We have deliberately simplified the data by reproducing the numbering of H. Diels' *Doxographi Graeci*, followed in parentheses by the name of the source or sources (generally Ps.-Plutarch and/or Stobaeus) on the basis of which the text of Aëtius has been reconstructed. We do not provide an exact reference for these sources, which the interested reader will be able to find in *Doxographi Graeci* and, for Book 2 of Aëtius,

24

in the edition by J. Mansfeld and D. Runia, or again by consulting the concordance prepared by G. Journée at http://www.placita.org/concordanceAetius.aspx. Whenever it was possible (this was not always the case), we have kept to the version of Ps.-Plutarch alone. The titles of the chapters of Aëtius are taken, with a few exceptions, from the collection of Ps.-Plutarch, even when Stobaeus is the principal or only source for the notice.

In the case of Sextus Empiricus, the titles of the books vary according to different editions and translations; we have adopted for the Greek text the global designation *Adv. Math.* and the correlative number, and for the English translation, for those books to which we refer, the following equivalences:

Adv. Math. 1–6: *Against the Professors*
Adv. Math. 7–8: *Against the Logicians*
Adv. Math. 9–10: *Against the Natural Philosophers*

EDITIONS OF PAPYROLOGICAL AND EPIGRAPHICAL FRAGMENTS

We have not replicated the arrangement in columns employed in most of the editions of reference, except in the case of the Derveni Papyrus, given the particular character of this text and of its editorial status (see the introduction to chap. 30). A vertical line | indicates the end of a line in the source text. We have maintained certain papyrological conventions: we use square brackets [$\alpha\beta\gamma$] to indicate letters that have been conjecturally restored in a lacuna, half square brackets ⌊$\alpha\beta\gamma$⌋ to indicate letters that are missing in the papyrus but that can be restored from a citation of the same text, and dots under letters to indicate that the restoration of the dotted letters is uncertain, because their traces are insufficient to render a restoration certain rather than merely probable. But we have simplified the editorial typography: iotas are always subscript, not adscript (except in the Derveni Papyrus and the Strasbourg Papyrus of Empedocles); we have not used parentheses indicating, in the edition of certain texts (like the Anonymous of London), the presence of an abbreviation in the papyrus that editors expand, but have simply expanded tacitly; in those texts present not only in the chapters **COSM.** and **MOR.** but also elsewhere in our collection (for example, passages from the Derveni Papyrus), we have suppressed most of the editorial signs that we use in the single-author chapters. In translating passages that have a lacuna that editors or we ourselves believe can be supplemented, we have tried to produce a visual equivalent of the condition of the papyrus or inscription by recurring to angle brackets ⟨ ⟩, to italics for the restored part, and to division of words. Thus, in the translation of the Strasbourg Papyrus of Empedocles, we write at **D73.267:** ⟨*But under the rule of Love we come tog*⟩**ether into one world.** This mode of presentation has of course a merely indicative value.

TRANSLATION

"He" or "this man" or similar expressions, without further explanation, always refers to the author to whom the chapter is devoted (for example, in the chapter on Xenophanes, "he" = Xenophanes), when no ambiguity is possible.

In the case of proper nouns, we have always used the Latinized form most common in English for better known names, and transliteration (indicating long vowels as *ê, ô*) for the others.

In a number of especially delicate cases, we have adopted a standard translation as far as possible: in particular, *phusikos* and *phusiologos* are systematically rendered "natural philosopher." When a term could not be rendered in the same way in all the passages in which it appeared, as for example in the case of *sophistês*, we have supplied a transcription of the Greek term in parentheses next to the translation we have adopted (sophist, 'sophist,' expert, sage). This is also the case with Greek terms that produce wordplays or assonances that are impossible to convey in translation. In general, particularly for transcribed terms, but more generally for questions of vocabulary, the reader should consult the glossary at the end of this volume.

LIST OF ABBREVIATIONS USED FOR CROSS-REFERENCES

ALCM. = Alcmaeon [23]

ANAXAG. = Anaxagoras [25]

ANAXIMAND. = Anaximander [6]

ANAXIMEN. = Anaximenes [7]

ANON. IAMBL. = The Anonymous of Iamblichus [40]

ANTIPH. = Antiphon [37]

ARCH. = Archelaus [26]

ARCHY. = Archytas [14]

ATOM. = Older Atomists: Leucippus, Democritus [27]

COSM. = Background: Cosmological Speculations [2]

DERV. = Derveni Papyrus [30]

DIOG. = Diogenes of Apollonia [28]

DISS. = *Pairs of Arguments* [41]

DOX. = Ancient Ways of Organizing and Presenting Early Greek Thought: Doxography and Successions [1]

DRAM. = Philosophy and Philosophers in Greek Comedy and Tragedy [43]

ECPH. = Ecphantus [16]

EMP. = Empedocles [22]

EUR. = Eurytus [13]

GORG. = Gorgias [32]

HER. = Heraclitus [9]

HIC. = Hicetas [15]

HIPPAS. = Hippasus [11]

HIPPIAS = Hippias [36]

HIPPO = Hippo [24]

LYC. = Lycophron [38]

MED. = Early Greek Medicine [29]

MEL. = Melissus [21]

MOR. = Background: Reflections on Gods and Men [3]

PARM. = Parmenides [19]

PHER. = Pherecydes [4]

PHILOL. = Philolaus [12]

PROD. = Prodicus [34]

PROT. = Protagoras [31]

PYTH. a = Pythagoras: The Person [10 a]

PYTH. b = Pythagoras: The Institution [10 b]

PYTH. c = Pythagoras: Doctrines Attributed by Name; Sayings and Precepts [10 c]

PYTHS. ANON. = Pythagorean Doctrines not Attrib-
uted by Name [17]
PYTHS. R = The Reception of Pythagoras and of Py-
thagoreanism [18]
SOC. = Socrates [33]
SOPH. = 'Sophists' and 'Sophistic': Collective Repre-
sentations and General Characterizations [42]
THAL. = Thales [5]
THRAS. = Thrasymachus [35]
XEN. = Xenophanes [8]
XENI. = Xeniades [39]
ZEN. = Zeno [20]

ABBREVIATIONS

Ach. Tat. *Introd. Arat.*	Achilles Tatius, *Introductio in Aratum,* ed. E. Maass. Berlin, 1898.
Ael. *Nat. anim.*	Aelianus, *De natura animalium,* ed. M. Garcia Valdés, L. A. Llera Fueyo, and L. Rodriguez-Noriega Guillén. Berlin, 2013.
Ael. *Var. hist.*	———, *Varia historia,* ed. M. R. Dilts. Leipzig, 1974.
Aesch.	Aeschylus, *Tragoediae,* ed. M. L. West. Stuttgart, 1990.
Aesch. Frag.	See *TrGF.*
Aeschin. Socr.	Aeschines Socraticus. See G².
Aët.	Aëtius. See *Dox. Gr.*
Aët. 2	———, Book 2 in J. Mansfeld and D. Runia, *Aëtiana,* vol. II.2. Leiden-Boston, 2009.
Aët. 5.30.1 (**ALCM. D30**)	D. T. Runia, "The *Placita* Ascribed to Doctors in Aëtius' Doxography on Physics," in P. J. van der Eijk, ed. *Ancient Histories of Medicine: Essays*

	in Medical Doxography and Historiography in Classical Antiquity. Leiden, 1999, pp. 191–250.
Agathem. *Geogr.*	Agathemerus, *Geographia.* See *GGM.*
Alb. Mag. *Veget.*	Albertus Magnus, *De vegetabilibus et plantis,* ed. A. Borgnet. Paris, 1891.
Alcid.	Alcidamas, *Orazioni e frammenti,* ed. G. Avezzù. Rome, 1982.
Alex. *Fat.*	Alexander Aphrodisiensis, *De fato,* ed. I. Bruns. Berlin, 1892.
Alex. *In Metaph.*	———, *In Aristotelis Metaphysica Commentaria,* ed. M. Hayduck. *CAG* 1.
Alex. *In Meteor.*	———, *In Aristotelis Meteorologicorum libros Commentaria,* ed. M. Hayduck. *CAG* 3.2.
Alex. *In Phys.*	———, *Commentaire perdu à la Physique d'Aristote (Livres IV–VIII). Les scholies byzantines,* ed. M. Rashed. Berlin-Boston, 2011.
Alex. *In SE*	———, *Quod fertur in Aristotelis sophisticos elenchos commentarium,* ed. M. Wallies. *CAG* 2.3.

Alex. *In Top.*	———, *In Aristotelis Topicorum libros octo commentaria,* ed. M. Wallies. *CAG* 2.2.
Alex. *Quaest.*	———, *Quaestiones,* in *Alexandri Aphrodisiensis praeter commentaria scripta minora,* ed. I. Bruns. Berlin, 1887.
Ps.-Alex. *Probl.*	———, *Quae feruntur. Problematorum liber III et IIII,* ed. H. Usener. Berlin, 1859.
Alex. Aet.	Alexander Aetolus, *Testimonia et fragmenta,* ed. E. Magnelli. Florence, 1999.
Amm. Marc.	Ammianus Marcellinus, *Rerum gestarum libri,* ed. W. Seyfarth et al. Leipzig, 1978.
Ammon. *In Interp.*	Ammonius, *In Aristotelis De interpretatione commentarius,* ed. A. Busse. *CAG* 4.4.
Anecd. Gr. Bachmann	*Anecdota Graeca,* ed. L. Bachmann. Leipzig, 1828.
Anecd. Gr. Bekker	*Anecdota Graeca,* ed. I. Bekker. Berlin, 1814–1821.
Anecd. Gr. Cramer	*Anecdota Graeca,* ed. J. A. Cramer. Oxford, 1839.
Anon. *Introd. Arat.*	Anonymus, *Introductio in Aratum (De caelestibus),* ed. E. Maass. Berlin, 1898.
Anon. Flor. *Inund. Nili*	Anonymus Florentinus, *De inundatione Nili* (cod. Laur. 56.1), ed. C. Landi. Florence-Rome, 1895.

Anon. Lond.	Anonymus Londiniensis, *De medicina,* ed. D. Manetti. Berlin-New York, 2011.
Anon. *Proleg. in Plat. Philos.*	*Prolégomènes à la philosophie de Platon,* ed. L. G. Westerink, trans. J. Trouillard, with A.-P. Segonds. Paris, 1990.
Anon. *Vit. Hom. Rom.*	*Vitae Homeri et Hesiodi in usum scholarum,* ed. U. von Wilamowitz-Moellendorff. Bonn, 1916, pp. 30–32.
Anth. Gr.	*Anthologia Graeca,* ed. H. Beckby. Munich, 1957.
Antisth.	See Sosicr.
Antisth. Socr.	Antisthenes Socraticus. See G^2.
Apoll. *Mir.*	Apollonius, *Mirabilia,* in *Paradoxographorum graecorum reliquiae,* ed. A. Giannini. Milan, 1966.
Apoll. Cit. *In Hipp. Artic.*	Apollonius Citieus, *Kommentar zu Hippokrates Über das Einrenken der Gelenke,* ed. J. Kollesch and F. Kudlien. *CMG* 11.1.1.
Apoll. Dysc. *Pronom.*	Apollonius Dyscolus, *De pronominibus,* ed. R. Schneider. *GG* 2.1.1.
Appon.	Apponius, *In Canticum Canticorum,* ed. B. de Vregille and L. Neyrand. Turnhout, 1986.

34

ABBREVIATIONS

Apul.	Apuleius, *Opera quae supersunt,* ed. R. Helm and P. Thomas. Leipzig, 1908–1912.
Archim.	Archimedes, *Opera omnia cum commentariis Eutocii,* ed. J. L. Heiberg and E. S. Simatis. Stuttgart, 1972.
Ar. Did.	Arius Didymus, *Epitome.* See *Dox. Gr.*
Arist. *An.*	Aristoteles, *De anima,* ed. W. D. Ross. Oxford, 1961.
Arist. *An. Post.*	———, *Prior and posterior analytics,* ed. W. D. Ross. Oxford, 1957.
Arist. *Ath. Pol.*	———, ΑΘΗΝΑΙΩΝ ΠΟΛΙΤΕΙΑ, ed. M. Chambers. Leipzig, 1986.
Arist. *Cael.*	———, *De caelo,* ed. P. Moraux. Paris, 1965.
Arist. *EE*	———, *Ethica Eudemia,* ed. R. R. Walzer and J. M. Mingay. Oxford, 1991.
Arist. *EN*	———, *Ethica Nicomachea,* ed. I. Bywater. Oxford, 1894.
Arist. *GA*	———, *De generatione animalium,* ed. P. Louis. Paris, 1961.
Arist. *GC*	———, *De generatione et corruptione,* ed. M. Rashed. Paris, 2005.

Arist. *HA* ———, *Historia animalium,* ed. D. M. Balme. Cambridge, 2002.

Arist. *Metaph.* ———, *Metaphysica,* ed. W. D. Ross. Oxford, 1924.

Arist. *Metaph.* A ———, *Metaphysica A,* ed. O. Primavesi, in C. Steel, ed., *Aristotle's Metaphysics Alpha: Symposium Aristotelicum* (Oxford, 2012), pp. 465–516.

Arist. *Meteor.* ———, *Meteorologica,* ed. F. H. Fobes. Cambridge, MA, 1919.

Arist. *PA* ———, *De partibus animalium,* ed. P. Louis. Paris, 1956.

Arist. *Parv. nat.* ———, *Parva naturalia,* ed. W. D. Ross. Oxford, 1955.

Arist. *Phys.* ———, *Physica,* ed. W. D. Ross. Oxford, 1936.

Arist. *Poet.* ———, *Poetics,* ed. L. Tarán and D. Gutas. Leiden-Boston, 2012.

Arist. *Pol.* ———, *Politica,* ed. W. D. Ross. Oxford, 1957.

Arist. *Resp.* ———, *De respiratione.* See Arist. *Parv. nat.*

Arist. *Rhet.* ———, *Ars rhetorica,* ed. R. Kassel. Berlin, 1976.

Arist. *SE* ———, *Sophistici elenchi,* ed. W. D. Ross. Oxford, 1958.

Arist. *Sens.* ———, *De sensu:* See Arist. *Parv. nat.*

Arist. *Top.*	———, *Topica,* ed. J. Brunschwig. Paris, 1967–2007.
Arist. Frag.	*Aristotelis qui ferebantur librorum fragmenta,* ed. V. Rose. Leipzig, 1886.
Ps.-Arist. *Lin.*	Ps.-Aristoteles, *De plantis, De mirabilibus auscultationibus, Mechanica, De lineis insecabilibus, Ventorum situs et nomina, De Melisso Xenophane Gorgia,* ed. O. Apelt. Leipzig, 1888.
Ps.-Arist. *Mir. ausc.*	See Ps.-Arist. *Lin.*
Ps.-Arist. *MM*	———, *Magna Moralia,* ed. F. Susemihl. Leipzig, 1883.
Ps.-Arist. *Mund.*	———, *De mundo,* ed. W. L. Lorimer. Paris, 1933.
Ps.-Arist. *MXG*	———, *De Melisso Xenophane Gorgia libellus,* ed. H. Diels. Berlin, 1900.
Ps.-Arist. *Oec.*	———, *Oeconomica,* ed. F. Susemihl. Leipzig 1887.
Ps.-Arist. *Plant.*	See Ps.-Arist. *Lin.*
Ps.-Arist. *Probl.*	———, *Problèmes,* ed. P. Louis. Paris, 1991–94.
Ps.-Arist. *Spirit.*	———, *De spiritu,* ed. A. Roselli. Pisa, 1992.
Arist. Quint. *Mus.*	Aristides Quintilianus, *De musica,* ed. R. P. Winnington-Ingram. Leipzig, 1963.
Aristippus	See G^2.

Aristocl.	Aristocles Messanius. *Testimonia and Fragments,* ed. M. L. Chiesara. Oxford, 2001.
Aristocl. *Philos.*	Aristocles, *De philosophia.* See Eus. *PE.*
Aristocr. *Theos.*	Aristocritus, *Theosophia,* ed. P. F. Beatrice. Leiden, 2001.
Aristoph.	Aristophanes, *Fabulae,* ed. N. G. Wilson. Oxford, 2008.
Aristoph. Frag.	See K–A.
Aristoph. Byz. *Epit.*	Aristophanes Byzantius, *Historiae animalium epitome,* ed. S. P. Lambros, in *Supplementum Aristotelicum* 1.1. Berlin, 1885.
Art. Script.	*Artium Scriptores: Reste der voraristotelischen Rhetorik,* ed. L. Radermacher. Vienna, 1951.
Artem. *Oneiro.*	Artemidorus, *Onirocritica,* ed. R. Pack. Leipzig, 1963.
Asclep. *In Metaph.*	Asclepius, *In Aristotelis Metaphysicorum libros A–Z Commentaria,* ed. M. Hayduck. *CAG* 6.2.
Athan. Alex. *In Hermog.*	*Ex Athanasii Prolegomenis in Hermogenis* ΠΕΡΙ ΣΤΑΣΕΩΝ, in *Prolegomenon Sylloge,* ed. H. Rabe. Leipzig, 1931, pp. 171–83.

ABBREVIATIONS

Athen. *Deipn.* Athenaeus, *Dipnosophistae,* ed.
G. Kaibel. Leipzig, 1887.

August. *Civ. Dei* Augustinus, *De civitate Dei,* ed.
B. Dombart and A. Kalb.
Stuttgart, 1981.

August. *Conf.* ———, *Confessiones,* ed. J. J.
O'Donnell. Oxford, 1992.

August. *Epist.* ———, *Epistulae CI–CXXXIX,*
ed. K. D. Daur. Turnhout,
2009.

Aul. Gell. *Noct.* Aulus Gellius, *Noctes Atticae,* ed.
P. K. Marshall. Oxford, 1968.

Bernabé *Poetae epici Graeci,* Pars II, ed.
A. Bernabé. Munich-Leipzig,
2004.

Boeth. *Arithm.* Boethius, *De institutione arith-
metica libri duo, De institu-
tione musica libri quinque,* ed.
G. Friedlein. Leipzig, 1867.

Boeth. *Mus.* See Boeth. *Arithm.*
Bollack J. Bollack. *Empédocle,* 4 vols.
Paris, 1965–1969, repr. 1992.

Cael. Aurel. Caelius Aurelianus, *Acutarum
sive celerum passionum libri
III, Chronicarum sive tar-
darum passionum libri V,* ed.
G. Bendz and I. Pape. *CMG*
VI 1.1–2.

Càffaro L. Càffaro, ed. *Encomio di
Elena, Apologia di Palamede.*
Florence, 1997.

CAG	*Commentaria in Aristotelem Graeca.* Berlin, 1882–1909.
Calcid. *In Tim.*	Calcidius, *In Platonis Timaeum,* ed. B. Bakhouche. Paris, 2011.
Callim.	Callimachus, ed. Pfeiffer. Oxford, 1949–1953.
Ps.-Call. *Hist. Alex.*	*Historia Alexandri Magni (Pseudo-Callisthenes). Volumen I, Recensio vetusta,* ed. W. Kroll. Berlin, 1926.
Carm. Aur.	*The Pythagorean Golden Verses,* ed. J. C. Thom. Leiden, 1995.
Ps.-Ceb. *Tab.*	*Cebetis Tabula,* ed. K. Praechter. Leipzig, 1893.
CEG	*Carmina Epigraphica Graeca,* ed. P. A. Hansen. Berlin-New York, 1983–1989.
Cels. *Medic.*	Aulus Cornelius Celsus, *De medicina,* ed. G. Serbat. Paris, 1995.
Cens. *Die nat.*	Censorinus, *De die natali,* ed. N. Sallmann. Leipzig, 1983. (Cf. ed. C. A. Rapisarda. Bologna, 1991.)
Christod. *Ecphr.*	Christodorus, *Ecphrasis* (*Anth. Gr.* lib. 2). See *Anth. Gr.*
Chron. Pasch.	*Chronicon Paschale,* ed. L. Dindorf. Bonn, 1832.
Cic. *Acad.*	Cicero, *Academica,* ed. O. Plasberg. Leipzig, 1922.
Cic. *Ad Q.*	———, *Epistulae ad Quintum fratrem,* ed. D. R. Shackleton Bailey. Leipzig, 1988.

Cic. *Brut.*	———, *Brutus,* in *M. Tulli Ciceronis Rhetorica,* ed. A. S. Wilkins. Oxford, 1969.
Cic. *De orat.*	———, *De oratore,* ed. K. F. Kumaniecki. Stuttgart-Leipzig, 1969.
Cic. *Div.*	———, *De divinatione, De fato, Timaeus,* ed. R. Giomini, Leipzig, 1975.
Cic. *Fat.*	———, *De fato.* See Cic. *Div.*
Cic. *Fin.*	———, *De finibus,* ed. C. Moreschini. Munich-Leipzig, 2005.
Cic. *Inv.*	———, *De inventione,* ed. G. Achard. Paris, 1994.
Cic. *Lael.*	———, *Laelius de amicitia.* See Cic. *Rep.*
Cic. *Leg.*	———, *De legibus.* See Cic. *Rep.*
Cic. *Luc.*	———, *Lucullus,* ed. O. Plasberg. Stuttgart, 1980.
Cic. *Nat. deor.*	———, *De natura deorum,* ed. A. S. Pease. Cambridge, MA, 1955–1958.
Cic. *Orat.*	———, *Orator,* in *M. Tulli Ciceronis Rhetorica,* ed. A. S. Wilkins. Oxford, 1969.
Cic. *Rep.*	———, *De re publica, De legibus, Cato Maior de senectute, Laelius de amicitia,* ed. J. G. F. Powell. Oxford, 2006.
Cic. *Sen.*	———, *Cato Maior de senectute.* See Cic. *Rep.*
Cic. *Tim.*	———, *Timaeus.* See Cic. *Div.*

41

Cic. *Tusc.*	————, *Tusculanae disputationes*, ed. G. Fohlen. Paris, 1931.
Claud. *Car.*	Claudius Claudianus, *Carmina*, ed. J. B. Hall. Leipzig, 1985.
Claud. Mam. *Stat. an.*	Claudianus Mamertus, *De statu animae*, ed. A. Engelbrecht. Vienna, 1885.
Clem. Alex.	Clemens Alexandrinus, ed. O. Stählin, L. Früchtel, and U. Treu. Berlin, 1970.
Ps.-Clem. Rom. *Homil.*	Ps.-Clemens Romanus, *Homiliae*, ed. B. Rehm, I. Irmscher, and F. Paschke. Berlin, 1965.
CMG	*Corpus Medicorum Graecorum.* Berlin, 1927–.
Cod. Brux. 1348–59 (**DIOG. D28b**)	M. Wellmann, *Die Fragmente der sikelischen Ärzte Akron, Philistion und des Diokles von Karystos.* Berlin, 1901, pp. 208–34.
Cod. Monac. 490 (**ANAXAG. P44**)	See DK. (Cf. I. Hardt, *Catalogus codicum manuscriptorum graecorum Bibliothecae Regiae Bavaricae.* Tom. 5. Munich, 1812.)
Coll. Alchim.	*Collection des anciens alchimistes grecs*, ed. M. Berthelot and C. E. Ruelle. Paris, 1887.
Colum.	Columella, *Opera quae exstant*, ed. V. Lundstrom. Uppsala-Goteborg, 1897–1940.

Corn. *Theol.*	Cornutus, *De natura deorum,* ed. C. Lang. Leipzig, 1881.
CPF	*Corpus dei papiri filosofici greci e latini.* Florence, 1989–.
Critias (?) Frag.	See *TrGF.*
Cyrill. Alex. *Jul.*	Cyrillus Alexandrinus, *Contre Julien,* ed. P. Burguière and P. Evieux. Paris, 1985.
Dam. *In Parm.*	Damascius, *Commentaire du Parmenide de Platon,* ed. L. G. Westerink. Paris, 1997–2003.
Dam. *In Phil.*	———, *In Platonis Philebum Scholia,* ed. L. G. Westerink. Amsterdam, 1959.
Dam. *Princ.*	———, *De principiis,* ed. L. G. Westerink. Paris, 1986–2002.
David. *Proleg.*	David, *Prolegomena et in Porphyrii Isagogen commentarium,* ed. A. Busse. *CAG* 18.2.
Demetr. *Eloc.*	Demetrius, *On Style,* ed. W. Rhys Roberts. Cambridge, 1902.
Demetr. Magn.	Jørgen Mejer, "Demetrius of Magnesia: On Poets and Authors of the Same Name," *Hermes* 109 (1981): 447–72.
Democrates	See DK.
Dio	Dio Prusaensis, *Quae extant omnia,* ed. J. de Arnim. Berlin, 1893–1896.

Diod. Sic.	Diodorus Siculus, *Bibliotheca historica,* ed. F. Vogel. Leipzig, 1888. (Cf. ed. P. Bertrac et al. Paris, 1993ff.)
Diog. Laert.	Diogenes Laertius, *Lives of Eminent Philosophers,* ed. T. Dorandi. Cambridge, 2013.
Diog. Oen.	Diogenes Oenoandensis, *The Epicurean Inscription,* ed. M. F. Smith. Naples, 1993; *Supplement to Diogenes of Oinoanda, The Epicurean Inscription,* Naples 2003.
Dion. Hal.	Dionysius Halicarnaseus, *Opuscula,* ed. H. Usener and L. Radermacher. Leipzig, 1899–1904.
Dion. Hal. *Imit.*	———, *Opuscules rhétoriques,* vol. 5, ed. G. Aujac. Paris, 1992.
DK	*Die Fragmente der Vorsokratiker,* ed. H. Diels and W. Kranz. 6. Auflage. Berlin, 1951–52.
Donadi	F. Donadi, *Gorgiae Leontini in Helenam laudatio.* Rome, 1982.
Dox. Gr.	*Doxographi Graeci,* ed. H. Diels. Berlin, 1879.
Elias *In Cat.*	Elias, *In Aristotelis Categorias Commentaria,* ed. A. Busse. *CAG* 18.1.

Epicur.	*Epicurea,* ed. H. Usener. Leipzig, 1887.
Epicur. *Nat.* 25 (**ATOM. R83**)	Epicurus, *De natura liber* 25, ed. S. Laursen, "The Later Parts of Epicurus, *On Nature,* 25th Book," *Cronache Ercolanesi* 27 (1997): 5–82.
Epimer. Hom.	*Epimerismi Homerici,* ed. A. R. Dyck. Berlin, 1983–1995.
Epiph.	Epiphanius, ed. K. Holl, H. Lietzmann, J. Dummer. Leipzig-Berlin, 1915–1985.
Erat.	*Die geographischen Fragmente des Eratosthenes,* ed. H. Berger. Leipzig, 1880.
Erot. *Lex. Hipp.*	Erotianus, *Vocum Hippocraticarum collectio cum fragmentis,* ed. E. Nachmanson. Uppsala, 1918.
Etym. Gen.	*Etymologicum Magnum Genuinum (usque ad β),* ed. F. Lasserre and N. Livadaras. Rome, 1976.
Etym. Gen. Calame	*Etymologicum Genuinum: Les Citations de poètes lyriques,* ed. C. Calame. Rome, 1970.
Etym. Gud.	*Etymologicum Gudianum,* ed. A. de Stefani. Leipzig, 1909–1920.
Etym. Mag.	*Etymologicon Magnum,* ed. T. Gaisford. Oxford, 1848.

Etym. Orion.   *Orioni Thebani Etymologicon,*
                         ed. F. W. Sturz. Leipzig, 1820.
Eucl. *Elem.*   Euclides, *Elementa,* ed. J. L.
                         Heiberg and E. S. Stamatis.
                         Leipzig, 1969–1977.
Eudox.   *Die Fragmente des Eudoxos von*
                         Knidos, ed. F. Lasserre. Berlin,
                         1966.
Eur.   Euripides, *Fabulae,* ed. J. Dig-
                         gle. Oxford, 1984–1994.
Eur. Frag.   See *TrGF.*
Eus. *Chron.* (Hier.)   Hieronymus, *Chronicon,* ed. R.
                         Helm. Berlin, 1984.
Eus. *PE*   Eusebius, *Praeparatio evangel-*
                         ica, ed. K. Mras. Berlin, 1954.
Eust. *In Dion. Per-*   Dionysius Periegetes, ed. G.
     ieg.   Bernhardy, vol. 1, pp. 65–316.
                         Leipzig, 1828.
Eust. *In Il.*   Eustathius, *Commentarii ad Ho-*
                         meri Iliadem pertinentes, ed.
                         M. van der Valk. Leiden,
                         1971–1987.
Eust. *In Od.*   ———, *Commentarii ad Homeri*
                         Odysseam, ed. G. Stallbaum.
                         Leipzig, 1825.
Eutoc. *In Arch.*   See Archim.
Excerpta Vind.   *Excerpta Vindobonensia,* in A.
                         Meineke, ed. *Ioannis Stobaei*
                         Florilegium, vol. IV, pp. 290–
                         96. Leipzig, 1857.

Favor.	Favorinus, *Œuvres,* ed. E. Amato. Paris, 2005–2010.
FGrHist	*Die Fragmente der griechischen Historiker,* ed. F. Jacoby. Leiden, 1923ff.
FHG	*Fragmenta historicorum Graecorum,* ed. C. Müller. Paris 1841–1870.
Flav. Jos. *Apion.*	Flavius Josephus, *Contra Apionem,* ed. F. Siegert. Göttingen, 2008.
Flav. Manl. Theod. *Metr.*	Flavius Manlius Theodorus, *De metris,* ed. F. Romanini. Hildesheim-Zurich-New York, 2007.
G^1	G. G. Giannantoni, *Socrate. Tutte le testimonianze: da Aristofane e Senofonte ai padri cristiani.* Bari, 1971.
G^2	———, ed. *Socratis et Socraticorum Reliquiae.* Naples, 1990.
Gal. ed. Kühn	Galenus, *Opera omnia,* ed. C. G. Kühn. Leipzig, 1821–1833.
Gal. *Diff. puls.*	———, *De pulsuum differentiis libri IV.* See Gal. ed. Kühn, vol. VIII, pp. 493–765.
Gal. *Elem. Hipp.*	———, *De elementis ex Hippocratis sententia,* ed. P. De Lacy. *CMG* V 1.2.

Gal. *Exper. med.*
(**ATOM D23a**)

H. Schöne, "Eine Streitschrift
Galen's gegen die empirischen
Ärzte," *Sitzungsberichte der
königlich Preussischen Akademie der Wissenschaften
zu Berlin, Philosophisch-
historischen Classe* 51 (1901):
1255–1263; cf. R. Walzer, *On
Medical Experience.* London,
1944, pp. 93–96, 113–14.

Gal. *In Hipp. Epid.*
2

———, *In Hippocratis Epide-
miarum librum secundum
commentarii V,* ed. F. Pfaff.
CMG V 10.1.

Gal. *In Hipp. Epid.*
3

———, *In Hippocratis Epi-
demiarum librum tertium commentarii III,* ed. E. Wenke-
bach. *CMG* V 10.2.1.

Gal. *In Hipp. Epid.*
6

———, *In Hippocratis Epide-
miarum librum sextum com-
mentarii I–II,* ed. E. Wenke-
bach. *CMG* V 10.2.2.

Gal. *In Hipp. Med.*
off.

———, *In Hippocratis librum de
officina medici commentarii
III.* See Gal. ed. Kühn, vol.
XVIII.2, pp. 629–925.

Gal. *In Hipp. Nat.*
hom.

———, *In Hippocratis De natura hominis commentaria
III,* ed. J. Mewaldt. *CMG* V
9.1.

Gal. *Nat. fac.* ————, *De naturalibus facultatibus libri III,* ed. G. Helmreich, in Galen, *Scripta minora,* ed. I. Marquardt, I. Mueller, G. Helmreich, vol. 3, pp. 101–257. Leipzig, 1893.

Gal. *Nom. med.* ————, *Über die medizinischen Namen,* ed. M. Meyerhof and J. Schacht. *Abhandlungen der Preussischen Akademie der Wissenschaften,* 1931, Phil. Hist. Kl. 3.

Gal. *Plac. Hipp. Plat.* ————, *De placitis Hippocratis et Platonis,* ed. P. De Lacy. *CMG* V 4.1.2.

Gal. *Quod animi mores* _____, *Quod animi mores corporis temperamenta sequantur.* See Gal. ed. Kühn, vol. IV, pp. 767–822.

Ps.-Gal. *An animal sit* H. Wagner, *Galeni qui fertur libellus* Εἰ ζῷον τὸ κατὰ γαστρός. Diss. Marburg, 1914.

Ps.-Gal. *Def. med.* Ps.-Galenus, *Definitiones medicae.* See Gal. ed. Kühn, vol. VIII, pp. 346–462.

Ps.-Gal. *Hist. phil.* ————, *Historia philosopha.* See *Dox. Gr.*

Ps.-Gal. *In Hipp. Hum.* ————, *In Hippocratis De humoribus librum commentarii III.* See Gal. ed. Kühn, vol. XVI, pp. 1–488.

Gemin. *Elem.* — Geminus, *Elementa astronomiae,* ed. K. Manitius. Leipzig, 1898.

Gentili-Prato — B. Gentili and C. Prato, ed. *Poetarum elegiacorum testimonia et fragmenta.* Leipzig, 1988–2002.

GG — *Grammatici Graeci.* Leipzig, 1878–1902.

GGM — *Geographi Graeci Minores,* ed. K. Müller. Paris, 1855–1861.

Glauc. Rheg. — Glaucus Rhegius, in G. Lanata, ed. *Poetica Pre-platonica.* Florence, 1963, pp. 270–77.

Gnomol. Mon. Lat. — *Gnomologium Monacense Latinum,* in Caecilius Balbus, *De Nugis Philosophorum quae supersunt,* ed. E. Wölfflin. Basel, 1855.

Gnomol. Par. — *Gnomologium Parisinum,* ed. L. Sternbach, in *Rozprawy Akademii Umiejętnosći. Wydział Filologiczny,* ser. 2, vol. 5. Cracow, 1894.

Gnomol. Vat. — *Gnomologium Vaticanum,* ed. L. Sternbach, in *Wiener Studien* 9–11. Vienna, 1887–1889.

Gnomol. Vind. — K. Wachsmuth, "Die Wiener Apophthegmen-Sammlung," in *Festschrift zur Begrüssung der XXXVI. Philologen-Versammlung.* Freiburg-Tübingen, 1882, pp. 3–36.

Greg. Cor. *Dial.* — *Gregorii Corinthii et aliorum grammaticorum libri de dialectis linguae Graecae,* ed. G. H. Schaefer. Leipzig, 1811.

Harpocr. — Harpocratio, *Lexicon in decem oratores Atticos,* ed. W. Dindorf. Oxford, 1854. (Cf. ed. J. J. Keaney. Amsterdam, 1991.)

Hdn. — Herodianus, ed. A. Lentz, *GG* 3.1 and 3.2.

Hdn. *Prosod. cath.* (**EMP. D37**) — O. Primavesi and K. Alpers, "Empedokles im Wiener Herodian-Palimpsest," *Zeitschrift für Papyrologie und Epigraphik* 156 (2006): 27–37.

Hdt. — Herodotus, *Historiae,* ed. C. Hude. Oxford, 1908. (Cf. ed. N. G. Wilson. Oxford, 2015.)

Heph. *Ench.* — Hephaestio, *Enchiridion,* ed. M. Consbruch. Stuttgart, 1906.

Heracl. *Alleg.* — Heraclitus, *Allegoriae Homericae,* ed. F. Buffière. Paris, 1962.

Heracl. Lemb. — Heraclides Lembus. See *FHG,* vol. III, pp. 167–71.

Heracl. Pont. — See Wehrli.

Hercher — *Epistolographi Graeci,* ed. R. Hercher. Paris, 1873.

Herm. *In Phaedr.* — Hermias, *In Platonis Phaedrum Scholia,* ed. C. M. Lucarini and C. Moreschini. Berlin, 2012.

Herm. *Irris.*	Hermias, *Irrisio gentilium philosophorum,* ed. R. P. C. Hanson. Paris, 1993.
Hermog.	Hermogenes, *Opera,* ed. H. Rabe. Leipzig, 1913.
Hes. *Th.*	Hesiodus, *Theogonia,* ed. M. L. West. Oxford, 1966.
Hes. *Op.*	———, *Opera et dies,* ed. M. L. West. Oxford, 1978.
Hes. Frag.	*Fragmenta Hesiodea,* ed. R. Merkelbach and M. L. West. Oxford, 1967.
Hesych.	Hesychius, *Lexicon,* ed. K. Latte and P. A. Hansen. Berlin, 1953–2005.
Hier. *Chron.*	Hieronymus, *Chronicon,* ed. R. Helm. Berlin, 1984.
Hierocl. *In Carm. Aur.*	Hierocles, *In Aureum Pythagoreorum Carmen Commentarius,* ed. F. W. Koehler. Stuttgart, 1974.
Hipp. ed. Littré	Hippocrates, ed. E. Littré. Paris-London, 1839–1861.
Hipp. *Aer.*	———, *Airs, eaux, lieux,* ed. J. Jouanna. Paris, 1966.
Hipp. *Art.*	———, *De l'art,* ed. J. Jouanna. Paris, 1988.
Hipp. *Carn.*	———, *Des chairs,* ed. R. Joly. Paris, 1978.
Hipp. *Flat.*	———, *Des vents,* ed. J. Jouanna. Paris, 1988.

Hipp. *Genit.* —————, *De la génération, De la nature de l'enfant, Des maladies IV,* ed. R. Joly. Paris, 1970.

Hipp. *Loc. Hom.* —————, *Des lieux dans l'homme,* ed. R. Joly. Paris, 1978.

Hipp. *Morb. sacr.* —————, *La maladie sacrée,* ed. J. Jouanna. Paris, 2003.

Hipp. *Nat. hom.* —————, *De natura hominis,* ed. J. Jouanna. *CMG* I 1.3.

Hipp. *Nat. puer.* See Hipp. *Genit.*

Hipp. *Nutrim.* —————, *De l'aliment,* ed. R. Joly. Paris, 1972.

Hipp. *Oct.* —————, *Du foetus de huit mois,* ed. R. Joly. Paris, 1970.

Hipp. *Vet. med.* —————, *De l'ancienne médecine,* ed. J. Jouanna. Paris, 1990.

Hipp. *Vict.* —————, *De diaeta,* ed. R. Joly and S. Byl. *CMG* I 2.4.

Ps.-Hipp. *Epist.* W. Putzger, ed. *Hippocratis quae feruntur epistulae.* Gymn. Progr. Wurzen, 1914.

Hippob. M. Gigante, "Frammenti di Ippoboto: Contributo alla storia della storiografia filosofica," in A. Mastrocinque, ed. *Omaggio a Piero Treves.* Padua, 1983, pp. 151–93.

(Ps.-?) Hippol. *Ref.* Hippolytus, *Refutatio omnium haeresium,* ed. P. Wendland. Leipzig, 1916. (Cf. ed. M. Marcovich. Berlin-New York, 1986.)

Hom. *Il.*	Homerus, *Ilias,* ed. M. L. West. Stuttgart, 1998–2000.
Hom. *Od.*	———, *Odyssea,* ed. H. van Thiel. Hildesheim, 1991.
Hor.	Horatius, *Opera,* ed. S. Borzsák. Leipzig, 1984.
Huffman	C. Huffman, ed. *Archytas of Tarentum: Pythagorean, Philosopher and Mathematician King.* Cambridge, 2005.
Iambl. *Comm.*	Iamblichus, *De communi mathematica scientia liber,* ed. N. Festa. Leipzig, 1891.
Iambl. *In Nic.*	———, *In Nicomachi arithmeticam introductionem liber,* ed. H. Pistelli. Leipzig, 1894.
Iambl. *Myst.*	———, *Réponse à Porphyre (De Mysteriis),* ed. A. Segonds and H. D. Saffrey. Paris, 2013.
Iambl. *Protr.*	———, *Protrepticus,* ed. H. Pistelli. Leipzig, 1888.
Iambl. *VP*	———, *Vita Pythagorica,* ed. L. Deubner. Stuttgart, 1975.
Ps.-Iambl. *Theol.*	Ps.-Iamblichus, *Theologoumena arithmeticae,* ed. V. De Falco and U. Klein. Stuttgart, 1975.
IEG	*Iambi et Elegi Graeci ante Alexandrum cantati,* ed. M. L. West. Oxford, 1992.
IG	*Inscriptiones Graecae.* Berlin, 1873–.

Io. Lyd. *Mens.*	Joannes Lydus, *De mensibus,* ed. R. Wünsch. Leipzig, 1898.
Io. Lyd. *Ost.*	———, *Liber de ostentis et calendaria graeca omnia,* ed. C. Wachsmuth. Leipzig, 1897.
Ioan. Diac. Galen. *in Theog.*	H. Flach, ed. *Glossen und Scholien zur hesiodischen Theogonie.* Leipzig, 1876.
Ioli	R. Ioli, ed. *Gorgia di Leontini, Su ciò che non è.* Hildesheim-Zurich-New York, 2010.
Ion Chius	A. von Blumenthal, ed. *Ion von Chios: Die Reste seiner Werke.* Stuttgart, 1939.
Iren. *Adv. haer.*	Irenaeus, *Adversus haereses,* ed. A. Rousseau and L. Doutreleau. Paris, 1982.
Isid. Pelus. *Epist.*	Isidorus Pelusiotes, *Lettres,* ed. P. Evieux. Paris, 1997–.
Isocr.	Isocrates, *Orationes,* ed. F. Blass and G. E. Benseler. Leipzig, 1927.
Jul. *Or.*	Julianus, *Orationes,* ed. J. Bidez. Paris, 1963–64.
Just. *Epitoma*	Justinus, *Epitoma historiarum Philippicarum Pompei Trogi,* ed. O. Seel. Leipzig, 1985.
Just. M. *Apol.*	Justinus Martyr, *Apologia,* ed. C. Munier. Paris, 2006.

Juv.   A. *Persi Flacci et D. Juni Juvenalis Saturae,* ed. W. V. Clausen. Oxford, 1959.

K–A   *Poetae Comici Graeci,* ed. R. Kassel and C. Austin. Berlin, 1983–2012.

Lact. *Div. inst.*   Lactantius, *Divinarum institutionum libri septem,* ed. E. Heck and A. Wlosok. Munich-Leipzig, 2005–2011.

Lact. *Ira Dei*   ———, *La colère de Dieu,* ed. C. Ingremeau. Paris, 1982.

Laks   A. Laks, ed. *Diogène d'Apollonie. Édition, traduction et commentaire des fragments et témoignages.* Second edition, Sankt-Augustin, 2008.

Lampr. *Libr. Plut.*   Lamprias, *Librorum Plutarchi index,* ed. J. Irigoin, in Plutarque, *Œuvres Morales,* vol. 1.1, pp. cccxi–cccxviii. Paris, 1987.

Lanza   D. Lanza, ed. *Anassagora. Testimonianze e frammenti.* Florence, 1966.

Leszl   W. Leszl, ed. *I Primi Atomisti.* Florence, 2009.

LGPN   P. M. Fraser and E. Matthews, ed. *A Lexicon of Greek Personal Names.* Oxford, 1987–.

Liban. *Declam.*   Libanius, *Opera,* ed. R. Förster. Leipzig, 1903–1927.

Liv.	Livius, *Ab urbe condita,* ed. R. S. Conway et al. Oxford, 1914–1999.
Lobon	*Il Περὶ ποιητῶν di Lobone di Argo,* ed. V. Garulli. Bologna, 2004.
Longin.	Cassius Longinus, *Fragments: Art rhétorique,* ed. M. Patillon and L. Brisson. Paris, 2001.
Ps.-Longin.	*Libellus de sublimitate Dionysio Longino fere adscriptus,* ed. D. A. Russell. Oxford, 1968.
Luc.	Lucianus, *Opera,* ed. M. D. MacLeod. Oxford, 1987.
Ps.-Luc.	Ps.-Lucianus. See Luc.
Lucr.	Lucretius, *De rerum natura,* ed. C. Bailey. Oxford, 1947.
Lysias	Lysias, *Orationes cum fragmentis,* ed. C. Carey. Oxford, 2007.
M. Aur.	Marcus Aurelius, *Ad se ipsum,* ed. J. Dalfen. Leipzig, 1979.
Macr. *In Somn.*	Macrobius, *Commentarii in Somnium Scipionis,* ed. J. Willis. Stuttgart-Leipzig, 1994.
Mansfeld/Primavesi	J. Mansfeld and O. Primavesi, ed. *Die Vorsokratiker.* Stuttgart, 2011.
Marcell. *Thuc.*	Marcellinus, *Vita Thucydidis;* Anonymus, *Vita Thucydidis,* ed. L. Piccirilli. Genoa, 1985.

Martin-Primavesi	A. Martin and O. Primavesi, ed. *L'Empédocle de Strasbourg* (P. Strasb. gr. Inv. 1665–1666). Strasbourg, 1999.
Max. Tyr. *Diss.*	Maximus Tyrius, *Dissertationes,* ed. M. Trapp. Berlin, 1994.
Ps.-Max. Conf. *Loc. comm.*	Ps.-Maximus Confessor, *Loci communes,* ed. S. Ihm. Stuttgart, 2001.
Mayhew	R. Mayhew. *Prodicus the Sophist: Texts, Translations, and Commentary.* Oxford, 2011.
Melamp.	Melampus, Περὶ παλμῶν, in H. Diels, *Beiträge zur Zuckungsliteratur des Okzidents und Orients,* vol. I. Berlin, 1908.
Men. Rh.	Menander Rhetor, ed. D. A. Russell and N. G. Wilson. Oxford, 1981.
Metrod.	Metrodorus Epicureus, *Fragmenta,* ed. A. Koerte. Leipzig, 1890.
Mich. Eph. *In PA*	Michael Ephesius, *In libros de Partibus Animalium,* ed. M. Hayduck. *CAG* 22.2.
Min. Fel. *Octav.*	Minucius Felix, *Octavius,* ed. B. Kytzler. Stuttgart, 1992.
Mouraviev	S. N. Mouraviev, ed. *Heraclitea. Édition critique complète des témoignages sur la vie et l'œuvre d'Héraclite et des vestiges de son livre.* Sankt Augustin, 1999–.

Nicom. *Harm.*	Nicomachus, *Harmonia,* in *Musici scriptores graeci,* ed. C. Janus. Leipzig, 1895.
Nicom. *Intr. arith.*	———, *Introductionis arithmeticae libri II,* ed. R. G. Hoche. Leipzig, 1866.
Numen.	Numenius, *Fragments,* ed. E. Des Places. Paris, 1973.
Olymp. *In Alc.*	Olympiodorus, *Commentary on the First Alcibiades of Plato,* ed. L. G. Westerink. Amsterdam, 1982.
Olymp. *In Gorg.*	———, *In Platonis Gorgiam commentaria,* ed. L. G. Westerink. Leipzig, 1970.
Olymp. *In Meteor.*	———, *In Aristotelis Meteora commentaria,* ed. G. Stüve. *CAG* 12.2.
Ps.-Olymp. *Ars sacra*	Ps.-Olympiodorus, *De arte sacra.* See *Coll. Alchim.*
Oribas. *Coll. med.*	Oribasius, *Collectionum medicarum reliquiae,* ed. J. Raeder. *CMG* 6.2.2.
Orig. *Cels.*	Origenes, *Contra Celsum,* ed. P. Koetschau. Berlin, 1899. (Cf. ed. M. Marcovich. Leiden, 2001.)
Ovid. *Met.*	Ovidius, *Metamorphoses,* ed. R. J. Tarrant. Oxford, 2004.

P. Derveni	*The Derveni Papyrus*, ed. T. Kouremenos, G. Parassoglou, K. Tsantsanoglou. Florence, 2006.
P. Herc. 1012 (**EMP. D12**)	O. Primavesi, "Die Häuser von Zeus und Hades: zu Text und Deutung von Empedokles B 142 D.-K.," *Cronache Ercolanesi* 33 (2003): 53–68.
Palaeph. *Incred.*	Palaephatus, Περὶ ἀπίστων, ed. N. Festa. Leipzig, 1902.
Pamph.	*Nicobule e Panfila: Frammenti di storiche greche,* ed. S. Cagnazzi. Bari, 1997.
Panaet.	Panaetius Rhodius, *Fragmenta,* ed. M. van Straaten. Leiden, 1962.
Paus.	Pausanias, *Graeciae Descriptio,* ed. M. H. Rocha-Pereira. Leipzig, 1989–90.
Pendrick	G. J. Pendrick, ed. *Antiphon the Sophist. The Fragments.* Cambridge, 2002.
Petron. *Sat.*	Petronius Arbiter, *Satyricon reliquiae,* ed. K. Müller. Munich, 2003. First edition, 1961.
PGM	*Papyri Graecae magicae.* Stuttgart, 1973–74.
Phil.	Philo Alexandrinus, *Opera,* ed. L. Cohn and P. Wendland. Berlin, 1896–1926.

Philod. *Acad. Ind.*	Philodemus, *Storia dei filosofi. Platone e l'Accademia (P. Herc. 1021 e 164)*, ed. T. Dorandi. Naples, 1991.
Philod. *Ira*	———, *L'ira*, ed. G. Indelli. Naples, 1988.
Philod. *Lib. dic.*	———, *On Frank Criticism*, ed. D. Konstan et al. Atlanta, 1998.
Philod. *Mort.*	———, *On Death*, ed. W. B. Henry. Atlanta, 2009.
Philod. *Music.*	———, *De la musique*, livre IV, ed. D. Delattre. Paris, 2007.
Philod. *Piet.*	———, *De pietate*, ed. T. Gomperz. Leipzig, 1886; cf. part 1, ed. D. Obbink. Oxford, 1996.
Philod. *Piet.* Henrichs (**PROD. D15, R8**)	A. Henrichs, "Die Kritik der stoischen Theologie im *PHerc. 1428*," *Cronache Ercolanesi* 4 (1974): 5–32.
Philod. *Poem.* (P. Herc. 994)	F. Sbordone, *Ricerche sui Papiri Ercolanesi*, vol. II, pp. 1–113. Naples, 1976.
Philod. *Poem.* (P. Herc. 1676)	See Philod. *Poem.* (P. Herc. 994), pp. 189–267.
Philod. *Rhet.*	Philodemus, *Rhetorica*, ed. S. Sudhaus. Leipzig, 1892.
Philop. *Aetern.*	Joannes Philoponus, *De aeternitate mundi contra Proclum*, ed. H. Rabe. Leipzig, 1899.

61

Philop. *In An.*   ————, *In Aristotelis De anima libros commentaria,* ed. M. Hayduck. *CAG* 15.

Philop. *In Phys.*   ————, *In Aristotelis Physica commentaria,* ed. H. Vitelli. *CAG* 16.

Φιλοσόφων λόγοι   H. Schenkl, "Florilegia duo Graeca," in *Jahres-Bericht über das K. K. Akademische Gymnasium in Wien für das Schuljahr 1887–88,* pp. 1–18. Vienna, 1888.

Philostr.   Flavius Philostratus, *Opera,* ed. C. L. Kayser. Leipzig, 1870–71.

Phot. *Bibl.*   Photius, *Bibliothèque,* ed. R. Henry. Paris, 1959–1991.

Phot. *Lex.*   ————, *Lexicon,* ed. C. Theodoridis, vols. I–III. Berlin, 1982–2012.

Phryn. *Ecl.*   E. Fisher, ed. *Die Ekloge des Phrynichos.* Berlin, 1974.

Pind.   Pindarus, *Carmina cum fragmentis,* ed. B. Snell and H. Maehler. Leipzig, 1987–1989.

Plan. *In Hermog.*   Maximus Planudes, Σχόλια εἰς Ἰδέων tom. α-β, in *Rhetores graeci,* ed. C. Walz, vol. V. Stuttgart-Tübingen, 1833, pp. 439–561.

Plat.	Plato, *Opera,* tom. I, ed. E. A. Duke et al. Oxford, 1995; tom. II–V, ed. J. Burnet. Oxford, 1900–1907.
Plat. *Rep.*	———, *De re publica,* ed. S. R. Slings. Oxford, 2003.
Ps.-Plat.	Ps.-Plato. See Plat.
Plin. *Nat. hist.*	Plinius, *Naturalis historiae libri XXXVII,* ed. K. Mayhoff. Stuttgart-Berlin, 1967–2002.
Plot.	Plotinus, *Opera,* ed. P. Henry and H.-R. Schwyzer. Paris-Brussels, 1951–1973.
Plut.	Plutarchus, *Moralia,* ed. W. R. Paton et al. Leipzig-Berlin, 1993ff.; *Vitae parallelae,* ed. K. Ziegler and H. Gärtner. Leipzig, 1998.
Plut. Frag.	———, *Fragmenta:* Plutarchus, *Moralia,* vol. VII, ed. F. H. Sandbach. Leipzig, 1967.
Ps.-Plut.	Ps.-Plutarchus. See Plut.
Ps.-Plut. *Plac.*	———, *Opinions des philosophes,* ed. G. Lachenaud. Paris, 1993.
Ps.-Plut. *Strom.*	———, *Stromata,* in Eusebius, *Praeparatio evangelica.* See *Dox. Gr.*
PMG	*Poetae melici Graeci,* ed. D. L. Page. Oxford, 1962.

63

PMGF   *Poetarum melicorum Graecorum fragmenta,* vol. 1, ed. M. Davies. Oxford, 1991.

Pollux *Onom.*   Pollux, *Onomasticon,* ed. E. Bethe. Leipzig, 1900.

Polyb.   Polybius, *Historiae,* ed. T. Büttner-Wobst. Stuttgart, 1995.

Porph. *Abst.*   Porphyrius, *De l'abstinence,* ed. J. Bouffartigue and M. Patillon. Paris, 1977, 1979.

Porph. *Antr.*   ———, *De antro nympharum,* ed. J. M. Duffy et al. Buffalo, NY, 1969.

Porph. Frag.   ———, *Fragmenta,* ed. A. Smith. Leipzig, 1993.

Porph. *Gaur.*   ———, *Ad Gaurum,* ed. T. Dorandi, in *Porphyre: Sur la manière dont l'embryon reçoit l'âme,* ed. L. Brisson. Paris, 2012.

Porph. *In Ptol. Harm.*   ———, *In Ptolemaei Harmonica Commentaria,* ed. I. Düring. Göteborg, 1934.

Porph. *Introd. Tetr.*   ———, *Introductio in Tetrabiblum Ptolemaei,* ed. E. Boer and S. Weinstock, in *Catalogus Codicum Astrologorum Graecorum,* vol. V, part 4, pp. 187–228. Brussels, 1940.

Porph. *Quaest. Hom.*   ———, *Quaestionum Homericarum reliquiae,* ed. H. Schrader. Leipzig, 1880.

Porph. *Sent.*	————, *Sentences,* ed. L. Brisson et al. Paris, 2005.
Porph. *VP*	————, *Vita Pythagorae,* ed. A. Nauck. Leipzig, 1886.
Porph. *Vit. Plot.*	————, *Vita Plotini.* See Plot., vol. I, pp. 1–41.
Posid.	Posidonius, ed. L. Edelstein and I. G. Kidd. Cambridge, 1972–1999.
PPF	*Poetarum Philosophorum Fragmenta,* ed. H. Diels. Berlin, 1901.
Primavesi	O. Primavesi, ed. *Empedokles, Physika I.* Berlin-New York, 2008.
Prisc. *Inst.*	Priscianus, *Institutiones grammaticae,* ed. M. Hertz and H. Keil, in *Grammatici Latini,* vols. II, pp. 1–597, and III, pp. 1–377. Leipzig, 1855–1859.
Procl. *Chrestom.*	*Homeri Opera,* ed. T. W. Allen, vol. V, pp. 102–9. Oxford, 1912.
Procl. *In Alc.*	Proclus, *In Platonis Alcibiadem commentaria,* ed. L. G. Westerink. Amsterdam, 1954.
Procl. *In Crat.*	————, *In Platonis Cratylum,* ed. G. Pasquali. Leipzig, 1908.
Procl. *In Eucl.*	————, *In primum Euclidis Elementorum librum commentarii,* ed. G. Friedlein. Leipzig, 1873.

Procl. *In Hes. Op.*   ———, *Scholia in Hesiodi Opera et Dies,* ed. P. Marzillo. Tübingen, 2010.

Procl. *In Parm.*   ———, *In Platonis Parmenidem commentaria,* ed. C. Steel. Oxford, 2007–8.

Procl. *In Remp.*   ———, *In Platonis Rem Publicam commentaria,* ed. G. Kroll. Leipzig, 1899.

Procl. *In Tim.*   ———, *In Platonis Timaeum commentaria,* ed. E. Diehl. Leipzig, 1903–1906.

Procl. *Theol.*   ———, *Théologie platonicienne,* ed. H. D. Saffrey and L. G. Westerink. Paris, 2003.

Procop. *Mel. et Ant.*   E. Amato, "Un discorso inedito di Procopio di Gaza: In Meletis et Antoninae nuptias," *Revue des études tardo-antiques* 1 (2011–2012): 15–69.

Psell. *Lapid.*   Michael Psellus, *De lapidibus,* in *Opuscula logica, physica, allegorica, alia,* ed. J. M. Duffy. Stuttgart-Leipzig, 1992.

Ptol. *Harm.*   Ptolemaeus, *De harmonia,* ed. I. Düring. Göteborg, 1930.

Quintil. *Inst. or.*   Quintilianus, *Institutio oratoria,* ed. M. Winterbottom. Oxford, 1970.

Robinson   T. M. Robinson, ed. *Contrasting Arguments. An Edition of the Dissoi Logoi.* New York, 1979.

Ruf. Ephes. *Part. corp.*	Rufus Ephesius, *De partibus corporis humani,* ed. C. Daremberg and E. Ruelle. Paris, 1879.
Sapph.	Sappho et Alcaeus, *Fragmenta,* ed. M. E. Voigt. Amsterdam, 1971.
Satyr.	S. Schorn, ed. *Satyros aus Kallatis: Sammlung der Fragmente mit Kommentar.* Basel, 2004.
Schibli	H. S. Schibli, *Pherekydes of Syros.* Oxford, 1990.
Schol. Genav. in *Il.*	See Schol. in *Il.*
Schol. in Aesch. *Prom.*	*Scholia vetera in Aeschyli Prometheum Vinctum,* ed. J. Herington. Leiden, 1972.
Schol. in Apoll. Rhod.	*Scholia in Apollonium Rhodium vetera,* ed. C. Wendel. Berlin, 1935.
Schol. in Arat.	*Commentariorum in Aratum reliquiae,* ed. E. Maass. Berlin, 1898.
Schol. in Arist. *Cat.* (**EMP. R98**)	S. Ebbesen, "Boethius as an Aristotelian Scholar," in J. Wiesner, ed., *Aristoteles Werk und Wirkung,* vol. II, pp. 286–311. Berlin-New York, 1987.
Schol. in Arist. *Cael.*	M. Rashed, "Vestiges d'un commentaire alexandrin au *De caelo* d'Aristote," *L'Héritage aristotélicien: textes inédits de l'Antiquité,* pp. 219–67. Paris, 2007.

Schol. in Arist. *Metaph.*	*Scholia in Aristotelem,* ed. C. G. Brandis, in *Aristotelis opera,* vol. IV. Berlin, 1836.
Schol. in Arist. *Phys.* et *GC, Laur.* 87.7 (**EMP. D84– D86, R8, R13**)	M. Rashed, "La chronographie du système d'Empédocle: addenda et corrigenda," *Études philosophiques* 110 (2014): 315–42; cf. O. Primavesi, "Empedokles in Florentiner Aristoteles-Scholien," *Zeitschrift für Papyrologie und Epigraphik* 157 (2006): 27–40.
Schol. in Aristoph.	*Scholia in Aristophanem,* ed. W. J. W. Koster et al. Groningen, 1969–.
Schol. in Bas. *Hex.*	*Scholia in Basilii Hexaemeron,* ed. G. Pasquali. Berlin, 1910.
Schol. in Clem. Alex.	See Clem. Alex., vol. I, pp. 295–340.
Schol. in Dion. Thrax	*Scholia in Dionysii Thracis Artem grammaticam,* ed. A. Hilgard. *GG* 3.
Schol. in Eucl.	See Eucl. *Elem.*
Schol. in Eur.	*Scholia in Euripidem,* ed. E. Schwartz. Berlin, 1887–1891.
Schol. in Greg. Naz. *Orat.*	*Basilii aliorumque scholia in S. Gregorii orationes,* in *Gregorii Theologi Opera quae exstant omnia,* ed. J.-P. Migne, vol. II (*Patrologia Graeca,* vol. XXXVI), pp. 903–16. Paris, 1858.

Schol. in Hes. *Op.*	*Scholia vetera in Hesiodi Opera et Dies,* ed. A. Pertusi. Milan, 1955.
Schol. in *Il.*	*Scholia Graeca in Homeri Iliadem (scholia vetera),* ed. H. Erbse. Berlin, 1969–1988.
Schol. in Juv.	*Scholia in Iuvenalem vetustiora,* ed. P. Wessner. Stuttgart, 1967.
Schol. in Luc.	*Scholia in Lucianum,* ed. H. Rabe. Leipzig, 1906.
Schol. in Nic. *Ther.*	*Scholia in Nicandri Theriaca,* ed. A. Crugnola. Milan, 1971.
Schol. in Pind.	*Scholia vetera in Pindari carmina,* ed. A. B. Drachmann. Leipzig, 1903–1927.
Schol. in Plat.	*Scholia Platonica,* ed. G. Chase Greene. Hildesheim-Zürich-New York, 1988.
SEG	*Supplementum Epigraphicum Graecum,* ed. J. J. E. Hondius et al. Amsterdam-Leiden, 1923–.
Sen. *Contr.*	L. Annaeus Seneca Maior, *Oratorum et rhetorum sententiae divisiones colores,* ed. L. Håkanson. Leipzig, 1989.
Sen. *Epist.*	L. Annaeus Seneca, *Ad Lucilium Epistulae morales,* ed. L. D. Reynolds. Oxford, 1965.
Sen. *Prov.*	———, *De providentia,* in *Dialogorum liber 1,* ed. E. Hermes, pp. 1–20. Leipzig, 1923.

Sen. *Quaest. nat.*	———, *Naturales quaestiones,* ed. H. M. Hine. Stuttgart, 1996.
Sext. Emp.	Sextus Empiricus, *Opera,* ed. H. Mutschmann and J. Mau. Leipzig, 1914–1954.
SH	*Supplementum Hellenisticum,* ed. H. Lloyd-Jones and P. Parsons. Berlin, 1983.
Simon.	Simonides. See *PMG.*
Simpl. *In An.*	Simplicius, *In libros Aristotelis De anima Commentaria,* ed. M. Hayduck. *CAG* 11.
Simpl. *In Cael.*	———, *In Aristotelis De caelo Commentaria,* ed. J. L. Heiberg. *CAG* 7.
Simpl. *In Cat.*	———, *In Aristotelis Categorias Commentarium,* ed. C. Kalbfleisch. *CAG* 8.
Simpl. *In Phys.*	———, *In Aristotelis Physica Commentaria,* ed. H. Diels. *CAG* 9–10.
Solon	See *IEG.*
Sopat. *Quaest. div.*	Sopater, *Quaestionum divisio,* ed. M. Weißenberger. Würzburg, 2010.
Soph.	Sophocles, *Fabulae,* ed. H. Lloyd-Jones and N. G. Wilson. Oxford, 1990.
Soph. Frag.	See *TrGF.*

Soran. *Gyn.*	Soranus, *Gynaecia,* ed. J. Ilberg. Leipzig-Berlin, 1927.
Sosicr.	*I frammenti delle "Successioni dei filosofi,"* ed. R. Giannattasio Andria. Naples, 1989.
Speus. Frag. Isnardi-Parente	Speusippus, *Frammenti,* ed. M. Isnardi-Parente. Naples, 1980.
Speus. Frag. Tarán	L. Tarán, *Speusippus of Athens: A Critical Study.* Leiden, 1981.
Städele	A. Städele, ed. *Die Briefe des Pythagoras und der Pythagoreer.* Meisenheim am Glan, 1980.
Steph. Byz.	Stephanus Byzantius, *Ethnica,* ed. M. Billerbeck. Berlin-New York, 2006.
Stephens-Winkler	*Ancient Greek Novels: The Fragments,* ed. S. A. Stephens and J. J. Winkler. Princeton, 1995.
Stesich.	Stesichorus. See *PMGF.*
Stob.	Joannes Stobaeus, *Anthologium,* ed. C. Wachsmuth and O. Hense. Berlin, 1884–1912.
Strab.	Strabo, *Geographika,* ed. S. L. Radt. Göttingen, 2002–2011.
Suda	*Suidae lexicon,* ed. A. Adler. Leipzig, 1928–1938.
SVF	*Stoicorum veterum fragmenta,* ed. I. von Arnim. Leipzig, 1905–1924.

71

Sync. *Chron.*	Georgius Syncellus, *Ecloga chronographica,* ed. A. A. Mosshammer. Leipzig, 1984.
Synes.	Synesius, *Opuscula,* ed. N. Terzaghi. Rome, 1944.
Syr. *In Hermog.*	Syrianus, *In Hermogenem Commentaria,* ed. H. Rabe. Leipzig, 1892–1893.
Syr. *In Met.*	———, *In Metaphysica Commentaria,* ed. W. Kroll. *CAG* 6.1.
Tat. *Or.*	Tatianus, *Oratio ad Graecos,* ed. E. Schwartz. Leipzig, 1888. (Cf. ed. M. Marcovich. Berlin, 1995.)
Tert. *An.*	Tertullianus, *De anima,* ed. J. H. Waszink. Amsterdam, 1947.
Tert. *Apol.*	———, *Apologeticum,* ed. E. Dekkers. Turnhout, 1954.
Tert. *Cor.*	———, *De corona militis,* ed. J. Fontaine. Paris, 1966.
Them. *In Phys.*	Themistius, *In Aristotelis Physica paraphrasis,* ed. H. Schenkl. *CAG* 5.2.
Them. *Orat.*	———, *Orationes,* ed. H. Schenkl et al. Leipzig, 1971.
Theod. *Cur.*	Theodoretus, *Graecarum affectionum curatio,* ed. I. Raeder. Leipzig, 1904.

Theod. Prodr. *Epist.* Theodorus Prodromus, *Epistu-lae,* ed. J. P. Migne, in *Patrolo-giae cursus completus,* vol. 133, pp. 1239–92. Paris, 1864.

Theogn. Theognis. See *IEG.*

Theon Al. *In Almag.* Theon Alexandrinus, *In Ptol-emaei Almagesten,* ed. A. Rome. Rome, 1936–1943.

Theon Sm. *Exp.* Theon Smyrnaeus, *Expositio re-rum mathematicarum ad leg-endum Platonem utilium,* ed. E. Hiller. Leipzig, 1878.

Theophr. Theophrastus, *Opera omnia,* ed. F. Wimmer. Leipzig, 1854–1862.

Theophr. *CP* ———, *Les causes des phénomè-nes végétaux,* lib. 1–4, ed. S. Amigues. Paris, 2012–2015.

Theophr. Frag. *Theophrastus of Eresus: Sources for His Life, Writings, Thought, and Influence,* ed. W. W. For-tenbaugh, R. W. Sharples, P. M. Huby, and D. Gutas. Leiden-New York, 1995–2014.

Theophr. *HP* Theophrastus, *Recherches sur les plantes,* ed. S. Amigues. Paris, 1988–2006.

Theophr. *Ign.* ———, *De igne: A Post-Aristotelian View of the Nature of Fire,* ed. V. Coutant. Assen, 1971.

Theophr. *Metaph.* ————, *On First Principles,* ed. D. Gutas. Leiden-Boston, 2010.

Theophr. *Odor.* ————, *De odoribus,* ed. U. Eigler and G. Wöhrle. Stuttgart, 1993.

Theophr. *Pisc.* ————, *On Fish,* ed. R. W. Sharples, in W. W. Fortenbaugh and D. Gutas, ed. *Theophrastus. His Psychological, Doxographical, and Scientific Writings,* pp. 347–85. New Brunswick, NJ, 1992.

Theophr. *Sens.* ————, *De sensu.* See *Dox. Gr.*

Theophr. *Vert.* ————, *On Dizziness,* ed. R. W. Sharples. Leiden-Boston, 2003.

Thesleff H. Thesleff, ed. *The Pythagorean Texts of the Hellenistic Period.* Åbo, 1965.

Thrasyll. H. Tarrant, "The Testimonia of Thrasyllus," in *Thrasyllan Platonism.* Ithaca, NY, 1993, pp. 215–49.

Thuc. Thucydides, *Historiae,* ed. H. S. Jones. Oxford, 1966–67.

Timo Timo Phliasius, *Silli,* ed. M. Di Marco. Rome, 1989.

TrGF *Tragicorum graecorum fragmenta,* ed. B. Snell, R. Kannicht, S. Radt. Göttingen, 1971–2004.

Tzetz. *Chil.*	Joannes Tzetzes, *Historiarum variarum chiliades,* ed. G. Kiessling. Leipzig, 1826.
Tzetz. *In Aristoph. Plut.*	———, *Scholia in Aristophanis Plutum.* See Schol. in Aristoph.
Tzetz. *In Dion. Perieg.*	———, *In Dionysium Periegetem,* in Dionysius Periegetes, ed. G. Bernhardy. Leipzig, 1828.
Tzetz. *In Il.*	———, *Exegesis in Homeri Iliadem, Scholia ad Exegesin,* ed. G. Hermann. Leipzig, 1812.
Tzetz. *In Il.* 1.427 (**ANAXAG. D66d; ARCH. D17**)	F. Lasserre, "Archelai philos. fragm. novum," *Museum Criticum* 21–22 (1986–87): 187–97.
Untersteiner (Sophists)	M. Untersteiner, ed. (vol. 4 ed. with A. M. Battegazzore). *Sofisti. Testimonianze e frammenti,* 4 vols. Florence, 1954–1962.
Untersteiner (Zeno)	M. Untersteiner, ed. *Zenone. Testimonianze e frammenti.* Florence, 1963.
Val. Max.	Valerius Maximus, *Facta et dicta memorabilia,* ed. J. Briscoe. Stuttgart, 1998.
Vitruv.	Vitruvius, *De architectura libri decem,* ed. F. Krohn. Leipzig, 1912.
Wehrli	*Die Schule des Aristoteles,* ed. F. Wehrli. Basel, 1945–1978.

Wöhrle

G. Wöhrle et al., ed. *The Milesians: Thales.* Berlin, 2014.

Xen.

Xenophon, *Omnia opera,* ed. E. C. Marchant. Oxford, 1900–1920.

Xenocr.

Senocrate-Ermodoro: Frammenti, ed. M. Isnardi Parente. Naples, 1982.

OTHER LANGUAGES

Arabic and Hebrew

al-Šahrazūrī, *Nuzhat al-arwāḥ wa-rawḍat al-afrāḥ* (**ZEN. P3**)

F. Rosenthal, "Arabische Nachrichten über Zenon den Eleaten," *Orientalia* 6 (1937): 21–67.

Muḥammad ibn Umayl al-Tamīmī, *Kitāb al-mā' al-waraqī wa al-arḍ al-naġmiyya* (**ANAXIMAND. R21b**)

See *Turba Phil.:* ed. Ruska, p. 313.

Nic. Dam. *Plant.*

Nicolaus Damascenus, *De plantis,* ed. H. J. Drossaart Lulofs and E. L. J. Poortmann. Amsterdam-New York, 1989.

Turba Phil.	M. Plessner, *Vorsokratische Philosophie und griechische Alchemie in arabisch-lateinischer Überlieferung.* Wiesbaden, 1975. (Cf. J. Ruska, *Turba Philosophorum. Ein Beitrag zur Geschichte der Alchemie.* Berlin, 1931)

Armenian

Phil. *Prov.*	Philo, "De Providentia," in *Philonis Iudaei sermones tres hactenus inediti,* ed. J. B. Aucher. Venice, 1822.
Phil. *Quaest. Gen.*	———, "Quaestiones in Genesim," in *Philonis Iudaei paralipomena Armena,* ed. J. B. Aucher. Venice, 1826.

Syriac

Ps.-Plut. *Discipl.* (**PROT. D13**)	Plutarchus, *De exercitatione,* in P. de Lagarde, *Analecta Syriaca.* Leipzig-London, 1858, pp. 177–86.
Studia Sinaitica	A. Smith Lewis, "Catalogue of the Syriac Manuscripts in the Convent of S. Catharine on Mount Sinai," *Studia Sinaitica* 1 (1894): 26–38.

Iconography

Flashar (1998)	H. Flashar, ed. *Ueberweg. Grundriss der Geschichte der Philosophie. Die Philosophie der Antike. Bd. 2/1, Sophistik; Sokrates; Mathematik; Medizin.* Basel, 1998.
Flashar, Bremer, Rechenauer (2013)	H. Flashar, D. Bremer, and G. Rechenauer, eds. *Ueberweg. Grundriss der Geschichte der Philosophie. Die Philosophie der Antike. Bd. 1, Frühgriechische Philosophie.* 2 vols. Basel, 2013.
Richter	Gisela M. A. Richter, *The Portraits of the Greeks.* London, 1965.
Richter-Smith	———, *The Portraits of the Greeks,* abridged and revised by R. R. R. Smith. Ithaca, 1984.

GENERAL BIBLIOGRAPHY

In addition to this basic bibliography, readers should consult the bibliographies in the various introductions for additional references to works on individual thinkers or groups of thinkers.

BIBLIOGRAPHIES

Bell, Jr., G. G. and J. B. Allis. *Resources in Ancient Philosophy: An Annotated Bibliography of Scholarship in English, 1965–1989,* chapters 2–9. Metuchen, N. J., 1991.

Navia, L. E. *The Presocratic Philosophers: An Annotated Bibliography.* New York-London, 1993.

(On these two bibliographies, see: Berryman, S., A. P. D. Mourelatos, and R. K. Sharma. "Two Annotated Bibliographies on the Presocratics: A Critique and User's Guide," *Ancient Philosophy* 15 (1995): 471–94.)

Paquet, L., M. Roussel, and Y. Lafrance. *Les Présocratiques: Bibliographie analytique* (1879–1980). 3 vols. Montreal, 1988, 1989, and 1995.

Šijakovič, B. *Bibliographia Praesocratica: A Bibliographical Guide to the Studies of Early Greek Philosophy in*

Its Religious and Scientific Contexts with an Introductory Bibliography on the Historiography of Philosophy.
Paris, 2001.

REFERENCE MANUALS

Flashar, H., ed. *Ueberweg. Grundriss der Geschichte der Philosophie. Die Philosophie der Antike. Bd. 2/1, Sophistik; Sokrates; Mathematik; Medizin.* Basel, 1998.

Flashar, H., D. Bremer, and G. Rechenauer, eds. *Ueberweg. Grundriss der Geschichte der Philosophie. Die Philosophie der Antike. Bd. 1, Frühgriechische Philosophie.* 2 vols. Basel, 2013.

Goulet, R., ed. *Dictionnaire des philosophes antiques.* 5 vols. (vol. 5 in two parts) and a supplement, hitherto A-P. Paris, 1989–2012.

HERMANN DIELS' COLLECTED EDITIONS OF THE EARLY GREEK PHILOSOPHERS

Diels' Standard Edition

Diels, H., ed. *Die Fragmente der Vorsokratiker.* 6th ed. rev. W. Kranz, 3 vols. Berlin, 1951–1952; 1st ed., 1903.

(For English translations of the "B" fragments, see: Freeman, K. *Ancilla to the Pre-Socratic Philosophers: A Complete Translation of the Fragments in Diels Fragmente der Vorsokratiker.* Oxford, 1962.)

GENERAL BIBLIOGRAPHY

*Diels' Earlier Collection of the Greek Poet-
Philosophers*

Diels, H., ed. *Poetarum Philosophorum Fragmenta.* Berlin, 1901.

PARTIAL EDITIONS AND
TRANSLATIONS OF EARLY GREEK
PHILOSOPHICAL AND RELATED
TEXTS

Barnes, J. *Early Greek Philosophy.* London, 1987.
Curd, P., and R. D. McKirahan, Jr. *A Presocratics Reader.* Indianapolis, 1996.
Gagarin, M., and P. Woodruff, eds. *Early Greek Political Thought from Homer to the Sophists.* Cambridge, 1995.
Gemelli Marciano, M. L., ed. *Die Vorsokratiker.* 3 vols. Düsseldorf-Mannheim, 2007–2010.
Graham, D. W., ed. *The Texts of Early Greek Philosophy: The Complete Fragments and Selected Testimonies of the Major Presocratics.* Cambridge, 2010.
Kirk, G. S., J. E. Raven, and M. Schofield. *The Presocratic Philosophers.* 2nd ed. Cambridge, 1982.
Lanata, G., ed. *Poetica pre-platonica. Testimonianze e frammenti.* Florence, 1963.
Mansfeld, J., and O. Primavesi, eds. *Die Vorsokratiker.* Stuttgart, 2011.
Sprague, R. K., ed. *The Older Sophists.* Columbia SC, 1972.
Untersteiner, M., ed. (vol. 4 ed. with A. M. Battegazzore). *Sofisti: Testimonianze e frammenti.* 4 vols. Florence, 1954–1962.

81

Waterfield, R. *The First Philosophers. The Presocratics and Sophists.* Oxford, 2000.

Wheelwright, P. *The Presocratics.* New York, 1966.

Wright, M. R. *The Presocratics.* Bristol, 1985.

GENERAL WORKS ON EARLY GREEK PHILOSOPHY

Barnes, J. *The Presocratic Philosophers.* 2nd ed. London, 1982.

Burnet, J. *Early Greek Philosophy.* 4th ed. London, 1930; 1st ed., 1892.

Fraenkel, H. *Early Greek Poetry and Philosophy. A History of Greek Epic, Lyric, and Prose to the Middle of the Fifth Century.* Oxford, 1975.

Guthrie, W. K. C. *A History of Greek Philosophy.* Vol. 1, *The Earlier Presocratics and the Pythagoreans,* Cambridge, 1962; vol. 2, *The Presocratic Tradition from Parmenides to Democritus,* Cambridge, 1965; vol. 3, *The Fifth-Century Enlightenment,* Cambridge, 1969.

Hussey, E. *The Presocratics.* London, 1972 (repr., Indianapolis, 1995).

Laks, A. *Introduction à la 'philosophie présocratique.'* Paris, 2006.

McKirahan, R. D. *Philosophy Before Socrates.* Indianapolis, 1994.

Osborne, C. *Presocratic Philosophy: A Very Short Introduction.* Oxford, 2004.

Robinson, J. M. *An Introduction to Early Greek Philosophy.* Boston, 1968.

Sassi, M. M. *Gli inizi della filosofia: in Grecia.* Turin, 2009.

Taylor, C. C. W., ed. *Routledge History of Philosophy.* Vol. 1, *From the Beginning to Plato.* London, 1997.

Zeller, E. *Die Philosophie der Griechen in ihrer geschichtlichen Entwicklung,* ed. W. Nestle. Vol. 1.1, 7th ed., Leipzig, 1923; vol. 1.2, 6th ed., Leipzig, 1920.

(Updated Italian translation in E. Zeller-R. Mondolfo, *La filosofia dei Greci nel suo sviluppo storico.* Parte I, vols. 1–5. Florence, 1932–1969.)

STUDIES OF PARTICULAR ASPECTS OF EARLY GREEK PHILOSOPHY

Bremmer, J. *The Early Greek Concept of the Soul.* Princeton, 1983.

Cherniss, H. *Aristotle's Criticism of Presocratic Philosophy.* Baltimore, 1935.

Curd, P. K. *The Legacy of Parmenides: Eleatic Monism and Later Presocratic Thought.* Princeton, 1998.

Dicks, D. R. *Early Greek Astronomy to Aristotle.* London, 1970.

Furley, D. J. *The Greek Cosmologists.* Vol. 1, *The Formation of the Atomic Theory and its Earliest Critics.* Cambridge, 1987.

Graham, D. W. *Explaining the Cosmos: The Ionian Tradition of Scientific Philosophy.* Princeton, 2006.

———. *Science Before Socrates: Parmenides, Anaxagoras and the New Astronomy.* Oxford, 2013.

Jaeger, W. *The Theology of the Early Greek Philosophers.* Oxford, 1947.

Kerferd, G. B. *The Sophistic Movement.* Cambridge, 1981.

Lloyd, G. E. R. *Polarity and Analogy: Two Types of Argumentation in Early Greek Thought.* Cambridge, 1966.

———. *Early Greek Science: Thales to Aristotle.* London, 1970.

———. *Magic, Reason and Experience: Studies in the Origin and Development of Greek Science.* Cambridge, 1979.

Osborne, C. *Rethinking Early Greek Philosophy: Hippolytus of Rome and the Presocratics.* London, 1987.

Solmsen, F. *Intellectual Experiments of the Greek Enlightenment.* Princeton, 1975.

Stokes, M. C. *One and Many in Presocratic Philosophy.* Washington, DC, 1971.

West, M. L. *Early Greek Philosophy and the Orient.* London, 1971.

Wright, M. R. *Cosmology in Antiquity.* London, 1995.

COLLECTIONS OF ARTICLES

Anton, J. P., and G. L. Kustas, eds. *Essays in Ancient Greek Philosophy.* Vols. 1–2, 6. Albany, NY, 1971, 1983, 2001.

Caston, V., and D. W. Graham, *Presocratic Philosophy, Essays in Honour of Alexander Mourelatos.* Aldershot, 2002.

Curd, P., and D. W. Graham, eds. *The Oxford Handbook of Presocratic Philosophy.* Oxford, 2008.

Furley, D. J., and R. E. Allen, eds. *Studies in Presocratic Philosophy.* 2 vols. London, 1970, 1975.

Kerferd, G. B., ed. *The Sophists and Their Legacy.* Wiesbaden, 1981.

Laks, A., and C. Louguet, eds. *Qu'est-ce que la philosophie présocratique/What Is Presocratic Philosophy?* Lille, 2002.

GENERAL BIBLIOGRAPHY

Long A. A., ed. *The Cambridge Companion to Early Greek Philosophy*. Cambridge, 1999.

Mourelatos, A. P. D., ed. *The Pre-Socratics. A Collection of Critical Essays*. 2nd ed. Princeton, 1993.

Primavesi, O., and K. Luchner, eds. *The Presocratics from the Latin Middle Ages to Hermann Diels*. Stuttgart, 2011.

Sassi, M. M., ed. *La costruzione del discorso filosofico nell'età dei Presocratici/The Construction of Philosophical Discourse in the Age of the Presocratics*. Pisa, 2006.

Stern-Gillet, S., and Corrigan, K., eds., *Reading Ancient Texts, Essays in Honour of D. O'Brien*. 2 vols. Leiden, 2007.

Vlastos, G. *Studies in Greek Philosophy*. Edited by D. W. Graham. Vol. 1, *The Presocratics*. Princeton, 1995.

OTHER WORKS OF REFERENCE

Barker, A. *Greek Musical Writings*. Vol. 2, *Harmonic and Acoustic Theory*. Cambridge, 1989.

Burkert, W. *Greek Religion*. Cambridge, MA, 1985.

Neugebauer, O. *The Exact Sciences in Antiquity*. 2nd ed. Providence, RI, 1957.

REFERENCE MATERIALS

CONCORDANCE

a
DIELS-KRANZ > LAKS-MOST

1 B2: [2] COSM. T2a, T10a,
  T15
1 B10: [2] COSM. T2a, T10a
1 B12: [2] COSM. T13
1 B13: [2] COSM. T2a, T10a,
  T16
1 B17: [3] MOR. T34
1 B18: [3] MOR. T34
1 B19: [3] MOR. T34
1 B20: [3] MOR. T34
2 B14: [2] COSM. T21
3 B1: [3] MOR. T17
3 B5: [2] COSM. T2a, T10a
7 A1: [4] PHER. P1, P5, P10,
  P14, D2, R9
7 A2: [4] PHER. P2, P6, P9,
  D1, R5a, R5b, R15
7 A2a: [4] PHER. R10
7 A4: [4] PHER. P15
7 A5: [4] PHER. P3, R14, R16,
  R29, [5] THAL. R43
7 A6: [4] PHER. R13
7 A7: [4] PHER. R3
7 A7a: [4] PHER. R17
7 A8: [4] PHER. D6, R23
7 A9: [4] PHER. R20, R25, R30
7 A10: [4] PHER. R21

7 A11: [4] PHER. D3
7 A12: [4] PHER. R19
7 B1: [4] PHER. D5, D16b
7 B1a: [2] COSM. T11, [4]
  PHER. D7, R22
7 B2: [2] COSM. T1, [4]
  PHER. D9, D10, R28
7 B3: [4] PHER. D8, R24
7 B4: [4] PHER. P7, D11, D12,
  R1
7 B5: [4] PHER. D13, R27a
7 B6: [4] PHER. D14, R26
7 B7: [4] PHER. D15, R18
7 B9: [4] PHER. D16a
7 B11: [4] PHER. R8a
7 B12: [4] PHER. D17
7 B13: [4] PHER. D19, R8b
7 B13a: [4] PHER. D18
9 B1: [2] COSM. T21, T22
9 B2: [2] COSM. T11
10.3: [3] MOR. T35
11 A1: [5] THAL. P1a, P1b, P2,
  P3, P8, P11, P16, P17, P17a,
  P17b, P17c, P17d, P19, P20,
  D1, D11b, R1, R4, R6, R8,
  R11, R14, R15, R20, R25,
  R27, R31a, R34b, R37

11 A4: [5] THAL. P7
11 A5: [5] THAL. P9, P10
11 A6: [5] THAL. P6
11 A9: [5] THAL. P12
11 A10: [5] THAL. P15
11 A11: [5] THAL. P4, P5, R5
11 A12: [2] COSM. T6, T10a,
   [5] THAL. D3, R9, R32a
11 A13: [1] DOX. T14, [24]
   HIPPO D20
11 A13b: [5] THAL. D5
11 A13c: [5] THAL. R23
11 A14: [5] THAL. D7, R33a,
   R33b
11 A15: [5] THAL. D8, R24
11 A16: [5] THAL. D9
11 A17: [5] THAL. R16
11 A17a: [5] THAL. D6a, D6b,
   R18
11 A17b: [5] THAL. R19
11 A18: [5] THAL. R21
11 A19: [5] THAL. P18, R13
11 A20: [5] THAL. R26, R28,
   R29, R30
11 A21: [5] THAL. R31b, R31c
11 A22: [5] THAL. D10, D11a,
   R34a
11 A22a: [5] THAL. R36
11 A23: [5] THAL. R35, R38
11 B1: [1] DOX. T14, [5]
   THAL. R7, R10
11 B2: [5] THAL. R22
11 B3: [5] THAL. R44
12 A1: [6] ANAXIMAND. P2,
   P4, P11, D2, D5, D11, D31,
   R14
12 A2: [6] ANAXIMAND. D3
12 A3: [6] ANAXIMAND. P8

12 A4: [6] ANAXIMAND.
   R15
12 A5: [6] ANAXIMAND. P3,
   R16
12 A5a: [6] ANAXIMAND. P9
12 A6: [6] ANAXIMAND. P6,
   D4
12 A7: [6] ANAXIMAND. D1
12 A8: [6] ANAXIMAND. P10
12 A9: [1] DOX. T14, [6]
   ANAXIMAND. P5, D6, D12,
   R2, R7, R9
12 A9a: [6] ANAXIMAND. R8,
   [25] ANAXAG. R19
12 A10: [6] ANAXIMAND. D8
12 A11: [6] ANAXIMAND. P1,
   D7
12 A14: [6] ANAXIMAND.
   D10, R12, R13
12 A15: [6] ANAXIMAND.
   D9
12 A16: [6] ANAXIMAND.
   D12, R3, R4, R11
12 A17: [6] ANAXIMAND.
   D13, D14, D15, D16, D17,
   D18, R6, [7] ANAXIMEN.
   D11
12 A17a: [6] ANAXIMAND.
   D19
12 A18: [6] ANAXIMAND.
   D20, D22
12 A19: [6] ANAXIMAND.
   R17, [17] PYTHS. ANON.
   D39
12 A20: [6] ANAXIMAND.
   D21
12 A21: [6] ANAXIMAND.
   D23, D24, D25

12 A22: [6] ANAXIMAND.
D26, D27, D28
12 A23: [6] ANAXIMAND.
D33 a, D33b
12 A24: [6] ANAXIMAND.
D34
12 A25: [6] ANAXIMAND.
D29
12 A26: [6] ANAXIMAND.
D30, D32
12 A27: [6] ANAXIMAND.
D35a, D35b, D36
12 A28: [7] ANAXIMEN. D29
12 A29: [6] ANAXIMAND.
D37
12 A30: [6] ANAXIMAND.
D38, D39, D40, R18
12 B1: [6] ANAXIMAND. D6
12 B2: [6] ANAXIMAND. D7
12 B3: [6] ANAXIMAND. D9
12 B4: [6] ANAXIMAND. D23
13 A1: [7] ANAXIMEN. P1, R2
13 A2: [7] ANAXIMEN. P4
13 A3: [7] ANAXIMEN. P3
13 A4: [7] ANAXIMEN. D4,
[28] DIOG. D7
13 A5: [7] ANAXIMEN. D1,
D7
13 A6: [7] ANAXIMEN. D2
13 A7: [7] ANAXIMEN. P2, D3
13 A10: [7] ANAXIMEN. D5,
D6, R6, R7, R13a
13 A11: [7] ANAXIMEN. D10,
[28] DIOG. D16b
13 A13: [7] ANAXIMEN. D12
13 A14: [7] ANAXIMEN. D13,
D14, D16, D17
13 A14a: [7] ANAXIMEN. R8

13 A15: [7] ANAXIMEN. D15,
D18
13 A16: [7] ANAXIMEN. R9
13 A17: [7] ANAXIMEN. D21,
D23
13 A18: [7] ANAXIMEN. D24,
D25
13 A19: [7] ANAXIMEN. D26
13 A20: [7] ANAXIMEN. D19,
D20a, D20b, [25] ANAXAG.
D58, [27] ATOM. D110
13 A21: [7] ANAXIMEN. D27,
D28
13 A23: [7] ANAXIMEN. D30
13 B1: [7] ANAXIMEN. D8, R4
13 B2: [7] ANAXIMEN. D31,
R5
13 B3: [7] ANAXIMEN. R14
14.1: [10c] PYTH. c D4
14.2: [10a] PYTH. a P30
14.3: [10a] PYTH. a P16
14.4: [10a] PYTH. a P18, P24,
[10b] PYTH. b T12
14.5: [10a] PYTH. a P45
14.6: [10a] PYTH. a P11, P31
14.7: [10a] PYTH. a P34, P36,
P42
14.8: [8] XEN. P6, [10a] PYTH.
a P1, P5, P6, P19, P23, P37,
P39, [18] PYTHS. R6e
14.8a: [10a] PYTH. a P25, [10c]
PYTH. c D5
14.9: [10a] PYTH. a P20a, [10b]
PYTH. b T4a
14.10: [10a] PYTH. a P3, [10b]
PYTH. b T1, T29, [13] EUR.
P3
14.11: [10a] PYTH. a P21

14.12: [10b] PYTH. b T24,
  [10c] PYTH. c D12
14.13: [10a] PYTH. a P11,
  P46b, P46c, [10b] PYTH. b
  T22
14.14: [10b] PYTH. b T23
14.16: [10b] PYTH. b T25, T26,
  T27, T28
14.19: [10c] PYTH. c D1b, [18]
  PYTHS. R45a, R45b
14.21: [10c] PYTH. c D13
15.: [10b] PYTH. b T31
17.1: [10a] PYTH. a P10, [18]
  PYTHS. R64
17.3: [11] HIPPAS. P3
18.1: [11] HIPPAS. D1
18.2: [10b] PYTH. b T16, T18,
  [11] HIPPAS. P1a, P1b
18.3: [11] HIPPAS. D2
18.4: [10b] PYTH. b T8, T20,
  [11] HIPPAS. P2
18.5: [10b] PYTH. b T33
18.7: [1] DOX. T14, [11] HIP-
  PAS. D3, D4
18.9: [11] HIPPAS. D5
18.12: [11] HIPPAS. D7
18.13: [11] HIPPAS. D8
18.14: [11] HIPPAS. D9
18.15: [11] HIPPAS. D6, [14]
  ARCHY. D8
19.1: [10b] PYTH. b T32
21 A1: [8] XEN. P1, P8, P14,
  P15, P21, P22, D1, D20,
  D24, R8a, R19
21 A2: [8] XEN. P9, P11
21 A4: [8] XEN. R8b
21 A5: [8] XEN. P12
21 A6: [8] XEN. P2
21 A7: [8] XEN. P3

21 A8: [8] XEN. P4, R3
21 A9: [8] XEN. P5a, P5b
21 A10: [8] XEN. P6
21 A11: [8] XEN. P13
21 A12: [8] XEN. P16
21 A13: [8] XEN. P17
21 A14: [8] XEN. P18
21 A15: [43] DRAM. T3
21 A16: [8] XEN. P19
21 A17: [8] XEN. P20
21 A19: [8] XEN. D7
21 A20: [8] XEN. D2
21 A22: [8] XEN. D3
21 A23: [8] XEN. D4
21 A24: [8] XEN. D5
21 A25: [8] XEN. R17, R27,
  [19] PARM. R1
21 A26: [8] XEN. R28
21 A27: [8] XEN. R29
21 A28: [8] XEN. R6, R14
21 A29: [1] DOX. T4, [8] XEN.
  D25, R1
21 A30: [8] XEN. P10, R2, R12,
  [21] MEL. R7
21 A31: [8] XEN. R4, R5
21 A32: [8] XEN. D23
21 A33: [8] XEN. P7, D22, R20
21 A34: [8] XEN. R23
21 A35: [8] XEN. R16, R21a,
  R22
21 A36: [8] XEN. D6c, D27,
  R11, R24, R25a, R25b, R26
21 A37: [8] XEN. R7
21 A38: [8] XEN. D36
21 A39: [8] XEN. D38
21 A40: [8] XEN. D28
21 A41: [8] XEN. D34
21 A41a: [8] XEN. D31, D35
21 A42: [8] XEN. D33

CONCORDANCE a (DK > LM)

21 A43: [8] XEN. D29
21 A44: [8] XEN. D37
21 A45: [8] XEN. D40
21 A46: [8] XEN. D32
21 A47: [8] XEN. D42, D43,
  R13a, R13b
21 A48: [8] XEN. D45
21 A49: [8] XEN. R10, R18
21 A50: [8] XEN. D47
21 A51: [8] XEN. D48
21 A52: [8] XEN. D15a, D15b
21 B1: [8] XEN. D59
21 B2: [8] XEN. D61
21 B3: [8] XEN. D62
21 B4: [8] XEN. D63
21 B5: [8] XEN. D60
21 B6: [8] XEN. D69
21 B7: [8] XEN. D64, [10a]
  PYTH. a P32
21 B8: [8] XEN. D66
21 B9: [8] XEN. D67
21 B10: [8] XEN. D10
21 B11: [8] XEN. D8
21 B12: [8] XEN. D9
21 B13: [8] XEN. D11
21 B14: [8] XEN. D12
21 B15: [8] XEN. D14
21 B16: [8] XEN. D13
21 B17: [8] XEN. D55
21 B18: [8] XEN. D53
21 B20: [8] XEN. D65
21 B21: [8] XEN. D68
21 B21a: [8] XEN. D56
21 B22: [8] XEN. D54
21 B23: [8] XEN. D16
21 B24: [8] XEN. D17
21 B25: [8] XEN. D18
21 B26: [8] XEN. D19
21 B27: [8] XEN. D27

21 B28: [8] XEN. D41
21 B29: [8] XEN. D25
21 B30: [8] XEN. D6a, D46
21 B31: [8] XEN. D30
21 B32: [8] XEN. D39
21 B33: [8] XEN. D26
21 B34: [8] XEN. D49
21 B35: [8] XEN. D50
21 B36: [8] XEN. D51
21 B37: [8] XEN. D44
21 B38: [8] XEN. D52
21 B39: [8] XEN. D6b, D57
21 B40: [8] XEN. D70
21 B41: [8] XEN. D58
21 C1: [43] DRAM. T72
21 C2: [43] DRAM. T73
22 A1: [9] HER. P1, P3, P4, P6,
  P9, P11, P13, P14, P16, R1a,
  R1c, R3a, R3b, R3c, R5b,
  R5c, R16, R46a, R46b, R93a,
  R94, R97, R98
22 A1a: [9] HER. P2, P5, P17,
  R11
22 A3: [9] HER. P8
22 A3b: [9] HER. P7
22 A4: [9] HER. R5a, R6, R7
22 A5: [1] DOX. T14, [9] HER.
  R45
22 A6: [1] DOX. T3, [9] HER.
  D65b, R29, R47
22 A7: [9] HER. R37
22 A9: [9] HER. P15
22 A10: [1] DOX. T4, [9] HER.
  R31, R35, [22] EMP. D79a
22 A11: [9] HER. R65
22 A13: [9] HER. R64
22 A14: [9] HER. D96
22 A15: [9] HER. R43, R48a,
  [43] DRAM. T44

93

22 A16: [9] HER. R59, R60, R73
22 A17: [9] HER. R48b
22 A18: [9] HER. R66
22 A19: [9] HER. D69
22 A20: [9] HER. R58
22 A21: [9] HER. D115
22 A22: [9] HER. D23
22 B1: [9] HER. D1, D110, R86
22 B2: [9] HER. D2
22 B3: [9] HER. D89b
22 B5: [9] HER. D15
22 B6: [9] HER. D91a
22 B7: [9] HER. D34
22 B8: [9] HER. D62
22 B9: [9] HER. D79
22 B10: [9] HER. D47, D90
22 B12: [9] HER. D65a, D102, R51
22 B13: [9] HER. D80a
22 B14: [9] HER. D18
22 B15: [9] HER. D16
22 B16: [9] HER. D83
22 B17: [9] HER. D3
22 B18: [9] HER. D37, R81
22 B19: [9] HER. D5
22 B20: [9] HER. D118
22 B21: [9] HER. D72
22 B22: [9] HER. D39, R79
22 B23: [9] HER. D55
22 B24: [9] HER. D122a, R87
22 B25: [9] HER. D122b, R87
22 B26: [9] HER. D71, R85
22 B27: [9] HER. D120, R87
22 B28: [9] HER. D19, D28, R83
22 B29: [9] HER. D13

22 B30: [9] HER. D85, R13, R63, R82
22 B31: [9] HER. D86, R82
22 B32: [9] HER. D45
22 B33: [9] HER. D108
22 B34: [9] HER. D4
22 B35: [9] HER. D40
22 B36: [9] HER. D100
22 B37: [9] HER. D80b
22 B39: [9] HER. D11
22 B40: [9] HER. D20, [10a] PYTH. a P27
22 B41: [9] HER. D44
22 B42: [9] HER. D21
22 B43: [9] HER. D112
22 B44: [9] HER. D106
22 B45: [9] HER. D98
22 B46: [9] HER. R108
22 B47: [9] HER. D107
22 B48: [9] HER. D53
22 B49: [9] HER. D12
22 B49a: [9] HER. R9
22 B50–B67: [9] HER. R86
22 B50: [9] HER. D46
22 B51: [9] HER. D49, R32, R90b
22 B52: [9] HER. D76
22 B53: [9] HER. D64
22 B54: [9] HER. D50
22 B55: [9] HER. D31
22 B56: [9] HER. D22
22 B57: [9] HER. D25a
22 B58: [9] HER. D57
22 B59: [9] HER. D52
22 B60: [9] HER. D51
22 B61: [9] HER. D78
22 B62: [9] HER. D70, R84
22 B63: [9] HER. D123

CONCORDANCE a (DK > LM)

22 B64: [9] HER. D82
22 B65: [9] HER. D88
22 B66: [9] HER. D84
22 B67: [9] HER. D48
22 B67a: [9] HER. R71b
22 B68: [9] HER. D17
22 B70: [9] HER. D6
22 B71: [9] HER. R54
22 B72: [9] HER. R54
22 B73: [9] HER. R54
22 B74: [9] HER. D7, R54,
 R96
22 B75: [9] HER. R55
22 B76: [9] HER. R54
22 B77: [9] HER. D101, R90a
22 B78: [9] HER. D74
22 B79: [9] HER. D75
22 B80: [9] HER. D63
22 B81: [9] HER. D27
22 B82: [9] HER. D81, R33
22 B83: [9] HER. D77, R33
22 B84a: [9] HER. D58, R88
22 B84b: [9] HER. D109, R88
22 B85: [9] HER. D116
22 B86: [9] HER. D38
22 B87: [9] HER. D8
22 B88: [9] HER. D68
22 B89: [9] HER. R56
22 B90: [9] HER. D87
22 B92: [9] HER. D42
22 B93: [9] HER. D41
22 B94: [9] HER. D89c
22 B95: [9] HER. D113, R102c,
 R102e
22 B96: [9] HER. D119, R89
22 B97: [9] HER. D9
22 B98: [9] HER. D121
22 B99: [9] HER. D94

22 B101: [9] HER. D36
22 B101a: [9] HER. D32
22 B102: [9] HER. D73
22 B103: [9] HER. D54
22 B104: [9] HER. D10
22 B105: [9] HER. D24
22 B106: [9] HER. D25b, R12
22 B107: [9] HER. D33
22 B108: [9] HER. D43
22 B110: [9] HER. D117
22 B111: [9] HER. D56
22 B112: [9] HER. D114a,
 D114b
22 B113: [9] HER. D29
22 B114: [9] HER. D105
22 B115: [9] HER. D99
22 B116: [9] HER. D30
22 B117: [9] HER. D104
22 B118: [9] HER. D103,
 R101a, R101b, R101c,
 R101d, R101e, R101f, R101g,
 R101h, R101i, R101j, R101l
22 B119: [9] HER. D111
22 B120: [9] HER. D93a, D93b
22 B121: [9] HER. D14
22 B122: [9] HER. D61
22 B123: [9] HER. D35, R100f,
 R100g
22 B124: [9] HER. D60
22 B125: [9] HER. D59
22 B125a: [9] HER. R114
22 B126: [9] HER. D67
22 B129: [9] HER. D26, [10a]
 PYTH. a P28
22 B130: [9] HER. R116
22 B131: [9] HER. R109
22 B132: [9] HER. R110
22 B133: [9] HER. R111

95

22 B134: [9] HER. R112
22 B135: [9] HER. R113
22 C1: [29] MED. T9, T14
22 C2: [29] MED. T12
22 C3.1: [9] HER. R93b
22 C4: [9] HER. R52
22 C5: [9] HER. R99
23 A6: [1] DOX. T2, [9] HER. R30
23 B1: [43] DRAM. T4
23 B2: [43] DRAM. T8
23 B4: [43] DRAM. T6
23 B5: [43] DRAM. T7
23 B9: [43] DRAM. T1
23 B12: [43] DRAM. T2
23 B17: [43] DRAM. T5
23 B56: [43] DRAM. T9
24 A1: [23] ALCM. P2, P3, D1a, D3, D4
24 A2: [23] ALCM. D1b, D2
24 A3: [1] DOX. T6, [23] ALCM. P1, D5, R1
24 A4: [23] ALCM. D6, D7, D8
24 A5: [1] DOX. T15, [23] ALCM. D11, D12a, D13a, D15a, D16, D18, D19a
24 A6: [23] ALCM. D12b
24 A7: [23] ALCM. D14, R2
24 A8: [23] ALCM. D13b, D19b
24 A9: [23] ALCM. D15b
24 A10: [23] ALCM. D17, R6
24 A11: [29] MED. T23
24 A12: [23] ALCM. D9, R3, R4, R5
24 A13: [19] PARM. D44, [23] ALCM. D21, D22, D23, D26, D27, [25] ANAXAG. D84, D85
24 A14: [23] ALCM. D25

24 A15: [23] ALCM. D20
24 A16: [23] ALCM. D29
24 A17: [23] ALCM. D28
24 A18: [23] ALCM. D32
24 B1: [23] ALCM. D4, D10
24 B1a: [23] ALCM. D11 n. 1
24 B2: [23] ALCM. D31
24 B3: [23] ALCM. D24
24 B4: [23] ALCM. D30
24 B5: [23] ALCM. P4
25.1: [10b] PYTH. b T34
27.: [10b] PYTH. b T35
28 A1: [10c] PYTH. c D14, [19] PARM. P1, P6a, P8, P20, D2, D22, D33a, D40, D53a, R40, R64, R68
28 A2: [19] PARM. P6b
28 A3: [19] PARM. P16
28 A4: [19] PARM. P10, R66, R67
28 A5: [19] PARM. P4a, P4b, P12a, P12b, P12c, R6, R62
28 A6: [19] PARM. P5
28 A7: [19] PARM. P7, R13
28 A8: [19] PARM. P18
28 A9: [19] PARM. P14
28 A11: [19] PARM. P2, P3
28 A12: [19] PARM. P9, P21, P22
28 A13: [19] PARM. D1, [21] MEL. D1a
28 A14: [19] PARM. D3, R7
28 A15: [19] PARM. R2a
28 A16: [19] PARM. R2b
28 A18: [19] PARM. R4
28 A19: [19] PARM. R51
28 A20: [19] PARM. R3a, R3b, R5b
28 A21: [19] PARM. R73

28 A22: [19] PARM. D32, R29
28 A23: [19] PARM. R30, R60
28 A24: [19] PARM. R12
28 A25: [19] PARM. R47
28 A26: [19] PARM. R25a
28 A28: [19] PARM. R27, R50
28 A29: [19] PARM. R28, [21]
  MEL. R24a
28 A31: [19] PARM. R36
28 A32: [19] PARM. R55a
28 A33: [19] PARM. R54
28 A34: [19] PARM. R17, R53b
28 A36: [19] PARM. R34, R35,
  [21] MEL. R24b, R24c
28 A37: [19] PARM. D15a,
  D15b, D17, D18, R59
28 A38: [19] PARM. D19
28 A39: [19] PARM. D20
28 A40: [19] PARM. D21
28 A40a: [19] PARM. D22, D23
28 A41: [19] PARM. D26
28 A42: [19] PARM. D29, D30
28 A43: [19] PARM. D25
28 A43a: [19] PARM. D24
28 A44: [19] PARM. D33b, D36
28 A44a: [19] PARM. D37,
  D38, D39
28 A45: [19] PARM. D53b,
  D54, D55, D56
28 A46: [9] HER. R44, [19]
  PARM. D52, R61
28 A46a: [19] PARM. D60
28 A46b: [19] PARM. D59
28 A47: [19] PARM. D57, [22]
  EMP. D212
28 A48: [19] PARM. R69
28 A49: [22] EMP. R30
28 A50: [19] PARM. D58
28 A51: [19] PARM. D41

28 A52: [19] PARM. D43, [22]
  EMP. D173b
28 A53: [19] PARM. D42, D45,
  D47
28 A54: [19] PARM. D48, D50
28 B1: [19] PARM. D4, R8,
  R16, R39, R52
28 B2: [19] PARM. D6
28 B3: [19] PARM. D6
28 B4: [19] PARM. D10, R72
28 B5: [19] PARM. D5
28 B6: [9] HER. R15, [19]
  PARM. D7
28 B7: [19] PARM. D8, R40,
  R42
28 B8: [19] PARM. D8, R11,
  R18, R21, R24, R26, R37,
  [21] MEL. R2a, [27] ATOM.
  R12
28 B9: [19] PARM. D13
28 B10: [19] PARM. D9, D12,
  R53a
28 B11: [19] PARM. D11
28 B12: [19] PARM. D14a,
  D14b
28 B13: [19] PARM. D16, D61,
  R56a, R57, R58
28 B14: [19] PARM. D27
28 B15: [19] PARM. D28
28 B15a: [19] PARM. D35
28 B16: [19] PARM. D51
28 B17: [19] PARM. D46
28 B18: [19] PARM. D49
28 B19: [19] PARM. D62, R16,
  R52
28 B21: [19] PARM. D31
29 A1: [20] ZEN. P1a, P4, P8,
  P9, P10, P17, R7, R39, [21]
  MEL. R19

29 A2: [20] ZEN. P1b, R35
29 A3: [20] ZEN. P2
29 A4: [20] ZEN. P7, P11, R6
29 A5: [20] ZEN. P12
29 A6: [20] ZEN. P13
29 A10: [20] ZEN. R4
29 A11: [20] ZEN. P5a, P5b,
    P6
29 A12: [20] ZEN. R2
29 A13: [20] ZEN. R3
29 A14: [20] ZEN. R36
29 A15: [20] ZEN. P14, D2,
    D3, R9, R27b
29 A16: [20] ZEN. D10
29 A19: [20] ZEN. P15
29 A20: [20] ZEN. P16
29 A21: [20] ZEN. D8, R11,
    R14
29 A22: [20] ZEN. D9, R30,
    R31
29 A23: [20] ZEN. R5, R37,
    [21] MEL. D18
29 A24: [20] ZEN. D13a, R22,
    R23
29 A25: [20] ZEN. D1, D14,
    D19, R17
29 A26: [20] ZEN. D15a
29 A27: [20] ZEN. D16a, D16b
29 A28: [20] ZEN. D18, R21
29 A29: [20] ZEN. D12a, D12b,
    R16
29 A30: [20] ZEN. R38
29 B1: [20] ZEN. D5, D6
29 B2: [20] ZEN. D7, R12
29 B3: [20] ZEN. D11
29 B4: [20] ZEN. D17, R15
30 A1: [19] PARM. P17, [21]
    MEL. P1, P2, P5, P6, D17,
    R27

30 A2: [21] MEL. P3, P7
30 A3: [21] MEL. P4, P8
30 A4: [21] MEL. D1b
30 A5: [2] COSM. T11, [21]
    MEL. D19, R3, R17a, R17b,
    R17c, R17d, R17e, R17f
30 A6: [21] MEL. R1, R28, [29]
    MED. T6
30 A7: [21] MEL. R5
30 A8: [21] MEL. D12a, D12b
30 A9: [21] MEL. D15, R24d
30 A10: [21] MEL. R9a, R9b,
    R9c, R10
30 A11: [21] MEL. R11
30 A12: [21] MEL. R25
30 A13: [21] MEL. R26
30 A14: [21] MEL. D14, R18
30 B1: [21] MEL. D2a
30 B2: [21] MEL. D3
30 B3: [21] MEL. D4
30 B4: [21] MEL. D5
30 B5: [21] MEL. D7
30 B6: [21] MEL. D6
30 B7: [21] MEL. D10
30 B8: [21] MEL. D11, R8
30 B9: [21] MEL. D8
30 B10: [21] MEL. D9
30 B11: [21] MEL. R29
30 B12: [21] MEL. R30
31 A1: [22] EMP. P1, P3a, P3b,
    P5a, P5b, P6, P7, P8a, P8b,
    P8c, P8d, P9, P10, P12, P13,
    P14, P15, P16, P18, P19, P20,
    P21, P22, P24, P25a, P25b,
    P27, P29, P30, P31, D1,
    D115, D128, D135b, R1b,
    R5a, R37, R91
31 A2: [19] PARM. P13, [22]
    EMP. P4, P26, D2

31 A4: [24] HIPPO D6

31 A8: [22] EMP. P11

31 A9: [22] EMP. P2

31 A12: [22] EMP. D3

31 A14: [22] EMP. R85

31 A15: [22] EMP. P17

31 A17: [22] EMP. P23

31 A19: [22] EMP. R5b

31 A20: [22] EMP. P28a, P28b

31 A21: [22] EMP. R31

31 A22: [22] EMP. R1a

31 A23: [22] EMP. R96

31 A24: [22] EMP. R3a, R3b

31 A25: [22] EMP. R1c, R2a

31 A27: [22] EMP. R36

31 A28: [22] EMP. D80

31 A29: [1] DOX. T4, [22]
EMP. D78

31 A30: [22] EMP. D97, D127,
D134c, D239

31 A31: [22] EMP. R41

31 A32: [22] EMP. R28a

31 A33: [22] EMP. D56, R89,
R90, R92

31 A35: [22] EMP. D103

31 A37: [22] EMP. R11a

31 A38: [22] EMP. D85a

31 A42: [22] EMP. D82, D83,
R13a

31 A43: [22] EMP. R10, R27

31 A43a: [22] EMP. R9

31 A45: [22] EMP. R28b

31 A46: [22] EMP. D81

31 A47: [22] EMP. R26

31 A49: [22] EMP. D99a, D99b

31 A50: [22] EMP. D114, D119,
D129

31 A51: [22] EMP. D118

31 A52: [22] EMP. D79b

31 A53: [22] EMP. D121a

31 A54: [22] EMP. D121b

31 A56: [22] EMP. D126a,
D126b

31 A57: [22] EMP. D221, R16

31 A58: [22] EMP. D120,
D130

31 A59: [22] EMP. D133

31 A60: [22] EMP. D134a,
D134b, D135a

31 A61: [22] EMP. D136

31 A62: [9] HER. R49, [22]
EMP. D142

31 A63: [22] EMP. D146a,
D146b

31 A64: [22] EMP. D145

31 A65: [22] EMP. D144

31 A66: [22] EMP. D100a,
D100b, D147c, D204

31 A67: [22] EMP. D117a,
D117b

31 A68: [22] EMP. D110

31 A69: [22] EMP. D111, D112

31 A69a: [22] EMP. D223

31 A70: [22] EMP. D150, D245,
D246, D250a, D250b,
D250c, D250d, D250e, R17,
[27] ATOM. D200

31 A71: [22] EMP. R6, [29]
MED. T7a, T7b

31 A72: [22] EMP. D151

31 A73: [22] EMP. D247, R21

31 A74: [22] EMP. D170a,
D170b, D202

31 A75: [22] EMP. D178a

31 A77: [22] EMP. D203b,
D205

31 A78: [22] EMP. D189, D194,
R23

31 A79: [22] EMP. D163
31 A80: [22] EMP. D161
31 A81: [22] EMP. D173a,
 D174, D175, D176, D180,
 D181, D182, D183, D184,
 R19
31 A82: [22] EMP. D186
31 A83: [22] EMP. D165, D166
31 A84: [22] EMP. D167
31 A85: [22] EMP. D206a,
 D206b, R29
31 A86: [1] DOX. T15, [9]
 HER. R44, [22] EMP. D211,
 D218, D226, D229, D233,
 D235, D237, R25
31 A87: [22] EMP. D210
31 A88: [22] EMP. D225
31 A89: [22] EMP. D148
31 A90: [22] EMP. D212, D220
31 A91: [22] EMP. D219, R24
31 A92: [22] EMP. D209, D222
31 A93: [22] EMP. D227
31 A94: [22] EMP. D230, D234,
 R18
31 A95: [22] EMP. D203a,
 D236a, D236b
31 A96: [22] EMP. D238b
31 A97: [22] EMP. D238a
31 B1: [22] EMP. D41
31 B2: [22] EMP. D42, R42
31 B3: [22] EMP. D44, R42, R74
31 B4: [22] EMP. D47
31 B5: [22] EMP. D258, R45
31 B6: [22] EMP. D57
31 B7: [22] EMP. D59
31 B8: [22] EMP. D53, R35
31 B9: [22] EMP. D54
31 B10: [22] EMP. D55

31 B11: [22] EMP. D51
31 B12: [22] EMP. D48
31 B13: [22] EMP. D49, D88
31 B14: [22] EMP. D50
31 B15: [22] EMP. D52
31 B16: [22] EMP. D63, R89
31 B17: [22] EMP. D73, R68
31 B18: [22] EMP. D65
31 B19: [22] EMP. D62, R93
31 B20: [22] EMP. D73, R79
31 B21: [22] EMP. D58b, D77a,
 R68
31 B22: [22] EMP. D101, R68
31 B23: [22] EMP. D60, R68
31 B24: [22] EMP. D46
31 B25: [22] EMP. D45
31 B26: [22] EMP. D77b, R68
31 B27: [2] COSM. T11, [22]
 EMP. D89, D96, D98, R74
31 B27a: [22] EMP. D91
31 B28: [22] EMP. D90
31 B29: [22] EMP. D87, D92,
 R79, R89
31 B30: [22] EMP. D94, R74
31 B31: [22] EMP. D95
31 B32: [22] EMP. D259
31 B33: [22] EMP. D72
31 B34: [22] EMP. D71
31 B35: [22] EMP. D75, R70
31 B36: [22] EMP. D104
31 B37: [22] EMP. D67
31 B38: [22] EMP. D122
31 B39: [22] EMP. D113
31 B40: [22] EMP. D125
31 B41: [22] EMP. D124
31 B42: [22] EMP. D132, D140
31 B43: [22] EMP. D140, D141
31 B44: [22] EMP. D123

31 B45: [22] EMP. D139
31 B46: [22] EMP. D137
31 B47: [22] EMP. D138
31 B48: [22] EMP. D131
31 B49: [22] EMP. D228
31 B51: [22] EMP. D102
31 B52: [22] EMP. D109
31 B53: [22] EMP. D105
31 B54: [22] EMP. D108
31 B55: [22] EMP. D147a
31 B56: [22] EMP. D147b
31 B57: [22] EMP. D154, R75
31 B58: [22] EMP. D153
31 B59: [22] EMP. D106, D149
31 B60: [22] EMP. D155
31 B61: [22] EMP. D152, D156
31 B62: [22] EMP. D157
31 B63: [22] EMP. D164, D171
31 B64: [22] EMP. D162
31 B65: [22] EMP. D172
31 B66: [22] EMP. D159
31 B67: [22] EMP. D158
31 B68: [22] EMP. D168
31 B69: [22] EMP. D179
31 B70: [22] EMP. D195
31 B71: [22] EMP. D61, R70
31 B72: [22] EMP. D187
31 B73: [22] EMP. D199, R70
31 B74: [22] EMP. D188
31 B75: [22] EMP. D200, R70
31 B76: [22] EMP. D74
31 B77: [22] EMP. D248, D251
31 B78: [22] EMP. D252, D253
31 B79: [22] EMP. D249, D254
31 B80: [22] EMP. D255, R4
31 B81: [22] EMP. D256
31 B82: [22] EMP. D198
31 B83: [22] EMP. D197

31 B84: [22] EMP. D215
31 B85: [22] EMP. D191, R69
31 B86: [22] EMP. D213, R70
31 B87: [22] EMP. D214, R70
31 B88: [22] EMP. D216
31 B89: [22] EMP. D208
31 B90: [22] EMP. D68
31 B91: [22] EMP. D69
31 B92: [22] EMP. D185, R22
31 B93: [22] EMP. D70
31 B94: [22] EMP. D224
31 B95: [22] EMP. D217, R70
31 B96: [22] EMP. D192
31 B97: [22] EMP. D177, R20
31 B98: [22] EMP. D58a, D190
31 B99: [22] EMP. D226
31 B100: [22] EMP. D201a,
    D201b
31 B101: [22] EMP. D232
31 B102: [22] EMP. D231
31 B103: [22] EMP. D242, R69
31 B104: [22] EMP. D107, R69
31 B105: [22] EMP. D240
31 B106: [22] EMP. D243
31 B107: [22] EMP. D241
31 B108: [22] EMP. D244a,
    D244b
31 B109: [1] DOX. T12, [22]
    EMP. D207
31 B110: [22] EMP. D257, R89
31 B111: [22] EMP. D43
31 B112: [22] EMP. D4
31 B113: [22] EMP. D5
31 B114: [22] EMP. D6, R83
31 B115: [2] COSM. T7, [22]
    EMP. D10, D11, R48, R50,
    R89
31 B116: [22] EMP. D23

31 B117: [22] EMP. D13
31 B118: [22] EMP. D14, R32
31 B119: [22] EMP. D15, R48, R81
31 B120: [22] EMP. D16, R50, R56
31 B121: [22] EMP. D24, R52, R53, R57
31 B122: [22] EMP. D21, R49
31 B123: [22] EMP. D22, R97
31 B124: [22] EMP. D17
31 B125: [22] EMP. D18
31 B126: [22] EMP. D19, R51
31 B127: [22] EMP. D36
31 B128: [22] EMP. D25, R64
31 B129: [10a] PYTH. a P33, [22] EMP. D38, R43
31 B130: [22] EMP. D26
31 B131: [22] EMP. D7, R88, R89
31 B132: [22] EMP. D8
31 B133: [22] EMP. D9
31 B134: [22] EMP. D93, R95
31 B135: [3] MOR. T30, [22] EMP. D27a, D27b
31 B136: [22] EMP. D28, R39
31 B137: [22] EMP. D29, R39, R86
31 B139: [22] EMP. D34, R65
31 B140: [22] EMP. D32
31 B141: [22] EMP. D31
31 B142: [22] EMP. D12
31 B143: [22] EMP. D35, R99
31 B144: [22] EMP. D33
31 B145: [22] EMP. D30, R80
31 B146: [3] MOR. T32a, T32d, [22] EMP. D39, R82
31 B147: [22] EMP. D40, R84
31 B148: [22] EMP. D20

31 B149: [22] EMP. D143
31 B150: [22] EMP. D196
31 B151: [22] EMP. D64
31 B153: [22] EMP. D160
31 B153a: [22] EMP. D169
31 B155: [10a] PYTH. a P10
31 B158: [22] EMP. R53
36 A6: [1] DOX. T6
36 B2: [10c] PYTH. c D1c
36 B4: [10a] PYTH. a P29
38 A1: [24] HIPPO P1, P2a, P4
38 A2: [43] DRAM. T15, T16a, T16b
38 A3: [24] HIPPO P5, D1
38 A4: [1] DOX. T14, [24] HIPPO D2, R3
38 A5: [24] HIPPO D4
38 A6: [24] HIPPO D3, D5, R4
38 A7: [24] HIPPO R1
38 A8: [24] HIPPO R5, R7a
38 A9: [24] HIPPO R6 n. 1
38 A10: [24] HIPPO D7
38 A11: [24] HIPPO P6, D8
38 A12: [24] HIPPO D9
38 A13: [24] HIPPO D10
38 A14: [24] HIPPO D11a, D11b, D12
38 A15: [24] HIPPO D15
38 A16: [24] HIPPO P2b, D16, D17
38 A17: [24] HIPPO D14
38 A18: [24] HIPPO D13
38 A19: [24] HIPPO D18a, D18b, R2
38 B1: [2] COSM. T10b, [24] HIPPO D19
38 B2: [24] HIPPO R6a, R7b
38 B4: [24] HIPPO P3, P7, R8
41.10: [17] PYTHS. ANON. D44

42.5: [1] DOX. T13, [17] PYTHS. ANON. D43

44 A1: [12] PHILOL. P1, P8, D1a, D1b

44 A1a: [12] PHILOL. P2, P4

44 A2: [12] PHILOL. P6

44 A3: [12] PHILOL. P5, [26] ARCH. P8

44 A4: [13] EUR. P3

44 A4a: [12] PHILOL. P3

44 A5: [13] EUR. P7a

44 A7: [12] PHILOL. P7, [26] ARCH. P14

44 A7a: [12] PHILOL. D6

44 A9: [12] PHILOL. D16

44 A10: [12] PHILOL. D10

44 A11: [12] PHILOL. D29

44 A13: [18] PYTHS. R6a, R7

44 A14: [12] PHILOL. D31, D33a, D33b, D34

44 A16: [12] PHILOL. D19, [17] PYTHS. ANON. D40a

44 A17: [12] PHILOL. D20

44 A18: [12] PHILOL. D18

44 A19: [12] PHILOL. D22

44 A20: [12] PHILOL. D23

44 A21: [12] PHILOL. D21

44 A22: [12] PHILOL. D24

44 A23: [12] PHILOL. D27, [17] PYTHS. ANON. D50

44 A24: [12] PHILOL. D13

44 A25: [12] PHILOL. D32

44 A26: [12] PHILOL. D35, [18] PYTHS. R50

44 A27: [12] PHILOL. D25a

44 A28: [12] PHILOL. D25b

44 A29: [12] PHILOL. D8, [22] EMP. R44

44 B1: [12] PHILOL. D2

44 B2: [12] PHILOL. D3

44 B3: [12] PHILOL. D4

44 B4: [12] PHILOL. D7

44 B5: [12] PHILOL. D9

44 B6: [12] PHILOL. D5, D14

44 B7: [12] PHILOL. D15

44 B11: [12] PHILOL. D12, [18] PYTHS. R48

44 B13: [12] PHILOL. D26

44 B14: [12] PHILOL. D30, [18] PYTHS. R4

44 B16: [12] PHILOL. D28

44 B17: [12] PHILOL. D17

44 B20: [12] PHILOL. D11

44 B21: [18] PYTHS. R51

44 B22: [10c] PYTH. c D3, [18] PYTHS. R47a, R47b

45.1: [13] EUR. P2, P4, P6, P7b, P8

45.2: [13] EUR. D2

45.3: [13] EUR. D1

47 A1: [14] ARCHY. P1, P4, P12, D3

47 A3: [14] ARCHY. P22

47 A4: [14] ARCHY. P6

47 A5: [14] ARCHY. P11a, P11b, P11c

47 A7: [14] ARCHY. P16

47 A8: [14] ARCHY. P18a

47 A9: [14] ARCHY. D24, [18] PYTHS. R6e

47 A10: [14] ARCHY. P18b

47 A11: [14] ARCHY. P19

47 A12: [14] ARCHY. D2

47 A13: [18] PYTHS. R6c, R11

47 A14: [14] ARCHY. D12

47 A16: [14] ARCHY. D17

47 A17: [17] PYTHS. ANON. D26

47 A18: [14] ARCHY. D16
47 A19: [14] ARCHY. D13
47 A19b: [14] ARCHY. D19
47 A20: [14] ARCHY. D6
47 A21: [17] PYTHS. ANON.
　D11, [14] ARCHY. D7
47 A22: [14] ARCHY. D1
47 A23: [14] ARCHY. D20
47 A23a: [14] ARCHY. D23
47 A24: [14] ARCHY. D21
47 A25: [14] ARCHY. D22
47 B1: [14] ARCHY. D14, [18]
　PYTHS. R1
47 B2: [14] ARCHY. D15
47 B3: [14] ARCHY. D4
47 B4: [14] ARCHY. D5
48.3: [18] PYTHS. R56a
50.1: [15] HIC. D1
50.2: [15] HIC. D2
51.1: [16] ECPH. D1
51.2: [16] ECPH. D2
51.3: [16] ECPH. D4
51.4: [16] ECPH. D3
51.5: [16] ECPH. D5
58A.: [10b] PYTH. b T30, [11]
　HIPPAS. P1b, [13] EUR.
　P1a, P1b, [16] ECPH. P1,
　[19] PARM. P11, [26] ARCH.
　P2b
58B.1: [10c] PYTH. c D11
58B.1a: [18] PYTHS. R33
58B.4: [10c] PYTH. c D6, [17]
　PYTHS. ANON. D1, D4,
　D20a, D40b
58B.5: [17] PYTHS. ANON. D6
58B.6: [17] PYTHS. ANON. D7
58B.7: [17] PYTHS. ANON. D8
58B.8: [17] PYTHS. ANON.
　D2, D3, [18] PYTHS. R15

58B.9: [17] PYTHS. ANON.
　D10, D27, [18] PYTHS. R23
58B.10: [18] PYTHS. R20
58B.11: [18] PYTHS. R14
58B.12: [17] PYTHS. ANON.
　D18, [18] PYTHS. R10
58B.13: [18] PYTHS. R9
58B.14: [18] PYTHS. R12
58B.15: [10c] PYTH. c D10,
　[17] PYTHS. ANON. D16,
　D19, [18] PYTHS. R72
58B.16: [17] PYTHS. ANON.
　D17
58B.17: [17] PYTHS. ANON.
　D15
58B.18: [17] PYTHS. ANON.
　D24
58B.19: [10c] PYTH. c D7b
58B.20: [17] PYTHS. ANON.
　D23
58B.21: [17] PYTHS. ANON.
　D22
58B.22: [17] PYTHS. ANON.
　D5, D41, [18] PYTHS. R18,
　R19
58B.26: [17] PYTHS. ANON.
　D13, D28, [18] PYTHS. R17
58B.28: [17] PYTHS. ANON.
　D12a, D12b, D12c
58B.29: [18] PYTHS. R22
58B.30: [17] PYTHS. ANON.
　D9, D29, D30, D31
58B.31: [17] PYTHS. ANON.
　D32, D33, D34
58B.32: [18] PYTHS. R13
58B.34: [17] PYTHS. ANON.
　D35, D38, [18] PYTHS. R27
58B.35: [17] PYTHS. ANON.
　D46

58B.36: [17] PYTHS. ANON.
D41, D42
58B.37: [17] PYTHS. ANON.
D36, [18] PYTHS. R16, R24
58B.37c: [17] PYTHS. ANON.
D45
58B.38: [18] PYTHS. R21
58B.39: [17] PYTHS. ANON.
D52, [18] PYTHS. R26
58B.40: [17] PYTHS. ANON.
D49
58B.41: [17] PYTHS. ANON.
D51, D53
58B.42: [17] PYTHS. ANON.
D48
58C.1: [10c] PYTH. c D21
58C.2: [10c] PYTH. c D23,
D25
58C.3: [10c] PYTH. c D22
58C.4: [3] MOR. T38, [10b]
PYTH. b T6, T17, [10c]
PYTH. c D15, D18, D20
58C.5: [10c] PYTH. c D24
58C.6: [10b] PYTH. b T4b ,
T4c, [10c] PYTH. c D16, [18]
PYTHS. R34
58D.: [18] PYTHS. R6e
58D.1: [10b] PYTH. b T10
58D.4: [17] PYTHS. ANON.
D54a, D54b
58D.5: [17] PYTHS. ANON.
D54e
58D.7: [10b] PYTH. b T3
58D.8: [17] PYTHS. ANON.
D54f, D54g
58D.10: [17] PYTHS. ANON.
D54c
58D.11: [17] PYTHS. ANON.
D54d, 18. [18] PYTHS. R6e

58E.1: [43] DRAM. T35a,
T35b, T36a, T36b
58E.2: [43] DRAM. T37a
58E.3: [43] DRAM. T37b,
T38a, T38b
59 A1: [25] ANAXAG. P1, P10,
P11, P14c, P23, P27, P31,
P40, P42, P46, D1a, D98,
R35, [27] ATOM. R10, [43]
DRAM. T75b
59 A3: [25] ANAXAG. P26b,
P45
59 A4: [25] ANAXAG. P4, P5
59 A5: [25] ANAXAG. P3, R1
59 A6: [25] ANAXAG. P8
59 A7: [25] ANAXAG. P12,
P13, P16, P17
59 A9: [25] ANAXAG. D96
59 A10: [25] ANAXAG. P9
59 A11: [25] ANAXAG. P6
59 A12: [25] ANAXAG. P7, D46
59 A13: [25] ANAXAG. P28,
P30
59 A15: [25] ANAXAG. P18,
P20, P43
59 A16: [25] ANAXAG. P21
59 A17: [25] ANAXAG. P24,
P25a
59 A18: [25] ANAXAG. P25b,
D38
59 A20: [43] DRAM. T43b,
T75a
59 A20a: [25] ANAXAG. P14e
59 A20b: [43] DRAM. T48
59 A20c: [25] ANAXAG. P14b
59 A21: [25] ANAXAG. P14a,
P32
59 A23: [25] ANAXAG. P47
59 A24: [25] ANAXAG. P48

59 A26: [25] ANAXAG. R28
59 A27: [25] ANAXAG. P49
59 A28: [25] ANAXAG. P33
59 A29: [25] ANAXAG. P36
59 A30: [5] THAL. P13, [25]
 ANAXAG. P29, P35, P37,
 [43] DRAM. T43a
59 A31: [25] ANAXAG. P39
59 A32: [25] ANAXAG. P22
59 A33: [25] ANAXAG. P14d,
 P38b, [43] DRAM. T80
59 A34: [25] ANAXAG. P41
59 A35: [25] ANAXAG. R4
59 A37: [25] ANAXAG. D1a
59 A38: [25] ANAXAG. P26a
59 A39: [25] ANAXAG. D97,
 [27] ATOM. D216
59 A40: [25] ANAXAG. P44
59 A41: [6] ANAXIMAND. R8,
 [25] ANAXAG. D2
59 A42: [25] ANAXAG. D4
59 A43: [25] ANAXAG. P2,
 D18, R8, R15
59 A44: [25] ANAXAG. R29
59 A45: [27] ATOM. D46, R15
59 A46: [25] ANAXAG. D3, R14
59 A47: [25] ANAXAG. R5, R10
59 A48: [25] ANAXAG. P34,
 [43] DRAM. T44, T81
59 A50: [25] ANAXAG. D17,
 R20
59 A52: [25] ANAXAG. D20
59 A53: [25] ANAXAG. R32
59 A54: [25] ANAXAG. D19
59 A55: [25] ANAXAG. R13
59 A56: [25] ANAXAG. R11
59 A58: [25] ANAXAG. R9
59 A59: [25] ANAXAG. R21

59 A61: [25] ANAXAG. R18a,
 R18b
59 A62: [43] DRAM. T77
59 A63: [25] ANAXAG. D33
59 A64: [25] ANAXAG. D34
59 A65: [7] ANAXIMEN. D9,
 [25] ANAXAG. D35a
59 A66: [25] ANAXAG. R27
59 A67: [25] ANAXAG. D32,
 R30, [28] DIOG. D17, R15
59 A68: [22] EMP. R15b, [25]
 ANAXAG. D59, D60
59 A69: [25] ANAXAG. D61,
 R22
59 A70: [25] ANAXAG. D11
59 A71: [25] ANAXAG. D36
59 A73: [25] ANAXAG. D37b,
 D37c, R7
59 A74: [25] ANAXAG. D76,
 D77
59 A75: [25] ANAXAG. D39
59 A76: [25] ANAXAG. D41
59 A77: [25] ANAXAG. D42,
 D43, D44, D45a, D45b
59 A78: [25] ANAXAG. D47
59 A79: [25] ANAXAG. D48
59 A80: [25] ANAXAG. D49
59 A81: [25] ANAXAG. D50,
 [27] ATOM. D99
59 A82: [25] ANAXAG. D52
59 A83: [25] ANAXAG. D51
59 A84: [25] ANAXAG. D53a,
 D53b
59 A85: [25] ANAXAG. D54a,
 D54b
59 A86: [25] ANAXAG. D56
59 A86a: [25] ANAXAG. D57,
 R25

59 A89: [25] ANAXAG. D62a, D62b, D63
59 A90: [25] ANAXAG. D64, D65, [43] DRAM. T76
59 A91: [25] ANAXAG. D66a, D66b, R3
59 A92: [1] DOX. T15, [25] ANAXAG. D70, D72, D73, D74, D78, D79b
59 A93: [25] ANAXAG. D69, R24a, R24b
59 A94: [25] ANAXAG. D79a, D79c
59 A95: [25] ANAXAG. R26, [27] ATOM. R100
59 A96: [25] ANAXAG. D8
59 A97: [25] ANAXAG. D7a
59 A98: [25] ANAXAG. D7b
59 A98a: [25] ANAXAG. D67
59 A100: [25] ANAXAG. R12
59 A102: [25] ANAXAG. D80
59 A103: [25] ANAXAG. D82
59 A106: [25] ANAXAG. D75
59 A107: [25] ANAXAG. D84, D85, D86
59 A108: [25] ANAXAG. D89
59 A109: [25] ANAXAG. D88
59 A110: [25] ANAXAG. D90
59 A111: [25] ANAXAG. D87
59 A112: [3] MOR. T4, [43] DRAM. T78
59 A113: [25] ANAXAG. D68
59 A114: [25] ANAXAG. D91
59 A115: [25] ANAXAG. D83
59 A116: [25] ANAXAG. D93, [27] ATOM. D199
59 A117: [1] DOX. T16, [25] ANAXAG. D94, D95

59 B1: [25] ANAXAG. D9, R34
59 B2: [25] ANAXAG. D10, R34
59 B3: [25] ANAXAG. D24
59 B4: [25] ANAXAG. D12, D13
59 B5: [25] ANAXAG. D16
59 B6: [25] ANAXAG. D25
59 B7: [25] ANAXAG. D23
59 B8: [25] ANAXAG. D22
59 B9: [25] ANAXAG. D14
59 B10: [25] ANAXAG. D21
59 B11: [25] ANAXAG. D26
59 B12: [25] ANAXAG. D27
59 B13: [25] ANAXAG. D29b
59 B14: [25] ANAXAG. D28
59 B15: [25] ANAXAG. D30, R33
59 B16: [25] ANAXAG. D31, R33
59 B17: [25] ANAXAG. D15
59 B18: [25] ANAXAG. D40
59 B19: [25] ANAXAG. D55
59 B21: [25] ANAXAG. D5
59 B21a: [25] ANAXAG. D6, R2
59 B21b: [25] ANAXAG. D81
59 B22: [25] ANAXAG. D92
59 B23: [25] ANAXAG. R36
60 A1: [26] ARCH. P1, D3, D7, D19, D22, R2, [33] SOC. P8c, D6a
60 A2: [26] ARCH. P3, D1
60 A3: [26] ARCH. P4, P5, P6a, P6b
60 A4: [26] ARCH. D2
60 A5: [26] ARCH. D4, R1

60 A6: [26] ARCH. D21
60 A7: [26] ARCH. D6
60 A9: [26] ARCH. D8
60 A10: [26] ARCH. D5
60 A11: [26] ARCH. D11
60 A12: [26] ARCH. D9
60 A13: [26] ARCH. D12
60 A14: [26] ARCH. D10, D14a
60 A15: [26] ARCH. D15
60 A16: [26] ARCH. D16
60 A17: [26] ARCH. D18, D20
60 A26: [26] ARCH. R3
60 B1: [26] ARCH. R5
60 B1a: [26] ARCH. D13
60 B2: [26] ARCH. R6
61.2: [25] ANAXAG. P27
62.2: [1] DOX. T15
62.3: [1] DOX. T16
63.: [28] DIOG. R5
64 A1: [28] DIOG. P1, P4,
  D14
64 A3: [28] DIOG. P3
64 A4: [28] DIOG. D1, R7
64 A5: [28] DIOG. P2, D8, R6,
  R9
64 A6: [28] DIOG. D15
64 A7: [28] DIOG. R1
64 A8: [28] DIOG. R14, R17,
  R19
64 A10: [21] MEL. R24e, [28]
  DIOG. D16a, R16
64 A11: [28] DIOG. D17, R15
64 A12: [28] DIOG. D18
64 A13: [28] DIOG. D19, D20
64 A14: [28] DIOG. D21
64 A15: [28] DIOG. D22
64 A16: [28] DIOG. D23a,
  D23b

64 A17: [28] DIOG. D24
64 A18: [28] DIOG. D25b
64 A19: [1] DOX. T15, [28]
  DIOG. D13, D34a, D34b,
  D35, D36, D38, D39, D41,
  D42, D43, D44, R10, [43]
  DRAM. T12
64 A20: [28] DIOG. D11
64 A21: [28] DIOG. D37
64 A22: [28] DIOG. D40
64 A24: [28] DIOG. D28a
64 A25: [28] DIOG. D32a,
  D32b, R2, R12
64 A26: [28] DIOG. D31b
64 A27: [28] DIOG. D29, D30
64 A29: [28] DIOG. D33
64 A30: [28] DIOG. D45
64 A31: [28] DIOG. D46, D47,
  R3
64 A32: [1] DOX. T16, [28]
  DIOG. D48
64 A33: [28] DIOG. D26
64 B1: [28] DIOG. D2
64 B2: [28] DIOG. D3
64 B3: [28] DIOG. D5b
64 B4: [28] DIOG. D9
64 B5: [28] DIOG. D10
64 B6: [28] DIOG. D27, D28b
64 B7: [28] DIOG. D4
64 B8: [28] DIOG. D6
64 B9: [28] DIOG. D31a
64 B10: [28] DIOG. D49
64 C1: [43] DRAM. T10a,
  T28a, T28b, T28c
64 C2: [29] MED. T10, [43]
  DRAM. T44
64 C3: [29] MED. T11
64 C3a: [29] MED. T23

64 C4: [43] DRAM. T40
65.1: [9] HER. R25
65.2: [9] HER. R26
65.3: [9] HER. R27a, R28a
65.4: [9] HER. R19, R23
65.5: [9] HER. R24a
66.2: [9] HER. R21
66.3: [9] HER. R17
67 A1: [27] ATOM. P1a, P2, D10, D80a, D80b, D93, D94, D103
67 A2: [27] ATOM. R80
67 A5: [27] ATOM. P4, P5
67 A6: [27] ATOM. D31, R38
67 A7: [27] ATOM. D30, R18
67 A8: [27] ATOM. P1b, D11, D32
67 A9: [27] ATOM. D56, D71
67 A10: [27] ATOM. P3, D81, D92
67 A11: [27] ATOM. D58
67 A13: [27] ATOM. R95
67 A14: [27] ATOM. D61
67 A15: [27] ATOM. D45, D47, D59, R13, R33
67 A16: [27] ATOM. R42
67 A18: [27] ATOM. R37
67 A19: [27] ATOM. D39, R39
67 A23: [27] ATOM. D86
67 A24: [27] ATOM. R86
67 A25: [27] ATOM. D117
67 A26: [27] ATOM. D111
67 A27: [27] ATOM. D89
67 A28: [27] ATOM. D132, D136
67 A29: [27] ATOM. D145
67 A31: [27] ATOM. D150
67 A34: [27] ATOM. D138

67 A35: [27] ATOM. D162
67 A36: [27] ATOM. D174
67 B1: [27] ATOM. D90
67 B2: [27] ATOM. D1a, D73
68 A1: [27] ATOM. P6, P10, P15, P16a, P16b, P21, P22, P23, P24, P26, P31, P32, P37b, P42, P50, P51, P55, D2a, D2b, D13, D229, D375, R11, R77, R99
68 A2: [27] ATOM. P8, P11, P17, R78
68 A3: [27] ATOM. R69, R76
68 A4: [27] ATOM. P12a, P12b, P12c
68 A5: [27] ATOM. P13, R73
68 A6: [27] ATOM. P14, P54, R70a
68 A7: [27] ATOM. R70b
68 A9: [27] ATOM. P27, R71
68 A10: [27] ATOM. P28
68 A12: [27] ATOM. D115
68 A13: [27] ATOM. P19
68 A15: [27] ATOM. P38
68 A16: [27] ATOM. P37a
68 A17: [27] ATOM. R72
68 A17a: [27] ATOM. P41
68 A18: [27] ATOM. P49
68 A21: [9] HER. P12, [27] ATOM. P46
68 A22: [27] ATOM. P33
68 A23: [27] ATOM. P34
68 A24: [27] ATOM. P53
68 A26: [27] ATOM. R111
68 A27: [27] ATOM. P35
68 A29: [27] ATOM. P52
68 A31: [27] ATOM. D3
68 A32: [27] ATOM. R2a, R2b

68 A34: [27] ATOM. R5, R6, R7, R8
68 A34a: [27] ATOM. R1a, R1b, R1c, R1d, R1e, R1f, R1g, R1h
68 A35: [27] ATOM. D71
68 A35a: [27] ATOM. D12
68 A36: [27] ATOM. D25a, D25b, R28
68 A37: [27] ATOM. D29
68 A38: [27] ATOM. D32, R47
68 A39: [27] ATOM. D77, D87
68 A40: [27] ATOM. P7, P18, D81, D92
68 A42: [27] ATOM. R23
68 A43: [27] ATOM. R96
68 A47: [27] ATOM. D37, D50, D51, D52, D53, D54, D62, R94
68 A48: [27] ATOM. D42
68 A48b: [27] ATOM. D41
68 A49: [27] ATOM. D23b, D43, D63
68 A50: [27] ATOM. R92
68 A51: [27] ATOM. R79a
68 A52: [27] ATOM. R81
68 A53: [27] ATOM. R82, R85
68 A57: [27] ATOM. D34a
68 A58: [27] ATOM. D36
68 A60: [27] ATOM. D40, D48, D68, R32a, R32b, R32c, R32d, R36, R44, R45
68 A60a: [27] ATOM. R33
68 A61: [27] ATOM. D49, R90
68 A62: [27] ATOM. D125
68 A63: [27] ATOM. D70
68 A65: [27] ATOM. R26

68 A66: [27] ATOM. D74, D75, R30
68 A67: [27] ATOM. D82, R31
68 A68: [27] ATOM. D76a, c
68 A69: [27] ATOM. R83
68 A70: [27] ATOM. R79b
68 A71: [27] ATOM. D78
68 A73: [27] ATOM. D124
68 A74: [27] ATOM. D209a, D209b
68 A75: [27] ATOM. D207
68 A76: [27] ATOM. D208
68 A77: [27] ATOM. D152, D153, R9
68 A81: [27] ATOM. D85
68 A82: [27] ATOM. D83a
68 A84: [27] ATOM. D84
68 A85: [27] ATOM. D91
68 A86: [27] ATOM. D95
68 A87: [27] ATOM. D101, D102
68 A88: [27] ATOM. D105
68 A89: [27] ATOM. D104
68 A89a: [27] ATOM. D106
68 A90: [27] ATOM. D107
68 A91: [27] ATOM. D98a, D98b
68 A92: [27] ATOM. P29, D100
68 A93: [27] ATOM. D117
68 A93a: [27] ATOM. D118
68 A94: [27] ATOM. D111
68 A95: [27] ATOM. D88
68 A96: [27] ATOM. D89
68 A97: [27] ATOM. D119a
68 A98: [27] ATOM. D119b
68 A99: [27] ATOM. D120a, D120b, D121
68 A99a: [27] ATOM. D123

68 A100: [27] ATOM. D122,
R49
68 A101: [27] ATOM. D130,
D133
68 A104: [27] ATOM. D131
68 A104a: [27] ATOM. R20b
68 A105: [27] ATOM. D135
68 A106: [27] ATOM. R29a,
R29b
68 A108: [27] ATOM. R91
68 A109: [27] ATOM. D139
68 A110: [27] ATOM. R98
68 A112: [27] ATOM. R53
68 A114: [27] ATOM. R107
68 A116: [27] ATOM. D144
68 A117: [27] ATOM. D140
68 A119: [27] ATOM. D159b,
R54
68 A120: [27] ATOM. D45,
D57a, R13
68 A121: [27] ATOM. D148
68 A122: [27] ATOM. D149,
R58
68 A123: [27] ATOM. D72
68 A126a: [27] ATOM. D155
68 A128: [27] ATOM. D156,
R61
68 A129: [27] ATOM. D160
68 A130: [27] ATOM. D161,
R63
68 A131: [27] ATOM. R64
68 A132: [27] ATOM. R65
68 A133: [27] ATOM. R66
68 A134: [27] ATOM. R104
68 A135: [1] DOX. T11, T15,
[27] ATOM. D64, D65, D66,
D67, D69, D134, D147,
D157, D158, D159a, R21,
R25, R46, R55, R56, R57,
R59, R60, R62
68 A136: [27] ATOM. D137,
D151
68 A138: [27] ATOM. D211,
D212
68 A139: [27] ATOM. D128
68 A140: [27] ATOM. D162
68 A141: [27] ATOM. D165
68 A142: [27] ATOM. D166
68 A143: [27] ATOM. D173,
D174, D177
68 A144: [27] ATOM. D169,
D175
68 A145: [27] ATOM. D170,
D171
68 A146: [27] ATOM. D168
68 A147: [27] ATOM. D185,
R67a
68 A148: [27] ATOM. D187
68 A149: [27] ATOM. D178
68 A150: [27] ATOM. D193a,
D193b
68 A151: [27] ATOM. D179
68 A152: [27] ATOM. D176
68 A153: [27] ATOM. D190
68 A154: [27] ATOM. D191
68 A155: [27] ATOM. D192
68 A155a: [27] ATOM. D197
68 A155b: [27] ATOM. D198
68 A156: [27] ATOM. D188a
68 A157: [27] ATOM. D189
68 A158: [27] ATOM. D194
68 A159: [27] ATOM. D180
68 A160: [27] ATOM. D141,
D142, R87
68 A162: [27] ATOM. D201a,
D201b

68 A163: [27] ATOM. D200,
    R56b
68 A165: [27] ATOM. D126,
    R50
68 A166: [27] ATOM. D376
68 A167: [27] ATOM. D231
68 A169: [27] ATOM. D230
68 A170: [27] ATOM. D388
68 B1: [27] ATOM. D8, D143,
    R68a, R68b
68 B1a: [27] ATOM. D281,
    D282
68 B2: [27] ATOM. D293a,
    D293b, R68b
68 B3: [27] ATOM. D228, R75
68 B4: [27] ATOM. R74
68 B5: [27] ATOM. P9, P23,
    D129, D202
68 B6: [27] ATOM. D5, D17,
    R108
68 B7: [27] ATOM. D18, R108
68 B8: [27] ATOM. D19, R108
68 B9: [27] ATOM. D4, D14,
    D15, D23a, R108
68 B10: [27] ATOM. D16
68 B10b: [27] ATOM. D27
68 B11: [27] ATOM. D6, D20,
    D21, R108, [29] MED. T13
68 B12: [27] ATOM. D96
68 B13: [27] ATOM. R3a
68 B14.3: [27] ATOM. D109
68 B14.6: [27] ATOM. D108
68 B15: [27] ATOM. P30,
    D112, D113
68 B16: [27] ATOM. D220
68 B17: [27] ATOM. D219
68 B18: [27] ATOM. D217
68 B19: [27] ATOM. R3d
68 B20: [27] ATOM. R3g

68 B21: [27] ATOM. D221
68 B22: [27] ATOM. D195
68 B23: [27] ATOM. D222
68 B24: [27] ATOM. D223
68 B25: [27] ATOM. D224
68 B26: [27] ATOM. D205
68 B26f: [27] ATOM. P45
68 B27: [27] ATOM. D400
68 B27a: [27] ATOM. D401
68 B28: [27] ATOM. D9, D402
68 B29: [27] ATOM. R4b
68 B29a: [27] ATOM. R3b
68 B30: [27] ATOM. D210
68 B31: [27] ATOM. D235
68 B32: [27] ATOM. D163a,
    D163b, D163c, D163d
68 B33: [27] ATOM. D403
68 B34: [27] ATOM. D225
68 B39: [27] ATOM. D311
68 B41: [27] ATOM. D387
68 B42: [27] ATOM. D300
68 B44: [27] ATOM. D347b
68 B46: [27] ATOM. D327
68 B47: [27] ATOM. D366
68 B48: [27] ATOM. D352
68 B49: [27] ATOM. D368
68 B51: [27] ATOM. D346
68 B52: [27] ATOM. D308
68 B53a: [27] ATOM. D339
68 B55: [27] ATOM. D340
68 B57: [27] ATOM. D305
68 B58: [27] ATOM. D301
68 B59: [27] ATOM. D412
68 B60: [27] ATOM. D337
68 B61: [27] ATOM. D304
68 B63: [27] ATOM. D345
68 B64: [9] HER. R103, [27]
    ATOM. D307
68 B65: [9] HER. R104

68 B73: [27] ATOM. D266
68 B75: [27] ATOM. D367
68 B77: [27] ATOM. D410
68 B78: [27] ATOM. D261
68 B81: [27] ATOM. D351
68 B85: [27] ATOM. D348
68 B86: [27] ATOM. D349
68 B88: [27] ATOM. D334
68 B98: [9] HER. R105
68 B108: [27] ATOM. D273
68 B111: [27] ATOM. D391
68 B116: [27] ATOM. P22, P39
68 B117: [27] ATOM. D24,
   R103
68 B118: [27] ATOM. P40
68 B119: [27] ATOM. D7,
   D274
68 B120: [27] ATOM. D181
68 B121: [27] ATOM. R4j
68 B122: [27] ATOM. R4k
68 B122a: [27] ATOM. D167
68 B123: [27] ATOM. D146
68 B124: [27] ATOM. D164
68 B125: [27] ATOM. D14,
   D23a
68 B126: [27] ATOM. D196
68 B127: [27] ATOM. D249
68 B128: [27] ATOM. R3e
68 B129: [27] ATOM. D218
68 B129a: [27] ATOM. R3c
68 B130: [27] ATOM. R4d
68 B131: [27] ATOM. R3f
68 B132: [27] ATOM. R4f
68 B133: [27] ATOM. R4g
68 B134: [27] ATOM. R4h
68 B135: [27] ATOM. D182
68 B136: [27] ATOM. R4i
68 B137: [27] ATOM. R4l
68 B138: [27] ATOM. D83b

68 B139: [27] ATOM. D38
68 B139a: [27] ATOM. R4c
68 B140: [27] ATOM. D232
68 B141: [27] ATOM. D34b
68 B142: [27] ATOM. D206
68 B143: [27] ATOM. D313
68 B144: [27] ATOM. P43,
   D204
68 B144a: [27] ATOM. R4e
68 B145: [27] ATOM. D338
68 B146: [27] ATOM. D245
68 B147: [9] HER. R107, [27]
   ATOM. D250
68 B148: [27] ATOM. D172
68 B149: [27] ATOM. D267
68 B150: [27] ATOM. D28
68 B151: [27] ATOM. D359
68 B152: [27] ATOM. D116
68 B153: [27] ATOM. D374
68 B154: [27] ATOM. D203
68 B155: [27] ATOM. D213,
   D214
68 B155a: [27] ATOM. D60a,
   D60b
68 B156: [27] ATOM. D33, R89
68 B157: [27] ATOM. D355
68 B158: [27] ATOM. D310
68 B159: [27] ATOM. D233a,
   D233b
68 B160: [27] ATOM. D280
68 B162: [27] ATOM. D215
68 B163: [27] ATOM. P25, [39]
   XENI. D1
68 B164: [27] ATOM. D55
68 B165: [27] ATOM. P44a,
   P44b, D26a, D26b, R24,
   R101, R105
68 B166: [27] ATOM. D154
68 B167: [27] ATOM. D82

113

68 B168: [27] ATOM. D36
68 B169: [27] ATOM. D309
68 B170: [27] ATOM. D237
68 B171: [27] ATOM. D238
68 B172: [27] ATOM. D268
68 B173: [27] ATOM. D269
68 B174: [27] ATOM. D320
68 B175: [27] ATOM. D303
68 B176: [27] ATOM. D252
68 B177: [27] ATOM. D341
68 B178: [27] ATOM. D404
68 B179: [27] ATOM. D405
68 B180: [27] ATOM. D406
68 B181: [27] ATOM. D385
68 B182: [27] ATOM. D407
68 B183: [27] ATOM. D408
68 B184: [27] ATOM. D312
68 B185: [27] ATOM. D409
68 B186: [27] ATOM. D358
68 B187: [27] ATOM. D236
68 B188: [27] ATOM. D241
68 B189: [27] ATOM. D227
68 B190: [27] ATOM. D342
68 B191: [27] ATOM. D226
68 B192: [27] ATOM. D343
68 B193: [27] ATOM. D306
68 B194: [27] ATOM. D243
68 B195: [27] ATOM. D353
68 B196: [27] ATOM. D272
68 B197: [27] ATOM. D297
68 B198: [27] ATOM. D260
68 B199: [27] ATOM. D286
68 B200: [27] ATOM. D283
68 B201: [27] ATOM. D284
68 B202: [27] ATOM. D298
68 B203: [27] ATOM. D288
68 B204: [27] ATOM. D299
68 B205: [27] ATOM. D285
68 B206: [27] ATOM. D287

68 B207: [27] ATOM. D242
68 B208: [27] ATOM. D396
68 B209: [27] ATOM. D255
68 B210: [27] ATOM. D277
68 B211: [27] ATOM. D244
68 B212: [27] ATOM. D183
68 B213: [27] ATOM. D326
68 B214: [27] ATOM. D325
68 B215: [27] ATOM. D322
68 B216: [27] ATOM. D295
68 B216bis: [27] ATOM. D323
68 B217: [27] ATOM. D321
68 B218: [27] ATOM. D263
68 B219: [27] ATOM. D257
68 B220: [27] ATOM. D271
68 B221: [27] ATOM. D270
68 B222: [27] ATOM. D330
68 B223: [27] ATOM. D234
68 B224: [27] ATOM. D251
68 B225: [27] ATOM. D347a
68 B226: [27] ATOM. D344
68 B226bis: [27] ATOM. D345
68 B227: [27] ATOM. D331
68 B228: [27] ATOM. D332
68 B229: [27] ATOM. D333
68 B230: [27] ATOM. D292
68 B231: [27] ATOM. D253
68 B232: [27] ATOM. D247
68 B233: [27] ATOM. D246
68 B234: [27] ATOM. D240
68 B235: [27] ATOM. D248
68 B236: [9] HER. R106, [27]
   ATOM. D296
68 B237: [27] ATOM. D335
68 B238: [27] ATOM. D372
68 B239: [27] ATOM. D350
68 B240: [27] ATOM. D314
68 B241: [27] ATOM. D315
68 B242: [27] ATOM. D411

68 B243: [27] ATOM. D316
68 B244: [27] ATOM. D336
68 B245: [27] ATOM. D380
68 B246: [27] ATOM. D254
68 B247: [27] ATOM. D354
68 B248: [27] ATOM. D379
68 B249: [27] ATOM. D360
68 B250: [27] ATOM. D357
68 B251: [27] ATOM. D361
68 B252: [27] ATOM. D356
68 B253: [27] ATOM. D369
68 B254: [27] ATOM. D362
68 B255: [27] ATOM. D364
68 B256: [27] ATOM. D319
68 B257: [27] ATOM. D381
68 B258: [27] ATOM. D382
68 B259: [27] ATOM. D383
68 B260: [27] ATOM. D384
68 B261: [27] ATOM. D377
68 B262: [27] ATOM. D378
68 B263: [27] ATOM. D324
68 B264: [27] ATOM. D386
68 B265: [27] ATOM. D370
68 B266: [27] ATOM. D363
68 B267: [27] ATOM. D365
68 B268: [27] ATOM. D373
68 B269: [27] ATOM. D275
68 B270: [27] ATOM. D390
68 B271: [27] ATOM. D265
68 B272: [27] ATOM. D399
68 B273: [27] ATOM. D328
68 B274: [27] ATOM. D329
68 B275: [27] ATOM. D392
68 B276: [27] ATOM. D393
68 B277: [27] ATOM. D394
68 B278: [27] ATOM. D395
68 B279: [27] ATOM. D398
68 B280: [27] ATOM. D397
68 B281: [27] ATOM. D264

68 B282: [27] ATOM. D262
68 B283: [27] ATOM. D258
68 B284: [27] ATOM. D259
68 B285: [27] ATOM. D256
68 B286: [27] ATOM. D278
68 B287: [27] ATOM. D371
68 B288: [27] ATOM. D389
68 B288*: [27] ATOM. D276
68 B289: [27] ATOM. D294
68 B290: [27] ATOM. D239
68 B291: [27] ATOM. D318
68 B292: [27] ATOM. D302
68 B293: [27] ATOM. D279
68 B294: [27] ATOM. D317
68 B295: [27] ATOM. D290
68 B296: [27] ATOM. D291
68 B297: [27] ATOM. D289
68 B298: [27] ATOM. R4a
68 B299: [27] ATOM. R115
68 B300.1: [27] ATOM. R118a,
    R118b
68 B300.3: [27] ATOM. R117
68 B300.4: [27] ATOM. R119a
68 B300.6: [27] ATOM. R126a
68 B300.7: [27] ATOM. R120a,
    R120b, R122
68 B300.10: [27] ATOM. R118c,
    R123a, R123b, R123c, [29]
    MED. T1
68 B300.14: [27] ATOM. R126b
68 B300.16: [27] ATOM. R125a
68 B300.17: [27] ATOM. R125b
68 B300.18: [27] ATOM. R125c
68 B300.19: [27] ATOM. R127a
68 B300.20: [27] ATOM. R124
68 B302.194: [27] ATOM. D263
68 B302.202: [27] ATOM. D261
68 B302.748: [27] ATOM. D259
68 B303: [27] ATOM. R128a

68 B304: [27] ATOM. R128b
68 C1: [43] DRAM. T34
68 C3: [27] ATOM. P48a, P48b, P48c
68 C6: [27] ATOM. R116
70 A24: [2] COSM. T2a, T10a, [31] PROT. R12
78.: [27] ATOM. R119b
79.1: [42] SOPH. R5
79.2: [42] SOPH. R27, R29, R32
79.2a: [42] SOPH. R25, R26
79.3: [42] SOPH. R34a
80 A1: [31] PROT. P1, P3, P5, P6a, P8, P12, P13b, P17, P19, P20, P23, D1, D4a, D15, D17, D20, D26, D29, R13, R19b, [43] DRAM. T18b
80 A2: [31] PROT. P7, P21, R3, R25
80 A3: [31] PROT. P6b, P13c, P16, D16
80 A4: [31] PROT. P4
80 A5: [31] PROT. P2a, P13a, D35, D36, D37, [42] SOPH. R11a, R11b, R12
80 A6: [31] PROT. P15
80 A7: [31] PROT. D14
80 A8: [31] PROT. P2b, P14
80 A9: [36] HIPPIAS P4
80 A10: [31] PROT. D30
80 A11: [31] PROT. P9a, P9b, [43] DRAM. T18a, T18b, T18c
80 A12: [31] PROT. P22, R19a
80 A14: [31] PROT. R21

80 A15: [31] PROT. R22, R9b
80 A16: [31] PROT. R28
80 A17: [31] PROT. R16
80 A19: [31] PROT. R10, R14a, R17
80 A20: [31] PROT. D27
80 A21: [31] PROT. D28, R18
80 A21a: [31] PROT. D38
80 A23: [31] PROT. R24
80 A24: [31] PROT. D5b, D21
80 A25: [3] MOR. T37, [31] PROT. P18, D31, D42
80 A26: [31] PROT. D22a
80 A27: [31] PROT. D23
80 A28: [31] PROT. D24
80 A29: [31] PROT. D25
80 A30: [31] PROT. D32
80 B1: [31] PROT. D3, D5a, D9, R4, R5, R7a, R20
80 B2: [31] PROT. D7, R2
80 B3: [31] PROT. D8, D11, R23, [43] DRAM. T71
80 B4: [31] PROT. D4b, D10, R29
80 B5: [31] PROT. R1a, R1b
80 B6: [31] PROT. D18, D19
80 B6a: [31] PROT. D26
80 B7: [31] PROT. D33
80 B7a: [31] PROT. D34
80 B8: [31] PROT. D2
80 B9: [31] PROT. P11
80 B10: [31] PROT. D12
80 B11: [31] PROT. D13
80 B12: [31] PROT. R30
80 C1: [31] PROT. D40
80 C2: [43] DRAM. T19a
80 C3: [43] DRAM. T19c

81.: [39] XENI. D1, R1

82 A1: [32] GORG. P1, P14, P26, P33d, D2b, D22, D27, R6c, R19

82 A1a: [32] GORG. D2a, D11a

82 A2: [32] GORG. P3, P10

82 A3: [32] GORG. P5, D6a

82 A4: [32] GORG. P13a, P13b, P17, D6b, D20, R2, R12, R13

82 A5: [32] GORG. P6

82 A5a: [43] DRAM. T20, T21

82 A6: [37] ANTIPH. P5

82 A7: [32] GORG. P2, P15, P33a, P33b, P33c, P34a, D3

82 A8: [32] GORG. P34b

82 A9: [32] GORG. P18, R4

82 A10: [32] GORG. P4, P25

82 A11: [32] GORG. P27, P28a

82 A12: [32] GORG. P29

82 A13: [32] GORG. P28b, P32

82 A14: [32] GORG. D5

82 A15: [32] GORG. P30

82 A15a: [32] GORG. P24, R1b

82 A16: [32] GORG. P7

82 A17: [32] GORG. P35

82 A18: [32] GORG. P16

82 A19: [32] GORG. P11, D9, D39

82 A20: [32] GORG. D8, D13

82 A21: [32] GORG. D47

82 A22: [32] GORG. D50

82 A23: [32] GORG. R10c

82 A24: [32] GORG. P21, D11b

82 A25: [32] GORG. D14, D15, D16

82 A26: [32] GORG. D10, D51

82 A27: [32] GORG. D7a, D7b, D49

82 A28: [32] GORG. D48a, D48b

82 A29: [32] GORG. D21b, R9

82 A30: [32] GORG. D19a

82 A31: [32] GORG. D19c

82 A32: [32] GORG. P8, D19b, R11, R14

82 A33: [32] GORG. R27

82 A34: [32] GORG. R28

82 A35: [32] GORG. P12, R3

82 B1: [1] DOX. T6, [32] GORG. R24a, R24b

82 B2: [32] GORG. P4, R23

82 B3: [32] GORG. D26b, R1a, R26

82 B4: [32] GORG. D45a

82 B5: [32] GORG. D45b

82 B5a: [32] GORG. D30a, D30b, R17, R20, R22

82 B5b: [32] GORG. D29

82 B6: [32] GORG. D1, D6c, D28

82 B7: [32] GORG. D31

82 B8: [32] GORG. D32

82 B8a: [32] GORG. P20

82 B10: [32] GORG. D33

82 B11: [32] GORG. D24

82 B11a: [32] GORG. D25

82 B12: [32] GORG. D18

82 B13: [32] GORG. D12

82 B14: [32] GORG. D4, D52, R8, R18

82 B15: [32] GORG. D43a, D43b, R10a

82 B16: [32] GORG. D44, R10b

82 B17: [32] GORG. D17
82 B19: [32] GORG. D53
82 B20: [32] GORG. D40
82 B21: [32] GORG. D41
82 B22: [32] GORG. D42
82 B23: [32] GORG. D35
82 B24: [32] GORG. D36
82 B25: [32] GORG. D37
82 B26: [32] GORG. D34
82 B27: [32] GORG. D38
82 B28: [32] GORG. R29
82 B29: [32] GORG. P22
82 B30: [32] GORG. P23
82 B31: [32] GORG. D46
82 C1: [32] GORG. R6a
82 C2: [32] GORG. D23a
83.1: [38] LYC. D2
83.2: [38] LYC. D1
83.3: [38] LYC. D3
83.4: [38] LYC. D4
83.5: [38] LYC. D6
83.6: [38] LYC. D5a, D5b
84 A1: [34] PROD. P1, P14
84 A1a: [34] PROD. P8, P11,
    D18b, D19a, R1a, R1b, R6
84 A2: [34] PROD. P3, [42]
    SOPH. R6
84 A3: [34] PROD. P2, P4
84 A4: [42] SOPH. R7
84 A4a: [34] PROD. P7
84 A4b: [34] PROD. R3
84 A5: [43] DRAM. T22, T23,
    T24
84 A6: [34] PROD. P13
84 A7: [34] PROD. P12
84 A8: [34] PROD. P10
84 A9: [34] PROD. R2

84 A10: [34] PROD. D12, R7
84 A11: [34] PROD. P5
84 A12: [34] PROD. D13
84 A13: [34] PROD. D21a,
    D21b
84 A14: [34] PROD. D21c,
    D21d
84 A15: [34] PROD. D22
84 A16: [34] PROD. D5b
84 A17: [34] PROD. D5c, D23
84 A18: [34] PROD. D5a, D24
84 A19: [34] PROD. D6a, R10
84 A20: [34] PROD. D11a
84 B1: [34] PROD. D3, D4,
    D18a
84 B2: [34] PROD. D20
84 B3: [31] PROT. D6, [34]
    PROD. D2
84 B4: [34] PROD. D1, D9, R9
84 B5: [34] PROD. D14, D15a,
    D15b, D16, D17, R8, R11,
    R12a
84 B6: [34] PROD. D7
84 B7: [34] PROD. D8
84 B8: [34] PROD. R4
84 B9: [34] PROD. P6, R5
84 B10: [34] PROD. D10
85 A1: [35] THRAS. P1, D2,
    D11
85 A2: [35] THRAS. D7
85 A3: [35] THRAS. P2, R3
85 A4: [43] DRAM. T25
85 A5: [35] THRAS. D20
85 A6: [35] THRAS. P4
85 A7: [35] THRAS. P5a, P5b
85 A8: [35] THRAS. P6
85 A9: [35] THRAS. D4

85 A10: [35] THRAS. P3
85 A11: [35] THRAS. D12
85 A12: [35] THRAS. D10, R1
85 A13: [35] THRAS. D1, D8, R2
85 A14: [35] THRAS. R5
85 B1: [35] THRAS. D9, D16, R4
85 B2: [35] THRAS. D18
85 B3: [35] THRAS. D3
85 B4: [35] THRAS. D19
85 B5: [35] THRAS. D6, D14
85 B6: [35] THRAS. D13a, D13b
85 B6a: [35] THRAS. D21a
85 B7: [35] THRAS. D5
85 B7a: [35] THRAS. R10
85 B8: [35] THRAS. D17
86 A1: [36] HIPPIAS P1, D1, D21
86 A2: [36] HIPPIAS P5, D5, D12b, D14b, R1
86 A3: [36] HIPPIAS P2
86 A5: [36] HIPPIAS R5
86 A5a: [36] HIPPIAS D13
86 A6: [36] HIPPIAS P3
86 A7: [36] HIPPIAS P4
86 A8: [36] HIPPIAS D8, D9
86 A9: [36] HIPPIAS D10
86 A10: [36] HIPPIAS D25
86 A11: [36] HIPPIAS D12a, D14a, D34, [42] SOPH. R6
86 A12: [36] HIPPIAS D2, D15
86 A13: [36] HIPPIAS R4
86 A14: [36] HIPPIAS D11
86 A15: [36] HIPPIAS P6
86 B1: [36] HIPPIAS D4

86 B2: [36] HIPPIAS D6, D30
86 B3: [36] HIPPIAS D7, R3
86 B4: [36] HIPPIAS D3, D33
86 B6: [1] DOX. T1, [36] HIP-PIAS D22
86 B7: [36] HIPPIAS D23
86 B8: [36] HIPPIAS D28
86 B9: [36] HIPPIAS D26
86 B10: [36] HIPPIAS R2
86 B11: [36] HIPPIAS D32
86 B12: [36] HIPPIAS D27
86 B13: [36] HIPPIAS D35
86 B14: [36] HIPPIAS D29
86 B15: [36] HIPPIAS D31
86 B16: [36] HIPPIAS D20
86 B17: [36] HIPPIAS D19
86 B18: [36] HIPPIAS D24
86 B21: [36] HIPPIAS D36
86 C1: [36] HIPPIAS D17
87 A1: [37] ANTIPH. P1a, P1c
87 A2: [37] ANTIPH. P2, R3, R8
87 A3: [37] ANTIPH. D83
87 A4: [37] ANTIPH. D84
87 A6: [37] ANTIPH. P8, P9, P10
87 A7: [37] ANTIPH. R12
87 A8: [37] ANTIPH. P7
87 A9: [37] ANTIPH. D75b
87 B1: [29] MED. T2, [37] AN-TIPH. D1a
87 B2: [37] ANTIPH. D1b
87 B3: [37] ANTIPH. D40
87 B4: [37] ANTIPH. D2
87 B5: [37] ANTIPH. D3
87 B6: [37] ANTIPH. D4
87 B7: [37] ANTIPH. D5

87 B8: [37] ANTIPH. D6
87 B9: [37] ANTIPH. D17
87 B10: [37] ANTIPH. D9a, D9b
87 B11: [37] ANTIPH. D10
87 B12: [37] ANTIPH. D37, R17
87 B13: [37] ANTIPH. D36a, D36b, R14, R15, R16a, R16b
87 B14: [37] ANTIPH. D14, R1
87 B15: [37] ANTIPH. D7, D8
87 B16: [37] ANTIPH. D82
87 B17: [37] ANTIPH. D11
87 B18: [37] ANTIPH. D12a, D12b
87 B19: [37] ANTIPH. D13a, D13b
87 B20: [37] ANTIPH. D15
87 B21: [37] ANTIPH. D16
87 B22: [37] ANTIPH. D18
87 B23: [37] ANTIPH. D19a
87 B24: [37] ANTIPH. D19b
87 B24a: [37] ANTIPH. D20, D41b
87 B25: [37] ANTIPH. D21
87 B26: [37] ANTIPH. D22
87 B27: [37] ANTIPH. D23
87 B28: [37] ANTIPH. D24
87 B29: [37] ANTIPH. D25
87 B29a: [37] ANTIPH. D28
87 B30: [37] ANTIPH. D26a
87 B31: [37] ANTIPH. D26b
87 B32: [37] ANTIPH. D27
87 B33: [37] ANTIPH. D29
87 B34: [37] ANTIPH. D31
87 B35: [37] ANTIPH. D33

87 B36: [37] ANTIPH. D34
87 B37: [37] ANTIPH. D35
87 B38: [37] ANTIPH. D30
87 B39: [37] ANTIPH. D32
87 B40: [37] ANTIPH. D79
87 B41: [37] ANTIPH. D80
87 B42: [37] ANTIPH. D81a
87 B43: [37] ANTIPH. D39a, D39b
87 B44a: [37] ANTIPH. D38, R7
87 B45: [37] ANTIPH. D43
87 B46: [37] ANTIPH. D44
87 B47: [37] ANTIPH. D45
87 B48: [37] ANTIPH. D42
87 B49: [37] ANTIPH. D57
87 B50: [37] ANTIPH. D51
87 B51: [37] ANTIPH. D50
87 B52: [37] ANTIPH. D48
87 B53: [37] ANTIPH. D52
87 B53a: [37] ANTIPH. D53
87 B54: [37] ANTIPH. D59
87 B55: [37] ANTIPH. D47a
87 B56: [37] ANTIPH. D47b
87 B57: [37] ANTIPH. D54
87 B58: [37] ANTIPH. D55
87 B59: [37] ANTIPH. D56
87 B60: [37] ANTIPH. D62
87 B61: [37] ANTIPH. D63
87 B62: [37] ANTIPH. D60
87 B63: [37] ANTIPH. D41a, R1
87 B64: [37] ANTIPH. D61
87 B65: [37] ANTIPH. D49
87 B66: [37] ANTIPH. D58
87 B67: [37] ANTIPH. D64
87 B67a: [37] ANTIPH. D65

CONCORDANCE a (DK > LM)

87 B68: [37] ANTIPH. D66
87 B69: [37] ANTIPH. D67
87 B70: [37] ANTIPH. D46
87 B71: [37] ANTIPH. D68
87 B72: [37] ANTIPH. D71
87 B73: [37] ANTIPH. D73
87 B74: [37] ANTIPH. D69
87 B75: [37] ANTIPH. D70
87 B76: [37] ANTIPH. D72
87 B77: [37] ANTIPH. D74
87 B78: [37] ANTIPH. D76
87 B79: [37] ANTIPH. D75a,
   R10

87 B80: [37] ANTIPH. D77a
87 B81: [37] ANTIPH. R11
87 B81a: [37] ANTIPH. D78
87 B93: [37] ANTIPH. P11
88 A1: [33] SOC. P17
88 B18: [43] DRAM. T49a
88 B19: [43] DRAM. T49b
88 B22: [43] DRAM. T67
88 B25: [43] DRAM. T63
89.: [40] ANON. IAMBL.
90.: [41] DISS., [43] DRAM.
   T66

CONCORDANCE

b
LAKS-MOST > DIELS-KRANZ (AND OTHER EDITIONS OF REFERENCE)

[1] DOX.

T1	86 B6	T15	24 B1a, 31 A86, 59 A92, 62.2, 64 A19, 68 A135
T2	23 A6		
T3	22 A6		
T4	21 A29, 22 A10, 31 A29	T16	59 A117, 62.3, 64 A32
T5	≠ DK	T17	*Dox. Gr.*, pp. 327–29
T6	24 A3, 36 A6, 82 B1		
T7	≠ DK	T18a	*Dox. Gr.*, pp. 364–66
T8	≠ DK		
T9	≠ DK	T18b	*Dox. Gr.*, pp. 381–82
T10	≠ DK		
T11	68 A135	T18c	*Dox. Gr.*, pp. 406–7
T12	31 B109		
T13	42.5	T19	*Dox. Gr.*, p. 327
T14	11 A13, 11 B1, 12 A9, 18.7, 22 A5, 38 A4	T20	≠ DK
		T21	≠ DK
		T22	*Dox. Gr.*, pp. 589–90

[2] COSM.

T1	7 B2	T11	7 B1a, 9 B2, 30
T2a	1 B2, 1 B10, 1		A5, 31 B27
	B13, 3 B5, 11	T12a	≠ DK
	A12, 70 A24	T12b	≠ DK
T2b	7 B2	T12c	≠ DK
T3	≠ DK	T12d	≠ DK
T4	28 A44	T12e	≠ DK
T5	31 B39	T13	1 B12
T6	11 A12	T14	≠ DK
T7	31 B115	T15	1 B2
T8	≠ DK	T16	1 B13
T9	≠ DK	T17	≠ DK
T10a	1 B2, 1 B10, 1	T18	≠ DK
	B13, 3 B5, 11	T19	≠ DK
	A12, 70 A24	T20	≠ DK
T10b	38 B1	T21	2 B14, 9 B1
T10c	≠ DK	T22	9 B1

[3] MOR.

(Only those entries are indicated for which there is a corresponding entry in DK)

T4	59 A112	T34	1 B17, 1 B18, 1
T17	3 B1		B19, 1 B20
T30	31 B135	T35	10.3
T32a	31 B146	T37	80 A25
T32d	31 B146	T38	58C.4

[4] PHER.

P1	7 A1	D15	7 B7
P2	7 A2	D16a	7 B9
P3	7 A5	D16b	7 B1
P4	8 Schibli	D17	7 B12
P5	7 A1	D18	7 B13a
P6	7 A2	D19	7 B13
P7	7 B4	R1	7 B4
P8	38 Schibli	R2	p. 88 Schibli
P9	7 A2	R3	7 A7
P10	7 A1	R4	9 Schibli
P11	23 Schibli	R5a	7 A2
P12	25 Schibli	R5b	7 A2
P13	32 Schibli	R6	13 Schibli
P14	7 A1	R7	38 Schibli
P15	7 A4	R8a	7 B11
P16	28 Schibli	R8b	7 B13
D1	7 A2	R9	7 A1
D2	7 A1	R10	7 A2a
D3	7 A11	R11	58 Schibli
D4	38 Schibli	R12	46b Schibli
D5	7 B1	R13	7 A6
D6	7 A8	R14	7 A5
D7	7 B1a	R15	7 A2
D8	7 B3	R16	7 A5
D9	7 B2	R17	7 A7a
D10	7 B2	R18	7 B7
D11	7 B4	R19	7 A12
D12	7 B4	R20	7 A9
D13	7 B5	R21	7 A10
D14	7 B6	R22	7 B1a

R23	7 A8	R28	7 B2
R24	7 B3	R29	7 A5
R25	7 A9	R30	7 A9
R26	7 B6	R31a	Hercher 740
R27a	7 B5	R31b	test. 238 Wöhrle
R27b	79 Schibli		

[5] THAL.

P1a	11 A1	P19	11 A1
P1b	11 A1	P20	11 A1
P2	11 A1	P21	≠ DK
P3	11 A1	D1	11 A1
P4	11 A11	D2	Th 184 Wöhrle
P5	11 A11	D3	11 A12
P6	11 A6	D4	Th 210 Wöhrle
P7	11 A4	D5	11 A13b
P8	11 A1	D6a	11 A17a
P9	11 A5	D6b	11 A17a
P10	11 A5	D7	11 A14
P11	11 A1	D8	11 A15
P12	11 A9	D9	11 A16
P13	59 A30	D10	11 A22
P14	Th 22 Wöhrle	D11a	11 A22
P15	11 A10	D11b	11 A1
P16	11 A1	R1	11 A1
P17	11 A1	R2	Th 20 Wöhrle
P17a	11 A1	R3	Th 110 Wöhrle
P17b	11 A1	R4	11 A1
P17c	11 A1	R5	11 A11
P17d	11 A1	R6	11 A1
P18	11 A19	R7	11 B1

R8	11 A1	R29	11 A20
R9	11 A12	R30	11 A20
R10	11 B1	R31a	11 A1
R11	11 A1	R31b	11 A21
R12	Th 210 Wöhrle	R31c	11 A21
R13	11 A19	R32a	11 A12
R14	11 A1	R32b	Th 191 Wöhrle
R15	11 A1	R33a	11 A14
R16	11 A17	R33b	11 A14
R17	Th 91 Wöhrle	R34a	11 A22
R18	11 A17a	R34b	11 A1
R19	11 A17b	R35	11 A23
R20	11 A1	R36	11 A22a
R21	11 A18	R37	11 A1
R22	11 B2	R38	11 A23
R23	11 A13c	R39	Th 210 Wöhrle
R24	11 A15	R40	Th 145 Wöhrle
R25	11 A1	R41	Th 213 Wöhrle
R26	11 A20	R42	Th 229 Wöhrle
R27	11 A1	R43	7 A5
R28	11 A20	R44	11 B3

[6] ANAXIMAND.

P1	12 A11	P9	12 A5a
P2	12 A1	P10	12 A8
P3	12 A5	P11	12 A1
P4	12 A1	P12	I, p. 90 App;
P5	12 A9		Nachtrag,
P6	12 A6		p. 487.3–4
P7	Ar 23 Wöhrle	D1	12 A7
P8	12 A3	D2	12 A1

D3	12 A2	D33b	12 A23
D4	12 A6	D34	12 A24
D5	12 A1	D35a	12 A27
D6	12 A9, 12 B1	D35b	12 A27
D7	12 A11, 12 B2	D36	12 A27
D8	12 A10	D37	12 A29
D9	12 A15, 12 B3	D38	12 A30
D10	12 A14	D39	12 A30
D11	12 A1	D40	12 A30
D12	12 A9, 12 A16	R1	≠ DK
D13	12 A17	R2	12 A9
D14	12 A17	R3	12 A16
D15	12 A17	R4	12 A16
D16	12 A17	R5	≠ DK
D17	12 A17	R6	12 A17
D18	12 A17	R7	12 A9
D19	12 A17a	R8	12 A9a, 59 A41
D20	12 A18	R9	12 A9
D21	12 A20	R10	Ar 12 Wöhrle
D22	12 A18	R11	12 A16
D23	12 A21, 12 B4	R12	12 A14
D24	12 A21	R13	12 A14
D25	12 A21	R14	12 A1
D26	12 A22	R15	12 A4
D27	12 A22	R16	12 A5
D28	12 A22	R17	12 A19
D29	12 A25	R18	12 A30
D30	12 A26	R19	Ar 52 Wöhrle
D31	12 A1	R20	Ar 216 Wöhrle
D32	12 A26	R21a	≠ DK
D33a	12 A23	R21b	Ar 242 Wöhrle

CONCORDANCE b (LM > DK et al.)

[7] ANAXIMEN.

P1	13 A1	D23	13 A17
P2	13 A7	D24	13 A18
P3	13 A3	D25	13 A18
P4	13 A2	D26	13 A19
P5	As 176 Wöhrle	D27	13 A21
P6	≠ DK	D28	13 A21
D1	13 A5	D29	12 A28
D2	13 A6	D30	13 A23
D3	13 A7	D31	13 B2
D4	13 A4	R1a	As 7 Wöhrle
D5	13 A10	R1b	As 14 Wöhrle
D6	13 A10	R2	13 A1
D7	13 A5	R3	As 1 Wöhrle
D8	13 B1	R4	13 B1
D9	59 A65	R5	13 B2
D10	13 A11	R6	13 A10
D11	12 A17	R7	13 A10
D12	13 A13	R8	13 A14a
D13	13 A14	R9	13 A16
D14	13 A14	R10	As 18 Wöhrle
D15	13 A15	R11a	As 73 Wöhrle
D16	13 A14	R11b	As 74 Wöhrle
D17	13 A14	R11c	As 77 Wöhrle
D18	13 A15	R12	As 59 Wöhrle
D19	13 A20	R13a	13 A10
D20a	13 A20	R13b	As 101 Wöhrle
D20b	13 A20	R14	13 B3
D21	13 A17	R15	As 232 Wöhrle
D22	As 24 Wöhrle		

[8] XEN.

P1	21 A1	D6c	21 A36
P2	21 A6	D7	21 A19
P3	21 A7	D8	21 B11
P4	21 A8	D9	21 B12
P5a	21 A9	D10	21 B10
P5b	21 A9	D11	21 B13
P6	14.8, 21 A10	D12	21 B14
P7	21 A33	D13	21 B16
P8	21 A1	D14	21 B15
P9	21 A2	D15a	21 A52
P10	21 A30	D15b	21 A52
P11	21 A2	D16	21 B23
P12	21 A5	D17	21 B24
P13	21 A11	D18	21 B25
P14	21 A1	D19	21 B26
P15	21 A1	D20	21 A1
P16	21 A12	D21	Frag. dub. 47
P17	21 A13		Gentili-Prato
P18	21 A14	D22	21 A33
P19	21 A16	D23	21 A32
P20	21 A17	D24	21 A1
P21	21 A1	D25	21 A29, 21 B29
P22	21 A1	D26	21 B33
D1	21 A1	D27	21 A36, 21 B27
D2	21 A20	D28	21 A40
D3	21 A22	D29	21 A43
D4	21 A23	D30	21 B31
D5	21 A24	D31	21 A41a
D6a	21 B30	D32	21 A46
D6b	21 B39	D33	21 A42

D34	21 A41	D66	21 B8
D35	21 A41a	D67	21 B9
D36	21 A38	D68	21 B21
D37	21 A44	D69	21 B6
D38	21 A39	D70	21 B40
D39	21 B32	R1	21 A29
D40	21 A45	R2	21 A30
D41	21 B28	R3	21 A8
D42	21 A47	R4	21 A31
D43	21 A47	R5	21 A31
D44	21 B37	R6	21 A28
D45	21 A48	R7	21 A37
D46	21 B30	R8a	21 A1
D47	21 A50	R8b	21 A4
D48	21 A51	R10	21 A49
D49	21 B34	R11	21 A36
D50	21 B35	R12	21 A30
D51	21 B36	R13a	21 A47
D52	21 B38	R13b	21 A47
D53	21 B18	R14	21 A28
D54	21 B22	R15	≠ DK
D55	21 B17	R16	21 A35
D56	21 B21a	R17	21 A25
D57	21 B39	R18	21 A49
D58	21 B41	R19	21 A1
D59	21 B1	R20	21 A33
D60	21 B5	R21a	21 A35
D61	21 B2	R21b	≠ DK
D62	21 B3	R21c	≠ DK
D63	21 B4	R22	21 A35
D64	21 B7	R23	21 A34
D65	21 B20	R24	21 A36

R25a	21 A36	R28	21 A26
R25b	21 A36	R29	21 A27
R26	21 A36	R30	≠ DK
R27	21 A25		

[9] HER.

P1	22 A1	D6	22 B70
P2	22 A1a	D7	22 B74
P3	22 A1	D8	22 B87
P4	22 A1	D9	22 B97
P5	22 A1a	D10	22 B104
P6	22 A1	D11	22 B39
P7	22 A3b	D12	22 B49
P8	22 A3	D13	22 B29
P9	22 A1	D14	22 B121
P10a	T143 Mouraviev	D15	22 B5
P10b	T144 Mouraviev	D16	22 B15
P11	22 A1	D17	22 B68
P12	68 A21	D18	22 B14
P13	22 A1	D19	22 B28
P14	22 A1	D20	22 B40
P15	22 A9	D21	22 B42
P16	22 A1	D22	22 B56
P17	22 A1a	D23	22 A22
P18	p. 144.25–30; II,	D24	22 B105
	p. 3	D25a	22 B57
D1	22 B1	D25b	22 B106
D2	22 B2	D26	22 B129
D3	22 B17	D27	22 B81
D4	22 B34	D28	22 B28
D5	22 B19	D29	22 B113

D30	22 B116	D62	22 B8
D31	22 B55	D63	22 B80
D32	22 B101a	D64	22 B53
D33	22 B107	D65a	22 B12
D34	22 B7	D65b	22 A6
D35	22 B123	D65c	T353 Mouraviev
D36	22 B101	D66	T156 Mouraviev
D37	22 B18	D67	22 B126
D38	22 B86	D68	22 B88
D39	22 B22	D69	22 A19
D40	22 B35	D70	22 B62
D41	22 B93	D71	22 B26
D42	22 B92	D72	22 B21
D43	22 B108	D73	22 B102
D44	22 B41	D74	22 B78
D45	22 B32	D75	22 B79
D46	22 B50	D76	22 B52
D47	22 B10	D77	22 B83
D48	22 B67	D78	22 B61
D49	22 B51	D79	22 B9
D50	22 B54	D80a	22 B13
D51	22 B60	D80b	22 B37
D52	22 B59	D81	22 B82
D53	22 B48	D82	22 B64
D54	22 B103	D83	22 B16
D55	22 B23	D84	22 B66
D56	22 B111	D85	22 B30
D57	22 B58	D86	22 B31
D58	22 B84a	D87	22 B90
D59	22 B125	D88	22 B65
D60	22 B124	D89a	F3–94 Mouraviev
D61	22 B122	D89b	22 B3

D89c	22 B94	D117	22 B110
D90	22 B10	D118	22 B20
D91a	22 B6	D119	22 B96
D91b	T135 Mouraviev	D120	22 B27
D92a	T212, F80A	D121	22 B98
	Mouraviev	D122a	22 B24
D93b	22 B120	D122b	22 B25
D94	22 B99	D123	22 B63
D95	T564 Mouraviev	R1a	22 A1
D96	22 A14	R1b	≠ DK
D97	22 A14, Nachtrag	R1c	22 A1
	I, p. 492.6	R1d	≠ DK
D98	22 B45	R1e	≠ DK
D99	22 B115	R2	T469 Mouraviev
D100	22 B36	R3a	22 A1
D101	22 B77	R3b	22 A1
D102	22 B12	R3c	22 A1
D103	22 B118	R4	T687 Mouraviev
D104	22 B117	R5a	22 A4
D105	22 B114	R5b	22 A1
D106	22 B44	R5c	22 A1
D107	22 B47	R6	22 A4
D108	22 B33	R7	22 A4
D109	22 B84b	R8	T301 Mouraviev
D110	22 B1	R9	22 B49a
D111	22 B119	R10	T609 Mouraviev
D112	22 B43	R11	22 A1a
D113	22 B95	R12	22 B106
D114a	22 B112	R13	22 B30
D114b	22 B112	R14	T574A Mouraviev,
D115	22 A21		T565 Mouraviev
D116	22 B85	R15	28 B6

R16	22 A1	R43	22 A15
R17	66.3	R44	28 A46, 31 A86
R18	T112 Mouraviev	R45	22 A5
R19	65.4	R46a	22 A1
R20	Nachtrag II, pp. 421–22	R46b	22 A1
R21	66.2	R47	22 A6
R22	T78 Mouraviev	R48a	22 A15
R23	65.4	R48b	22 A17
R24a	65.5	R48c	T782 Mouraviev
R24b	T57 Mouraviev	R49	31 A62
R25	65.1	R50	T256 Mouraviev
R26	65.2	R51	22 B12
R27a	65.3	R52	22 C4
R27b	T99 Mouraviev	R53	T262 Mouraviev
R28a	65.3	R54	22 B71, 22 B72, 22 B73, 22 B74, 22 B76
R28b	T712 Mouraviev		
R29	22 A6	R55	22 B75
R30	23 A6	R56	22 B89
R31	22 A10	R57	T270 Mouraviev
R32	22 B51	R58	22 A20
R33	22 B82, 22 B83	R59	22 A16
R34	T134 Mouraviev	R60	22 A16
R35	22 A10	R61	T303 Mouraviev
R36	T172 Mouraviev	R62	T260, T940 Mouraviev
R37	22 A7		
R38a	T148 Mouraviev	R63	22 B30
R38b	T148 Mouraviev	R64	22 A13
R39	T149 Mouraviev	R65	22 A11
R40	T152 Mouraviev	R66	22 A18
R41	T151 Mouraviev	R67	T279 Mouraviev
R42	T143 Mouraviev		

R68	Nachtrag I, p. 491.37	R92	T901 Mouraviev
R69	T376 Mouraviev	R93a	22 A1
R70	T694 Mouraviev	R93b	22 C3.1
R71a	T651 Mouraviev	R94	22 A1
R71b	ad 22 B67a	R95	T294 Mouraviev
R72	T694 Mouraviev	R96	ad 22 B74
R73	22 A16	R97	22 A1
R74	Nachtrag I, p. 491.42	R98	22 A1
R75a	T339 Mouraviev	R99	22 C5
R75b	T338 Mouraviev	R100a	T326 Mouraviev
R76	Nachtrag I, p. 491.39	R100b	T328 Mouraviev
R77	T601 Mouraviev	R100c	T327 Mouraviev
R78	T604 Mouraviev	R100d	T330 Mouraviev
R79	22 B22	R100e	T329 Mouraviev
R80	T643b Mouraviev	R100f	22 B123
R81	22 B18	R100g	22 B123, T736 Mouraviev
R82	22 B30, 22 B31	R100h	T772 Mouraviev
R83	22 B28	R101a	22 B118, T358 Mouraviev
R84	22 B62	R101b	22 B118, T818 Mouraviev
R85	22 B26	R101c	22 B118, T342 Mouraviev
R86	22 B1, 22 B50–67	R101d	22 B118, T510 Mouraviev
R87	22 B24, 22 B25, 22 B27	R101e	22 B118, T509 Mouraviev
R88	22 B84a–b	R101f	22 B118, T511 Mouraviev
R89	22 B96	R101g	22 B118, T623 Mouraviev
R90a	22B77		
R90b	22 B51		
R91	Nachtrag I, p. 494.15		

136

R101h	22 B118, T578	R104	68 B65
	Mouraviev	R105	68 B98
R101i	22 B118, T290	R106	68 B236
	Mouraviev	R107	68 B147
R101j	22 B118, T591	R108	22 B46
	Mouraviev	R109	22 B131
R101k	T735 Mouraviev	R110	22 B132
R101l	22B118, T734	R111	22 B133
	Mouraviev	R112	22 B134
R102a	T479 Mouraviev	R113	22 B135
R102b	T478 Mouraviev	R114	22 B125a
R102c	22 B95	R115	T1044 Mouraviev
R102d	T481 Mouraviev	R116	22 B130
R102e	22B95	R117a	T705 Mouraviev
R103	68 B64	R117b	T705 Mouraviev

[10] PYTH. a

P1	14.8	P15	≠ DK
P2	≠ DK	P16	14.3
P3	14.10	P17a	≠ DK
P4	≠ DK	P17b	≠ DK
P5	14.8	P18	14.4
P6	14.8	P19	14.8
P7	≠ DK	P20a	14.9
P8	≠ DK	P20b	≠ DK
P9	≠ DK	P21	14.11
P10	17.1, 31 B155	P22	≠ DK
P11	14.13, 14.6	P23	14.8
P12	≠ DK	P24	14.4
P13	53b Schibli	P25	14.8a
P14	≠ DK	P26	≠ DK

P27	22 B40	P40	≠ DK
P28	22 B129	P41	≠ DK
P29	36 B4	P42	14.7
P30	14.2	P43	≠ DK
P31	14.6	P44a	≠ DK
P32	21 B7	P44b	≠ DK
P33	31 B129	P44c	≠ DK
P34	14.7	P44d	≠ DK
P35	≠ DK	P45	14.5
P36	14.7	P46a	≠ DK
P37	14.8	P46b	14.13
P38	≠ DK	P46c	14.13
P39	14.8	P47	I, p. xii

[10] PYTH. b

T1	14.10	T15	21 Mansfeld
T2	16 Mansfeld	T16	18.2
T3	58D.7	T17	58C.4
T4a	14.9	T18	18.2
T4b	58C.6	T19	20 Mansfeld
T4c	58C.6	T20	18.4
T5	≠ DK	T21	15 Mansfeld
T6	58C.4	T22	14.13
T7	≠ DK	T23	14.14
T8	18.4	T24	14.12
T9	12 Mansfeld	T25	14.16
T10	58D.1	T26	14.16
T11	≠ DK	T27	14.16
T12	14.4	T28	14.16
T13	16 Mansfeld	T29	14.10
T14	≠ DK	T30	58A.

T31	15.	T34	25.1
T32	19.1	T35	27.
T33	18.5	T36	46.3

[10] PYTH. c

D1a	≠ DK	D11	58B.1
D1b	14.19	D12	14.12
D1c	36 B2	D13	14.21
D1d	≠ DK	D14	28 A1
D2	46.2	D15	58C.4
D3	44 B22	D16	58C.6
D4	14.1	D17	≠ DK
D5	14.8a	D18	58C.4
D6	58B.4	D19	≠ DK
D7a	≠ DK	D20	58C.4
D7b	58B.19	D21	58C.1
D8	≠ DK	D22	58C.3
D9a	≠ DK	D23	58C.2
D9b	≠ DK	D24	58C.5
D10	58B.15	D25	58C.2

[11] HIPPAS.

P1a	18.2	D5	18.9
P1b	18.2, 58A.	D6	18.15
P2	18.4	D7	18.12
P3	17.3	D8	18.13
D1	18.1	D9	18.14
D2	18.3		
D3	18.7		
D4	18.7		

[12] PHILOL.

P1	44 A1	D15	44 B7
P2	44 A1a	D16	44 A9
P3	44 A4a	D17	44 B17
P4	44 A1a	D18	44 A18
P5	44 A3	D19	44 A16
P6	44 A2	D20	44 A17
P7	44 A7	D21	44 A21
P8	44 A1	D22	44 A19
D1a	44 A1	D23	44 A20
D1b	44 A1	D24	44 A22
D2	44 B1	D25a	44 A27
D3	44 B2	D25b	44 A28
D4	44 B3	D26	44 B13
D5	44 B6	D27	44 A23
D6	44 A7a	D28	44 B16
D7	44 B4	D29	44 A11
D8	44 A29	D30	44 B14
D9	44 B5	D31	44 A14
D10	44 A10	D32	44 A25
D11	44 B20	D33a	44 A14
D12	44 B11	D33b	44 A14
D13	44 A24	D34	44 A14
D14	44 B6	D35	44 A26

[13] EUR.

P1a	58A.	P4	45.1
P1b	58A.	P5	≠ DK
P2	45.1	P6	45.1
P3	14.10, 44 A4	P7a	44 A5

P7b	45.1	D1	45.3
P8	45.1	D2	45.2

[14] ARCHY.

P1	47 A1	P22	47 A3
P2a	A6b Huffman	D1	47 A22
P2b	58A.	D2	47 A12
P3a	A6b Huffman	D3	47 A1
P3b	A6b Huffman	D4	47 B3
P4	47 A1	D5	47 B4
P5	A1d Huffman	D6	47 A20
P6	47 A4	D7	47 A21
P7	A5c4 Huffman	D8	18.15
P8	44 A3	D9	A15 Huffman
P9a	A5b9 Huffman	D10	A15a Huffman
P9b	A5b10 Huffman	D11	A14a Huffman
P10	A5c3 Huffman	D12	47 A14
P11a	47 A5	D13	47 A19
P11b	47 A5	D14	47 B1
P11c	47 A5	D15	47 B2
P12	47 A1	D16	47 A18
P13	A6c Huffman	D17	47 A16
P14	44 A7	D18	A19c Huffman
P15	A6g Huffman	D19	47 A19b
P16	47 A7	D20	47 A23
P17	A7a Huffman	D21	47 A24
P18a	47 A8	D22	47 A25
P18b	47 A10	D23	47 A23a
P19	47 A11	D24	47 A9
P20	A11a Huffman	D25a	≠ DK
P21	≠ DK	D25b	≠ DK

[15] HIC.

D1	50.1	D2	50.2

[16] ECPH.

P1	58A	D3	51.4
D1	51.1	D4	51.3
D2	51.2	D5	51.5

[17] PYTHS. ANON.

D1	58B.4	D18	58B.12
D2	58B.8	D19	58B.15
D3	58B.8	D20a	58B.4
D4	58B.4	D20b	≠ DK
D5	58B.22	D21	63 Mansfeld/
D6	58B.5		Primavesi
D7	58B.6	D22	58B.21
D8	58B.7	D23	58B.20
D9	58B.30	D24	58B.18
D10	58B.9	D25	≠ DK
D11	47 A21	D26	47 A17
D12a	58B.28	D27	58B.9
D12b	58B.28	D28	58B.26
D12c	58B.28	D29	58B.30
D13	58B.26	D30	58B.30
D14	43 Mansfeld/	D31	58B.30
	Primavesi	D32	58B.31
D15	58B.17	D33	58B.31
D16	58B.15	D34	58B.31
D17	58B.16	D35	58B.34

D36	58B.37	D48	58B.42
D37	≠ DK	D49	58B.40
D38	58B.34	D50	44 A23
D39	12 A19	D51	58B.41
D40a	44 A16	D52	58B.39
D40b	58B.4	D53	58B.41
D41	58B.22, 58B.36	D54a	58D.4
D42	58B.36	D54b	58D.4
D43	42.5	D54c	58D.10
D44	41.10	D54d	58D.11
D45	58B.37c	D54e	58D.5
D46	58B.35	D54f	58D.8
D47	≠ DK	D54g	58D.8

[18] PYTHS. R

R1	47 B1	R12	58B.14
R2	≠ DK	R13	58B.32
R3	≠ DK	R14	58B.11
R4	44 B14	R15	58B.8
R5	≠ DK	R16	58B.37
R6a	44 A13	R17	58B.26
R6b	≠ DK	R18	58B.22
R6c	47 A13	R19	58B.22
R6d	≠ DK	R20	58B.10
R6e	14.8, 58D.11, 47 A9	R21	58B.38
R7	44 A13	R22	58B.29
R8	≠ DK	R23	58B.9
R9	58B.13	R24	58B.37
R10	58B.12	R25a	≠ DK
R11	47 A13	R25b	≠ DK
		R26	58B.39

R27	58B.34	R49	F8a Huffmann
R28	≠ DK	R50	44 A26
R29a	≠ DK	R51	44 B21
R29b	≠ DK	R52	pp. 21–32 Thesleff
R29c	≠ DK	R53	pp. 15–19 Thesleff
R30	≠ DK	R54	pp. 111, 114
R31	≠ DK		Thesleff
R32	p. 237 Thesleff	R55a	p. 207 Thesleff
R33	58B.1a	R55b	p. 205 Thesleff
R34	58C.6	R56a	48.3
R35a	≠ DK	R56b	p. 126 Thesleff
R35b	≠ DK	R56c	p. 135 Thesleff
R35c	≠ DK	R57a	p. 79 Thesleff
R36	≠ DK	R57b	pp. 79–80 Thesleff
R37	≠ DK	R58	p. 71 Thesleff
R38	≠ DK	R59	p. 187 Thesleff
R39	≠ DK	R60	≠ DK
R40	≠ DK	R61	pp. 225–26
R41a	≠ DK		Thesleff
R41b	≠ DK	R62a	p. 226 Thesleff
R42	≠ DK	R62b	p. 60 Thesleff
R43	≠ DK	R63	pp. 195–96
R44	≠ DK		Thesleff
R45a	14.19	R64	17.1
R45b	14.19	R65	p. 194.27 Thesleff
R45c	≠ DK	R66	p. 142 Thesleff
R45d	≠ DK	R67	≠ DK
R46a	p. 164 Thesleff	R68	≠ DK
R46b	p. 164 Thesleff	R69	≠ DK
R47a	44 B22	R70	≠ DK
R47b	44 B22	R71a	≠ DK
R48	44 B11	R71b	≠ DK

R72	58B.15	R73b	≠ DK
R73a	≠ DK		

[19] PARM.

P1	28 A1	P23	≠ DK
P2	28 A11	D1	28 A13
P3	28 A11	D2	28 A1
P3b	≠ DK	D3	28 A14
P4a	28 A5	D4	28 B1
P4b	28 A5	D5	28 B5
P5	28 A6	D6	28 B2, 28 B3
P6a	28 A1	D7	28 B6
P6b	28 A2	D8	28 B7, 28 B8
P7	28 A7	D9	28 B10
P8	28 A1	D10	28 B4
P9	28 A12	D11	28 B11
P10	28 A4	D12	28 B10
P11	58A.	D13	28 B9
P12a	28 A5	D14a	28 B12
P12b	28 A5	D14b	28 B12
P12c	28 A5	D15a	28 A37
P13	31 A2	D15b	28 A37
P14	28 A9	D16	28 B13
P15	≠ DK	D17	28 A37
P16	28 A3	D18	28 A37
P17	30 A1	D19	28 A38
P18	28 A8	D20	28 A39
P19	≠ DK	D21	28 A40
P20	28 A1	D22	28 A1, 28 A40a
P21	28 A12	D23	28 A40a
P22	28 A12	D24	28 A43a

D25	28 A43
D26	28 A41
D27	28 B14
D28	28 B15
D29	28 A42
D30	28 A42
D31	28 B21
D32	28 A22
D33a	28 A1
D33b	28 A44
D34	≠ DK
D35	28 B15a
D36	28 A44
D37	28 A44a
D38	28 A44a
D39	28 A44a
D40	28 A1
D41	28 A51
D42	28 A53
D43	28 A52
D44	24 A13
D45	28 A53
D46	28 B17
D47	28 A53
D48	28 A54
D49	28 B18
D50	28 A54
D51	28 B16
D52	28 A46
D53a	28 A1
D53b	28 A45

D54	28 A45
D55	28 A45
D56	28 A45
D57	28 A47
D58	28 A50
D59	28 A46b
D60	28 A46a
D61	28 B13
D62	28 B19
R1	21 A25
R2a	28 A15
R2b	28 A16
R3a	28 A20
R3b	28 A20
R4	28 A18
R5a	≠ DK
R5b	28 A20
R6	28 A5
R7	28 A14
R8	28 B1
R9	≠ DK
R10a	≠ DK
R10b	≠ DK
R11	28 B8
R12	28 A24
R13	28 A7
R14	≠ DK
R15	≠ DK
R16	28 B1, 28 B19
R17	28 A34
R18	28 B8

R19	≠ DK	R48	≠ DK
R20	≠ DK	R49	≠ DK
R21	28 B8	R50	28 A28
R22	≠ DK	R51	28 A19
R23	≠ DK	R52	28 B1, 28 B19
R24	28 B8	R53a	28 B10
R25a	28 A26	R53b	28 A34
R25b	≠ DK	R54	28 A33
R26	28 B8	R55a	28 A32
R27	28 A28	R55b	≠ DK
R28	28 A29	R56a	28 B13
R29	28 A22	R56b	≠ DK
R30	28 A23	R57	28 B13
R31	≠ DK	R58	28 B13
R32	≠ DK	R59	28 A37
R33	≠ DK	R60	28 A23
R34	28 A36	R61	28 A46
R35	28 A36	R62	28 A5
R36	28 A31	R63	≠ DK
R37	28 B8	R64	28 A1
R38	≠ DK	R65	≠ DK
R39	28 B1	R66	28 A4
R40	28 A1, 28 B7	R67	28 A4
R41	≠ DK	R68	28 A1
R42	28 B7	R69	28 A48
R43	≠ DK	R70	≠ DK
R44	≠ DK	R71	≠ DK
R45	≠ DK	R72	28 B4
R46	≠ DK	R73	28 A21
R47	28 A25		

[20] ZEN.

P1a	29 A1	D11	29 B3
P1b	29 A2	D12a	29 A29
P2	29 A3	D12b	29 A29
P3	≠ DK	D13a	29 A24
P4	29 A1	D13b	Nachtrag I,
P5a	29 A11		p. 498
P5b	29 A11	D14	29 A25
P6	29 A11	D15a	29 A26
P7	29 A4	D15b	≠ DK
P8	29 A1	D16a	29 A27
P9	29 A1	D16b	29 A27
P10	29 A1	D17	29 B4
P11	29 A4	D18	29 A28
P12	29 A5	D19	29 A25
P13	29 A6	R1	I, p. 252.2–3
P14	29 A15	R2	29 A12
P15	29 A19	R3	29 A13
P16	29 A20	R4	29 A10
P17	29 A1	R5	29 A23
P18	≠ DK	R6	29 A4
D1	29 A25	R7	29 A1
D2	29 A15	R8	≠ DK
D3	29 A15	R9	29 A15
D4	A12 Untersteiner	R10a	≠ DK
D5	29 B1	R10b	≠ DK
D6	29 B1	R11	29 A21
D7	29 B2	R12	29 B2
D8	29 A21	R13	≠ DK
D9	29 A22	R14	29 A21
D10	29 A16	R15	29 B4

CONCORDANCE b (LM > DK et al.)

R16	29 A29	R28	≠ DK
R17	29 A25	R29	≠ DK
R18	≠ DK	R30	29 A22
R19	≠ DK	R31	29 A22
R20	≠ DK	R32	≠ DK
R21	29 A28	R33	≠ DK
R22	29 A24	R34	≠ DK
R23	29 A24	R35	29 A2
R24	≠ DK	R36	29 A14
R25	≠ DK	R37	29 A23
R26	≠ DK	R38	29 A30
R27a	≠ DK	R39	29 A1
R27b	29 A15		

[21] MEL.

P1	30 A1	D7	30 B5
P2	30 A1	D8	30 B9
P3	30 A2	D9	30 B10
P4	30 A3	D10	30 B7
P5	30 A1	D11	30 B8
P6	30 A1	D12a	30 A8
P7	30 A2	D12b	30 A8
P8	30 A3	D13	≠ DK
D1a	28 A13	D14	30 A14
D1b	30 A4	D15	30 A9
D2a	30 B1	D16	≠ DK
D2b	≠ DK	D17	30 A1
D3	30 B2	D18	29 A23
D4	30 B3	D19	30 A5
D5	30 B4	D20	I, pp. 268–73
D6	30 B6	R1	30 A6

R2a	28 B8	R19	29 A1
R2b	≠ DK	R20	≠ DK
R3	30 A5	R21a	≠ DK
R4	≠ DK	R21b	≠ DK
R5	30 A7	R21c	≠ DK
R6	≠ DK	R21d	≠ DK
R7	21 A30	R21e	≠ DK
R8	30 B8	R22a	≠ DK
R9a	30 A10	R22b	≠ DK
R9b	30 A10	R22c	≠ DK
R9c	30 A10	R22d	≠ DK
R10	30 A10	R23a	≠ DK
R11	30 A11	R23b	≠ DK
R12	≠ DK	R24a	28 A29
R13	≠ DK	R24b	28 A36
R14	≠ DK	R24c	28 A36
R15	≠ DK	R24d	30 A9
R16	≠ DK	R24e	64 A10
R17a	30 A5	R25	30 A12
R17b	30 A5	R26	30 A13
R17c	30 A5	R27	30 A1
R17d	30 A5	R28	30 A6
R17e	30 A5	R29	30 B11
R17f	30 A5	R30	30 B12
R18	30 A14		

[22] EMP.

P1	31 A1	P4	31 A2
P2	31 A9	P5a	31 A1
P3a	31 A1	P5b	31 A1
P3b	31 A1	P6	31 A1

CONCORDANCE b (LM > DK et al.)

P7	31 A1	D3	31 A12
P8a	31 A1	D4	31 B112
P8b	31 A1	D5	31 B113
P8c	31 A1	D6	31 B114
P8d	31 A1	D7	31 B131
P9	31 A1	D8	31 B132
P10	31 A1	D9	31 B133
P11	31 A8	D10	31 B115
P12	31 A1	D11	31 B115
P13	31 A1	D12	31 B142
P14	31 A1	D13	31 B117
P15	31 A1	D14	31 B118
P16	31 A1	D15	31 B119
P17	31 A15	D16	31 B120
P18	31 A1	D17	31 B124
P19	31 A1	D18	31 B125
P20	31 A1	D19	31 B126
P21	31 A1	D20	31 B148
P22	31 A1	D21	31 B122
P23	31 A17	D22	31 B123
P24	31 A1	D23	31 B116
P25a	31 A1	D24	31 B121
P25b	31 A1	D25	31 B128
P26	31 A2	D26	31 B130
P27	31 A1	D27a	31 B135
P28a	31 A20	D27b	31 B135
P28b	31 A20	D28	31 B136
P29	31 A1	D29	31 B137
P30	31 A1	D30	31 B145
P31	31 A1	D31	31 B141
D1	31 A1	D32	31 B140
D2	31 A2	D33	31 B144

D34	31 B139	D64	31 B151
D35	31 B143	D65	31 B18
D36	31 B127	D66	146 Bollack
D37	26 Mansfeld/	D67	31 B37
	Primavesi	D68	31 B90
D38	31 B129	D69	31 B91
D39	31 B146	D70	31 B93
D40	31 B147	D71	31 B34
D41	31 B1	D72	31 B33
D42	31 B2	D73	31 B17, 31 B20
D43	31 B111	D74	31 B76
D44	31 B3	D75	31 B35
D45	31 B25	D76	≠ DK
D46	31 B24	D77a	31 B21
D47	31 B4	D77b	31 B26
D48	31 B12	D78	31 A29
D49	31 B13	D79a	22 A10
D50	31 B14	D79b	31 A52
D51	31 B11	D80	31 A28
D52	31 B15	D81	31 A46
D53	31 B8	D82	31 A42
D54	31 B9	D83	31 A42
D55	31 B10	D84a	Nachtrag I,
D56	31 A33		p. 500
D57	31 B6	D84b	≠ DK
D58a	31 B98	D85a	31 A38
D58b	31 B21	D85b	≠ DK
D59	31 B7	D86a	≠ DK
D60	31 B23	D86b	≠ DK
D61	31 B71	D87	31 B29
D62	31 B19	D88	31 B13
D63	31 B16	D89	31 B27

CONCORDANCE b (LM > DK et al.)

D90	31 B28	D118	31 A51
D91	31 B27a	D119	31 A50
D92	31 B29	D120	31 A58
D93	31 B134	D121a	31 A53
D94	31 B30	D121b	31 A54
D95	31 B31	D122	31 B38
D96	31 B27	D123	31 B44
D97	31 A30	D124	31 B41
D98	31 B27	D125	31 B40
D99a	31 A49	D126a	31 A56
D99b	31 A49	D126b	31 A56
D100a	31 A66	D127	31 A30
D100b	31 A66	D128	31 A1
D101	31 B22	D129	31 A50
D102	31 B51	D130	31 A58
D103	31 A35	D131	31 B48
D104	31 B36	D132	31 B42
D105	31 B53	D133	31 A59
D106	31 B59	D134a	31 A60
D107	31 B104	D134b	31 A60
D108	31 B54	D134c	31 A30
D109	31 B52	D135a	31 A60
D110	31 A68	D135b	31 A1
D111	31 A69	D136	31 A61
D112	31 A69	D137	31 B46
D113	31 B39	D138	31 B47
D114	31 A50	D139	31 B45
D115	31 A1	D140	31 B42, 31 B43
D116	Nachtrag I, p. 499	D141	31 B43
D117a	31 A67	D142	31 A62
D117b	31 A67	D143	31 B149
		D144	31 A65

D145	31 A64	D173a	31 A81
D146a	31 A63	D173b	28 A52
D146b	31 A63	D174	31 A81
D147a	31 B55	D175	31 A81
D147b	31 B56	D176	31 A81
D147c	31 A66	D177	31 B97
D148	31 A89	D178a	31 A75
D149	31 B59	D178b	≠ DK
D150	31 A70	D179	31 B69
D151	31 A72	D180	31 A81
D152	31 B61	D181	31 A81
D153	31 B58	D182	31 A81
D154	31 B57	D183	31 A81
D155	31 B60	D184	31 A81
D156	31 B61	D185	31 B92
D157	31 B62	D186	31 A82
D158	31 B67	D187	31 B72
D159	31 B66	D188	31 B74
D160	31 B153	D189	31 A78
D161	31 A80	D190	31 B98
D162	31 B64	D191	31 B85
D163	31 A79	D192	31 B96
D164	31 B63	D193	464 Bollack
D165	31 A83	D194	31 A78
D166	31 A83	D195	31 B70
D167	31 A84	D196	31 B150
D168	31 B68	D197	31 B83
D169	31 B153a	D198	31 B82
D170a	31 A74	D199	31 B73
D170b	31 A74	D200	31 B75
D171	31 B63	D201a	31 B100
D172	31 B65	D201b	31 B100

D202	31 A74		D232	31 B101
D203a	31 A95		D233	31 A86
D203b	31 A77		D234	31 A94
D204	31 A66		D235	31 A86
D205	31 A77		D236a	31 A95
D206a	31 A85		D236b	31 A95
D206b	31 A85		D237	31 A86
D207	31 B109		D238a	31 A97
D208	31 B89		D238b	31 A96
D209	31 A92		D239	31 A30
D210	31 A87		D240	31 B105
D211	31 A86		D241	31 B107
D212	31 A90, 28 A47		D242	31 B103
D213	31 B86		D243	31 B106
D214	31 B87		D244a	31 B108
D215	31 B84		D244b	31 B108
D216	31 B88		D245	31 A70
D217	31 B95		D246	31 A70
D218	31 A86		D247	31A73
D219	31 A91		D248	31 B77
D220	31 A90		D249	31 B79
D221	31 A57		D250a	31 A70
D222	31 A92		D250b	31 A70
D223	31 A69a		D250c	31 A70
D224	31 B94		D250d	31 A70
D225	31 A88		D250e	31 A70
D226	31 A86, 31 B99		D251	31 B77
D227	31 A93		D252	31 B78
D228	31 B49		D253	31 B78
D229	31 A86		D254	31 B79
D230	31 A94		D255	31 B80
D231	31 B102		D256	31 B81

D257	31 B110	R21	31 A73
D258	31 B5	R22	31 B92
D259	31 B32	R23	31 A78
R1a	31 A22	R24	31 A91
R1b	31 A1	R25	31 A86
R1c	31 A25	R26	31 A47
R2a	31 A25	R27	31 A43
R2b	≠ DK	R28a	31 A32
R3a	31 A24	R28b	31 A45
R3b	31 A24	R29	31 A85
R4	31 B80	R30	28 A49
R5a	31 A1	R31	31 A21
R5b	31 A19	R32	31 B118
R6	31 A71	R33	≠ DK
R7	≠ DK	R34	≠ DK
R8a	≠ DK	R35	31 B8
R8b	≠ DK	R36	31 A27
R9	31 A43a	R37	31 A1
R10	31 A43	R38	≠ DK
R11a	31 A37	R39	31 B136, 31 B137
R11b	318 Bollack	R40a	SVF vol. 2,
R12	≠ DK		p. 255.15–20
R13a	31 A42	R40b	SVF vol. 2,
R13b	≠ DK		p. 237.23–25
R14	202 Bollack	R41	31 A31
R15a	202 Bollack	R42	31 B2, 31 B3
R15b	59 A68	R43	31 B129
R16	31 A57	R44	44 A29
R17	31 A70	R45	31 B5
R18	31 A94	R46	≠ DK
R19	31 A81	R47	≠ DK
R20	31 B97	R48	31 B115, 31 B119

R49	31 B122	R73	≠ DK
R50	31 B115, 31 B120	R74	31 B3, 31 B27, 31 B30
R51	31 B126		
R52	31 B121	R75	31 B57
R53	31 B121, 31 B158	R76	≠ DK
R54	≠ DK	R77	≠ DK
R55	≠ DK	R78	≠ DK
R56	31 B120	R79	31 B20, 31 B29
R57	31 B121	R80	31 B145
R58	≠ DK	R81	31 B119
R59	PPF 31 B115	R82	31 B146
R60	≠ DK	R83	31 B114
R61	≠ DK	R84	31 B147
R62	≠ DK	R85	31 A14
R63	103 Bollack	R86	31 B137
R64	31 B128	R87	≠ DK
R65	31 B139	R88	31 B131
R66a	≠ DK	R89	31 A33, 31 B16, 31 B29, 31 B110, 31 B115, 31 B131
R66b	≠ DK		
R66c	≠ DK		
R67	≠ DK	R90	31 A33
R68	31 B17, 31 B21, 31 B22, 31 B23, 31 B26	R91	31 A1
		R92	31 A33
		R93	31 B19
R69	31 B85, 31 B103, 31 B104	R94	PPF 31 B27
		R95	31 B134
R70	31 B35, 31 B71, 31 B73, 31 B75, 31 B86, 31 B87, 31 B95	R96	31 A23
		R97	31 B123
		R98	65 Mansfeld / Primavesi
R71	≠ DK	R99	31 B143
R72	≠ DK	R100	≠ DK

R101	≠ DK	R103	≠ DK
R102a	≠ DK	R104	≠ DK
R102b	≠ DK		

[23] ALCM.

P1	24 A3	D17	24 A10
P2	24 A1	D18	24 A5
P3	24 A1	D19a	24 A5
P4	24 B5	D19b	24 A8
D1a	24 A1	D20	24 A15
D1b	24 A2	D21	24 A13
D2	24 A2	D22	24 A13
D3	24 A1	D23	24 A13
D4	24 A1, 24 B1	D24	24 B3
D5	24 A3	D25	24 A14
D6	24 A4	D26	24 A13
D7	24 A4	D27	24 A13
D8	24 A4	D28	24 A17
D9	24 A12	D29	24 A16
D10	24 B1	D30	24 B4
D11	24 A5	D31	24 B2
D12a	24 A5	D32	24 A18
D12b	24 A6	D33	≠ DK
D13a	24 A5	R1	24 A3
D13b	24 A8	R2	24 A7
D14	24 A7	R3	24 A12
D15a	24 A5	R4	24 A12
D15b	24 A9	R5	24 A12
D16	24 A5	R6	24 A10

[24] HIPPO

P1	38 A1	D13	38 A18
P2a	38 A1	D14	38 A17
P2b	38 A16	D15	38 A15
P3	38 B4	D16	38 A16
P4	38 A1	D17	38 A16
P5	38 A3	D18a	38 A19
P6	38 A11	D18b	38 A19
P7	38 B4	D19	38 B1
D1	38 A3	D20	11 A13
D2	38 A4	R1	38 A7
D3	38 A6	R2	38 A19
D4	38 A5	R3	38 A4
D5	38 A6	R4	38 A6
D6	31 A4	R5	38 A8
D7	38 A10	R6a	38 B2
D8	38 A11	R6b	≠ DK
D9	38 A12	R6c	≠ DK
D10	38 A13	R7a	38 A8
D11a	38 A14	R7b	38 B2
D11b	38 A14	R8	38 B4
D12	38 A14		

[25] ANAXAG.

P1	59 A1	P7	59 A12
P2	59 A43	P8	59 A6
P3	59 A5	P9	59 A10
P4	59 A4	P10	59 A1
P5	59 A4	P11	59 A1
P6	59 A11	P12	59 A7

P13	59 A7	P38b	59 A33
P14a	59 A21	P39	59 A31
P14b	59 A20c	P40	59 A1
P14c	59 A1	P41	59 A34
P14d	59 A33	P42	59 A1
P14e	59 A20a	P43	59 A15
P15	≠ DK	P44	59 A40
P16	59 A7	P45	59 A3
P17	59 A7	P46	59 A1
P18	59 A15	P47	59 A23
P19	A15* Lanza	P48	59 A24
P20	59 A15	P49	59 A27
P21	59 A16	D1a	59 A37
P22	59 A32	D1b	59 A1
P23	59 A1	D2	59 A41
P24	59 A17	D3	59 A46
P25a	59 A17	D4	59 A42
P25b	59 A18	D5	59 B21
P26a	59 A38	D6	59 B21a
P26b	59 A3	D7a	59 A97
P27	59 A1, 61.2	D7b	59 A98
P28	59 A13	D8	59 A96
P29	59 A30	D9	59 B1
P30	59 A13	D10	59 B2
P31	59 A1	D11	59 A70
P32	59 A21	D12	59 B4
P33	59 A28	D13	59 B4
P34	59 A48	D14	59 B9
P35	59 A30	D15	59 B17
P36	59 A29	D16	59 B5
P37	59 A30	D17	59 A50
P38a	A7* Lanza	D18	59 A43

D19	59 A54	D46	59 A12
D20	59 A52	D47	59 A78
D21	59 B10	D48	59 A79
D22	59 B8	D49	59 A80
D23	59 B7	D50	59 A81
D24	59 B3	D51	59 A83
D25	59 B6	D52	59 A82
D26	59 B11	D53a	59 A84
D27	59 B12	D53b	59 A84
D28	59 B14	D54a	59 A85
D29a	A59* Lanza	D54b	59 A85
D29b	59 B13	D55	59 B19
D30	59 B15	D56	59 A86
D31	59 B16	D57	59 A86a
D32	59 A67	D58	13 A20, A88*
D33	59 A63		Lanza
D34	59 A64	D59	59 A68
D35a	59 A65	D60	59 A68
D35b	≠ DK	D61	59 A69
D36	59 A71	D62a	59 A89
D37a	A73* Lanza	D62b	59 A89
D37b	59 A73	D63	59 A89
D37c	59 A73	D64	59 A90
D38	59 A18	D65	59 A90
D39	59 A75	D66a	59 A91
D40	59 B18	D66b	59 A91
D41	59 A76	D66c	A91* Lanza
D42	59 A77	D66d	≠ DK
D43	59 A77	D67	59 A98a
D44	59 A77	D68	59 A113
D45a	59 A77	D69	59 A93
D45b	59 A77	D70	59 A92

D71	A93* Lanza	R3	59 A91
D72	59 A92	R4	59 A35
D73	59 A92	R5	59 A47
D74	59 A92	R6	≠ DK
D75	59 A106	R7	59 A73
D76	59 A74	R8	59 A43
D77	59 A74	R9	59 A58
D78	59 A92	R10	59 A47
D79a	59 A94	R11	59 A56
D79b	59 A92	R12	59 A100
D79c	59 A94	R13	59 A55
D80	59 A102	R14	59 A46
D81	59 B21b	R15	59 A43
D82	59 A103	R16	A52* Lanza
D83	59 A115	R17	≠ DK
D84	24 A13, 59 A107	R18a	59 A61
D85	24 A13, 59 A107	R18b	59 A61
D86	59 A107	R19	12 A9a
D87	59 A111	R20	59 A50
D88	59 A109	R21	59 A59
D89	59 A108	R22	59 A69
D90	59 A110	R23	≠ DK
D91	59 A114	R24a	59 A93
D92	59 B22	R24b	59 A93
D93	59 A116	R25	59 A86a
D94	59 A117	R26	59 A95
D95	59 A117	R27	59 A66
D96	59 A9	R28	59 A26
D97	59 A39	R29	59 A44
D98	59 A1	R30	59 A67
R1	59 A5	R31	≠ DK
R2	59 B21a	R32	59 A53

R33	59 B15, 59 B16	R36	59 B23
R34	59 B1, 59 B2	R37	≠ DK
R35	59 A1		

[26] ARCH.

P1	60 A1	D13	60 B1a
P2	≠ DK	D14a	60 A14
P3	60 A2	D14b	≠ DK
P4	60 A3	D15	60 A15
P5	60 A3	D16	60 A16
P6a	60 A3	D17	≠ DK
P6b	60 A3	D18	60 A17
D1	60 A2	D19	60 A1
D2	60 A4	D20	60 A17
D3	60 A1	D21	60 A6
D4	60 A5	D22	60 A1
D5	60 A10	R1	60 A5
D6	60 A7	R2	60 A1
D7	60 A1	R3	60 A26
D8	60 A9	R4	≠ DK
D9	60 A12	R5	60 B1
D10	60 A14	R6	60 B2
D11	60 A11	R7a	≠ DK
D12	60 A13	R7b	≠ DK

[27] ATOM.

P1a	67 A1	P4	67 A5
P1b	67 A8	P5	67 A5
P2	67 A1	P6	68 A1
P3	67 A10	P7	68 A40

P8	68 A2	P37a	68 A16
P9	68 B5	P37b	68 A1
P10	68 A1	P38	68 A15
P11	68 A2	P39	68 B116
P12a	68 A4	P40	68 B118
P12b	68 A4	P41	68 A17a
P12c	68 A4	P42	68 A1
P13	68 A5	P43	68 B144
P14	68 A6	P44a	68 B165
P15	68 A1	P44b	68 B165
P16a	68 A1	P45	68 B26f
P16b	68 A1	P46	68 A21
P17	68 A2	P47	0.3.11 Leszl
P18	68 A40	P48a	68 C3
P19	68 A13	P48b	68 C3
P20	0.3.21 Leszl	P48c	68 C3
P21	68 A1	P49	68 A18
P22	68 A1, 68 B116	P50	68 A1
P23	68 A1, 68 B5	P51	68 A1
P24	68 A1	P52	68 A29
P25	68 B163	P53	68 A24
P26	68 A1	P54	68 A6
P27	68 A9	P55	68 A1
P28	68 A10	P56	≠ DK
P29	68 A92	D1a	67 B2
P30	68 B15	D1b	≠ DK
P31	68 A1	D2a	68 A1
P32	68 A1	D2b	68 A1
P33	68 A22	D3	68 A31
P34	68 A23	D4	68 B9
P35	68 A27	D5	68 B6
P36	0.3.17 Leszl	D6	68 B11

D7	68 B119	D35	≠ DK
D8	68 B1	D36	68 A58, 68 B168
D9	68 B28	D37	68 A47
D10	67 A1	D38	68 B139
D11	67 A8	D39	67 A19
D12	68 A35a	D40	68 A60
D13	68 A1	D41	68 A48b
D14	68 B9, 68 B125	D42	68 A48
D15	68 B9	D43	68 A49
D16	68 B10	D44	≠ DK
D17	68 B6	D45	67 A15, 68 A120
D18	68 B7	D46	59 A45
D19	68 B8	D47	67 A15
D20	68 B11	D48	68 A60
D21	68 B11	D49	68 A61
D22	≠ DK	D50	68 A47
D23a	68 B9, 68 B125	D51	68 A47
D23b	68 A49	D52	68 A47
D24	68 B117	D53	68 A47
D25a	68 A36	D54	68 A47
D25b	68 A36	D55	68 B164
D26a	68 B165	D56	67 A9
D26b	68 B165	D57a	68 A120
D27	68 B10b	D57b	≠ DK
D28	68 B150	D58	67 A11
D29	68 A37	D59	67 A15
D30	67 A7	D60a	68 B155a
D31	67 A6	D60b	68 B155a
D32	67 A8, 68 A38	D61	67 A14
D33	68 B156	D62	68 A47
D34a	68 A57	D63	68 A49
D34b	68 B141	D64	68 A135

D65	68 A135	D93	67 A1
D66	68 A135	D94	67 A1
D67	68 A135	D95	68 A86
D68	68 A60	D96	68 B12
D69	68 A135	D97	68 A91
D70	68 A63	D98a	68 A91
D71	67 A9, 68 A35	D98b	68 A91
D72	68 A123	D99	59 A81
D73	67 B2	D100	68 A92
D74	68 A66	D101	68 A87
D75	68 A66	D102	68 A87
D76a	68 A68	D103	67 A1
D76b	≠ DK	D104	68 A89
D76c	68 A68	D105	68 A88
D77	68 A39	D106	68 A89a
D78	68 A71	D107	68 A90
D79	42.1 Leszl	D108	68 B14.6
D80a	67 A1	D109	68 B14.3
D80b	67 A1	D110	13 A20
D81	67 A10, 68 A40	D111	67 A26, 68 A94
D82	68 A67, 68 B167	D112	68 B15
D83a	68 A82	D113	68 B15
D83b	68 B138	D114	187.1.1 Leszl
D84	68 A84	D115	68 A12
D85	68 A81	D116	68 B152
D86	67 A23	D117	67 A25, 68 A93
D87	68 A39	D118	68 A93a
D88	68 A95	D119a	68 A97
D89	67 A27, 68 A96	D119b	68 A98
D90	67 B1	D120a	68 A99
D91	68 A85	D120b	68 A99
D92	67 A10, 68 A40	D121	68 A99

D122	68 A100	D154	68 B166
D123	68 A99a	D155	68 A126a
D124	68 A73	D156	68 A128
D125	68 A62	D157	68 A135
D126	68 A165	D158	68 A135
D127	90.1 Leszl	D159a	68 A135
D128	68 A139	D159b	68 A119
D129	68 B5	D160	68 A129
D130	68 A101	D161	68 A130
D131	68 A104	D162	67 A35, 68 A140
D132	67 A28	D163a	68 B32
D133	68 A101	D163b	68 B32
D134	68 A135	D163c	68 B32
D135	68 A105	D163d	68 B32
D136	67 A28	D164	68 B124
D137	68 A136	D165	68 A141
D138	67 A34	D166	68 A142
D139	68 A109	D167	68 B122a
D140	68 A117	D168	68 A146
D141	68 A160	D169	68 A144
D142	68 A160	D170	68 A145
D143	68 B1	D171	68 A145
D144	68 A116	D172	68 B148
D145	67 A29	D173	68 A143
D146	68 B123	D174	67 A36, 68 A143
D147	68 A135	D175	68 A144
D148	68 A121	D176	68 A152
D149	68 A122	D177	68 A143
D150	67 A31	D178	68 A149
D151	68 A136	D179	68 A151
D152	68 A77	D180	68 A159
D153	68 A77	D181	68 B120

D182	68 B135	D209b	68 A74
D183	68 B212	D210	68 B30
D184	≠ DK	D211	68 A138
D185	68 A147	D212	68 A138
D186a	98.3 Leszl	D213	68 B155
D186b	98.3 Leszl	D214	68 B155
D187	68 A148	D215	68 B162
D188a	68 A156	D216	68 B15b
D188b	99.4.2 Leszl	D217	68 B18
D189	68 A157	D218	68 B129
D190	68 A153	D219	68 B17
D191	68 A154	D220	68 B16
D192	68 A155	D221	68 B21
D193a	68 A150	D222	68 B23
D193b	68 A150	D223	68 B24
D194	68 A158	D224	68 B25
D195	68 B22	D225	68 B34
D196	68 B126	D226	68 B191
D197	68 A155a	D227	68 B189
D198	68 A155b	D228	68 B3
D199	59 A116	D229	68 A1
D200	31 A70, 68 A163	D230	68 A169
D201a	68 A162	D231	68 A167
D201b	68 A162	D232	68 B140
D202	68 B5	D233a	68 B159
D203	68 B154	D233b	68 B159
D204	68 B144	D234	68 B223
D205	68 B26	D235	68 B31
D206	68 B142	D236	68 B187
D207	68 A75	D237	68 B170
D208	68 A76	D238	68 B171
D209a	68 A74	D239	68 B290

D240	68 B234	D269	68 B173
D241	68 B188	D270	68 B221
D242	68 B207	D271	68 B220
D243	68 B194	D272	68 B196
D244	68 B211	D273	68 B108
D245	68 B146	D274	68 B119
D246	68 B233	D275	68 B269
D247	68 B232	D276	68 B288*
D248	68 B235	D277	68 B210
D249	68 B127	D278	68 B286
D250	68 B147	D279	68 B293
D251	68 B224	D280	68 B160
D252	68 B176	D281	68 B1a
D253	68 B231	D282	68 B1a
D254	68 B246	D283	68 B200
D255	68 B209	D284	68 B201
D256	68 B285	D285	68 B205
D257	68 B219	D286	68 B199
D258	68 B283	D287	68 B206
D259	68 B284, 68 B302.748	D288	68 B203
D260	68 B198	D289	68 B297
D261	68 B78, 68 B302.202	D290	68 B295
		D291	68 B296
D262	68 B282	D292	68 B230
D263	68 B218, 68 B302.194	D293a	68 B2
		D293b	68 B2
D264	68 B281	D294	68 B289
D265	68 B271	D295	68 B216
D266	68 B73	D296	68 B236
D267	68 B149	D297	68 B197
D268	68 B172	D298	68 B202
		D299	68 B204

D300	68 B42	D332	68 B228
D301	68 B58	D333	68 B229
D302	68 B292	D334	68 B88
D303	68 B175	D335	68 B237
D304	68 B61	D336	68 B244
D305	68 B57	D337	68 B60
D306	68 B193	D338	68 B145
D307	68 B64	D339	68 B53a
D308	68 B52	D340	68 B55
D309	68 B169	D341	68 B177
D310	68 B158	D342	68 B190
D311	68 B39	D343	68 B192
D312	68 B184	D344	68 B226
D313	68 B143	D345	68 B63, 68
D314	68 B240		B226bis
D315	68 B241	D346	68 B51
D316	68 B243	D347a	68 B225
D317	68 B294	D347b	68 B44
D318	68 B291	D348	68 B85
D319	68 B256	D349	68 B86
D320	68 B174	D350	68 B239
D321	68 B217	D351	68 B81
D322	68 B215	D352	68 B48
D323	68 B216bis	D353	68 B195
D324	68 B263	D354	68 B247
D325	68 B214	D355	68 B157
D326	68 B213	D356	68 B252
D327	68 B46	D357	68 B250
D328	68 B273	D358	68 B186
D329	68 B274	D359	68 B151
D330	68 B222	D360	68 B249
D331	68 B227	D361	68 B251

D362	68 B254		D394	68 B277
D363	68 B266		D395	68 B278
D364	68 B255		D396	68 B208
D365	68 B267		D397	68 B280
D366	68 B47		D398	68 B279
D367	68 B75		D399	68 B272
D368	68 B49		D400	68 B27
D369	68 B253		D401	68 B27a
D370	68 B265		D402	68 B28
D371	68 B287		D403	68 B33
D372	68 B238		D404	68 B178
D373	68 B268		D405	68 B179
D374	68 B153		D406	68 B180
D375	68 A1		D407	68 B182
D376	68 A166		D408	68 B183
D377	68 B261		D409	68 B185
D378	68 B262		D410	68 B77
D379	68 B248		D411	68 B242
D380	68 B245		D412	68 B59
D381	68 B257		R1a	68 A34a
D382	68 B258		R1b	68 A34a
D383	68 B259		R1c	68 A34a
D384	68 B260		R1d	68 A34a
D385	68 B181		R1e	68 A34a
D386	68 B264		R1f	68 A34a
D387	68 B41		R1g	68 A34a
D388	68 A170		R1h	68 A34a
D389	68 B288		R2a	68 A32
D390	68 B270		R2b	68 A32
D391	68 B111		R3a	68 B13
D392	68 B275		R3b	68 B29a
D393	68 B276		R3c	68 B129a

R3d	68 B19	
R3e	68 B128	
R3f	68 B131	
R3g	68 B20	
R4a	68 B298	
R4b	68 B29	
R4c	68 B139a	
R4d	68 B130	
R4e	68 B144a	
R4f	68 B132	
R4g	68 B133	
R4h	68 B134	
R4i	68 B136	
R4j	68 B121	
R4k	68 B122	
R4l	68 B137	
R5	68 A34	
R6	68 A34	
R7	68 A34	
R8	68 A34	
R9	68 A77	
R10	59 A1	
R11	68 A1	
R12	28 B8	
R13	67 A15, 68 A120	
R14a	101.1 Leszl	
R14b	101.4 Leszl	
R15	59 A45	
R16	57 Leszl	
R17	57.3 Leszl	
R18	67 A7	
R19	47.3 Leszl	

R20a	≠ DK
R20b	68 A104a
R21	68 A135
R22	24.3 Leszl
R23	68 A42
R24	68 B165
R25	68 A135
R26	68 A65
R27	42.1 Leszl
R28	68 A36
R29a	68 A106
R29b	68 A106
R30	68 A66
R31	68 A67
R32a	68 A60
R32b	68 A60
R32c	68 A60
R32d	68 A60
R33	67 A15, 68 A60a
R34	8.2 Leszl
R35	30.4 Leszl
R36	68 A60
R37	67 A18
R38	67A6
R39	67 A19
R40	36.1 Leszl
R41	30.6 Leszl
R42	67 A16
R43	64.1 Leszl
R44	68 A60
R45	68 A60
R46	68 A135

R47	68 A38	R75	68 B3
R48a	≠ DK	R76	68 A3
R48b	78.7 Leszl	R77	68 A1
R49	68 A100	R78	68 A2
R50	68 A165	R79a	68 A51
R51	103.3 Leszl	R79b	68 A70
R52	57 Leszl	R80	67 A2
R53	68 A112	R81	68 A52
R54	68 A119	R82	68 A53
R55	68 A135	R83	68 A69
R56	68 A135, 68 A163	R84	0.9.4 Leszl
R57	68 A135	R85	68 A53
R58	68 A122	R86	67 A24
R59	68 A135	R87	68 A160
R60	68 A135	R88	8.1. Leszl
R61	68 A128	R89	68 B156
R62	68 A135	R90	68 A61
R63	68 A130	R91	68 A108
R64	68 A131	R92	68 A50
R65	68 A132	R93	8.4 Leszl
R66	68 A133	R94	68 A47
R67a	68 A147	R95	67 A13
R67b	98.3 Leszl	R96	68 A43
R68a	68 B1	R97	53.1 Leszl
R68b	68 B1, 68 B2	R98	68 A110
R69	68 A3	R99	68 A1
R70a	68 A6	R100	59 A95
R70b	68 A7	R101	68 B165
R71	68 A9	R102	0.8.36 Leszl
R72	68 A17	R103	68 B117
R73	68 A5	R104	68 A134
R74	68 B4	R105	68 B165

R106	58.1 Leszl	R120a	68 B300.7
R107	68 A114	R120b	68 B300.7
R108	68 B6, 68 B7, 68	R121	188.5 Leszl
	B8, 68 B9, 68 B11	R122	68 B300.7
R109a	46.1 Leszl	R123a	68 B300.10
R109b	46.2 Leszl	R123b	68 B300.10
R110	≠ DK	R123c	68 B300.10
R111	68 A26	R124	68 B300.20
R112	9.4 Leszl	R125a	68 B300.16
R113	9.5 Leszl	R125b	68 B300.17
R114	112.5 Leszl	R125c	68 B300.18
R115	68 B299	R126a	68 B300.6
R116	68 C6	R126b	68B300.14
R117	68 B300.3	R127a	68 B300.19
R118a	68 B300.1	R127b	p. 192.97–107
R118b	68 B300.1		Martelli
R118c	68 B300.10	R128a	68 B303
R119a	68 B300.4	R128b	68 B304
R119b	78.	R129	≠ DK

[28] DIOG.

P1	64 A1	D6	64 B8
P2	64 A5	D7	13 A4
P3	64 A3	D8	64 A5
P4	64 A1	D9	64 B4
D1	64 A4	D10	64 B5
D2	64 B1	D11	64 A20
D3	64 B2	D12	5b Laks
D4	64 B7	D13	64 A19
D5a	3 Laks	D14	64 A1
D5b	64 B3	D15	64 A6

CONCORDANCE b (LM > DK et al.)

D16a	64 A10	D40	64 A22
D16b	13 A11	D41	64 A19
D17	59 A67, 64 A11	D42	64 A19
D18	64 A12	D43	64 A19
D19	64 A13	D44	64 A19
D20	64 A13	D45	64 A30
D21	64 A14	D46	64 A31
D22	64 A15	D47	64 A31
D23a	64 A16	D48	64 A32
D23b	64 A16	D49	64 B10
D24	64 A17	R1	64 A7
D25a	T35c Laks	R2	64 A25
D25b	64 A18	R3	64 A31
D25c	T35b Laks	R4	T35c Laks
D26	64 A33	R5	63.
D27	64 B6	R6	64 A5
D28a	64 A24	R7	64 A4
D28b	64 B6	R8	II, p. 52.28
D29	64 A27	R9	64 A5
D30	64 A27	R10	64 A19
D31a	64 B9	R11	p. 160 Laks
D31b	64 A26	R12	64 A25
D32a	64 A25	R13	≠ DK
D32b	64 A25	R14	64 A8
D33	64 A29	R15	59 A67, 64 A11
D34a	64 A19	R16	64 A10
D34b	64 A19	R17	64 A8
D35	64 A19	R18	T7b Laks
D36	64 A19	R19	64 A8
D37	64 A21	R20	≠ DK
D38	64 A19	R21	≠ DK
D39	64 A19		

[29] MED.

T1	68 B300.10	T18a	≠ DK
T2	87 B1	T18b	≠ DK
T3	≠ DK	T18c	≠ DK
T4	≠ DK	T19	≠ DK
T5a	≠ DK	T20	≠ DK
T5b	≠ DK	T21	≠ DK
T6	30 A6	T22	≠ DK
T7a	31 A71	T23	24 A11, 64 C3a
T7b	31 A71	T24	≠ DK
T8	≠ DK	T25	≠ DK
T9	22 C1	T26	≠ DK
T10	64 C2	T27	≠ DK
T11	64 C3	T28	≠ DK
T12	22 C2	T29a	≠ DK
T13	68 B11	T29b	≠ DK
T14	22 C1	T29c	≠ DK
T15	≠ DK	T30	≠ DK
T16	≠ DK	T31	≠ DK
T17	≠ DK		

[30] DERV.

≠ DK

[31] PROT.

P1	80 A1	P4	80 A4
P2a	80 A5	P5	80 A1
P2b	80 A8	P6a	80 A1
P3	80 A1	P6b	80 A3

P7	80 A2	D9	80 B1
P8	80 A1	D10	80 B4
P9a	80 A11	D11	80 B3
P9b	80 A11	D12	80 B10
P10	≠ DK	D13	80 B11
P11	80 B9	D14	80 A7
P12	80 A1	D15	80 A1
P13a	80 A5	D16	80 A3
P13b	80 A1	D17	80 A1
P13c	80 A3	D18	80 B6
P14	80 A8	D19	80 B6
P15	80 A6	D20	80 A1
P16	80 A3	D21	80 A24
P17	80 A1	D22a	80 A26
P18	80 A25	D22b	≠ DK
P19	80 A1	D23	80 A27
P20	80 A1	D24	80 A28
P21	80 A2	D25	80 A29
P22	80 A12	D26	80 A1, B6a
P23	80 A1	D27	80 A20
P24	≠ DK	D28	80 A21
D1	80 A1	D29	80 A1
D2	80 B8	D30	80 A10
D3	80 B1	D31	80 A25
D4a	80 A1	D32	80 A30
D4b	80 B4	D33	80 B7
D5a	80 B1	D34	80 B7a
D5b	80 A24	D35	80 A5
D5c	≠ DK	D36	80 A5
D6	84 B3	D37	80 A5
D7	80 B2	D38	80 A21a
D8	80 B3	D39	≠ DK

D40	80 C1	R14b	≠ DK
D41	≠ DK	R15	*13b
D42	80 A25		Untersteiner
R1a	80 B5	R16	80 A17
R1b	80 B5	R17	80 A19
R2	80 B2	R18	80 A21
R3	80 A2	R19a	80 A12
R4	80 B1	R19b	80 A1
R5	80 B1	R20	80 B1
R6	≠ DK	R21	80 A14
R7a	80 B1	R22	80 A15
R7b	≠ DK	R23	80 B3
R8	≠ DK	R24	80 A23
R9a	≠ DK	R25	80 A2
R9b	80 A15	R26	≠ DK
R10	80 A19	R27	≠ DK
R11	≠ DK	R28	80 A16
R12	70 A24	R29	80 B4
R13	80 A1	R30	80 B12
R14a	80 A19		

[32] GORG.

P1	82 A1	P10	82 A2
P2	82 A7	P11	82 A19
P3	82 A2	P12	82 A35
P4	82 A10, 82 B2	P13a	82 A4
P5	82 A3	P13b	82 A4
P6	82 A5	P14	82 A1
P7	82 A16	P15	82 A7
P8	82 A32	P16	82 A18
P9	≠ DK	P17	82 A4

P18	82 A9	D6b	82 A4
P19	Nachtrag II,	D6c	82 B6
	p. 425.26–28	D7a	82 A27
P20	82 B8a	D7b	82 A27
P21	82 A24	D8	82 A20
P22	82 B29	D9	82 A19
P23	82 B30	D10	82 A26
P24	82 A15a	D11a	82 A1a
P25	82 A10	D11b	82 A24
P26	82 A1	D12	82 B13
P27	82 A11	D13	82 A20
P28a	82 A11	D14	82 A25
P28b	82 A13	D15	82 A25
P29	82 A12	D16	82 A25
P30	82 A15	D17	82 B17
P31	≠ DK	D18	82 B12
P32	82 A13	D19a	82 A30
P33a	82 A7	D19b	82 A32
P33b	82 A7	D19c	82 A31
P33c	82 A7	D20	82 A4
P33d	82 A1	D21a	≠ DK
P34a	82 A7	D21b	82 A29
P34b	82 A8	D22	82 A1
P35	82 A17	D23a	82 C2
P36	≠ DK	D23b	≠ DK
D1	82 B6	D24	82 B11
D2a	82 A1a	D25	82 B11a
D2b	82 A1	D26a	≠ DK
D3	82 A7	D26b	82 B3
D4	82 B14	D27	82 A1
D5	82 A14	D28	82 B6
D6a	82 A3	D29	82 B5b

D30a	82 B5a	R4	82 A9
D30b	82 B5a	R5	≠ DK
D31	82 B7	R6a	82 C1
D32	82 B8	R6b	≠ DK
D33	82 B10	R6c	82 A1
D34	82 B26	R7a	≠ DK
D35	82 B23	R7b	≠ DK
D36	82 B24	R8	82 B14
D37	82 B25	R9	82 A29
D38	82 B27	R10a	82 B15
D39	82 A19	R10b	82 B16
D40	82 B20	R10c	82 A23
D41	82 B21	R11	82 A32
D42	82 B22	R12	82 A4
D43a	82 B15	R13	82 A4
D43b	82 B15	R14	82 A32
D44	82 B16	R15	≠ DK
D45a	82 B4	R16	≠ DK
D45b	82 B5	R17	82 B5a
D46	82 B31	R18	82 B14
D47	82 A21	R19	82 A1
D48a	82 A28	R20	82 B5a
D48b	82 A28	R21	≠ DK
D49	82 A27	R22	82 B5a
D50	82 A22	R23	82 B2
D51	82 A26	R24a	82 B1
D52	82 B14	R24b	82 B1
D53	82 B19	R25	≠ DK
R1a	82 B3	R26	82 B3
R1b	82 A15a	R27	82 A33
R2	82 A4	R28	82 A34
R3	82 A35	R29	82 B28

[33] SOC.

P1	I D1 G^2	P21	B2 G^1
P2	I B41 G^2	P22a	I D1 G^2
P3	I D1 G^2	P22b	$\neq$ G
P4	I B8 G^2, I D1 G^2	P23	B3 G^1
P5	I B41 G^2	P24	$\neq$ G
P6a	I C9 G^2	P25	$\neq$ G
P6b	I D1 G^2	P26	$\neq$ G
P7	I D1 G^2	P27	I D1 G^2
P8a	I D1 G^2	P28	$\neq$ G
P8b	I D1 G^2	P29	$\neq$ G
P8c	60 A1, I D1 G^2	P30	$\neq$ G
P8d	I D2 G^2	P31	$\neq$ G
P9	$\neq$ G	P32	I C410 G^2
P10	VI A66 G^2	P33	$\neq$ G
P11	$\neq$ G	P34a	B1 G^1
P12	I C15 G^2	P34b	D109 G^1
P13a	$\neq$ G	P35	B1 G^1
P13b	$\neq$ G	P36	I D1 G^2
P13c	I H1 G^2	P37	B1 G^1
P14	B1 G^1	P38	I E1 G^2
P15	I D1 G^2	P39	I D1 G^2
P16a	$\neq$ G	P40	I C133 G^2
P16b	$\neq$ G	P41	I D1 G^2
P17	88 A1, I C105 G^2	P42	I C155 G^2
P18a	$\neq$ G	P43	$\neq$ DK
P18b	I B.3 G^1	D1	I D2 G^2
P18c	I C49 G^2	D2	I B24 G^2
P19	$\neq$ G	D3	B1 G^1
P20a	$\neq$ G	D4	I C458 G^2
P20b	$\neq$ G	D5	I C465 G^2

D6a	I 60A1 G², I C12	D32	≠ G
	G²	D33a	B1 G¹
D6b	I D1 G²	D33b	B1 G¹
D7	≠ G	D33c	B1 G¹
D8	I D1 G²	D34a	≠ G
D9	B1 G¹	D34b	≠ G
D10a	I B24 G²	D35	B1 G¹
D10b	I B26 G²	D36	≠ G
D11a	≠ G	D37a	I B28 G²
D11b	≠ G	D37b	I B29 G²
D12	≠ G	D38	I B30 G²
D13	≠ G	D39	≠ G
D14	≠ G	D40a	I B34 G²
D15	I B20 G²	D40b	I B35 G².
D16	I B23 G²	D40c	I B36 G²
D17	I C440 G²	D41	≠ G
D18	B1 G¹	D42a	≠ G
D19	≠ G	D42b	≠ G
D20	≠ G	D43	≠ G
D21	B1 G¹	D44	≠ G
D22	I B26 G²	D45	≠ G
D23	I C434 G²	D46	I B38 G²
D24	I C446 G²	D47	I B17 G²
D25	≠ G	D48	B1 G¹
D26	≠ G	D49	≠ G
D27	≠ G	D50	I B39 G²
D28	B1 G¹	D51	I B340 G²
D29	≠ G	D52	≠ G
D30a	≠ G	D53a	≠ G
D30b	≠ G	D53b	≠ G
D31a	≠ G	D54	B1 G¹
D31b	≠ G	D55	B1 G¹

D56	B1 G^1		D61b	B1 G^1
D57	I B16 G^2		D61c	B1 G^1
D58	≠ G		D62	I H4 G^2
D59	B1 G^1		D63	I H8 G^2
D60	≠ G		D64	I H5 G^2
D61a	B1 G^1		D65	I H7 G^2

[34] PROD.

P1	84 A1		D7	84 B6
P2	84 A3		D8	84 B7
P3	84 A2		D9	84 B4
P4	84 A3		D10	84 B10
P5	84 A11		D11a	84 A20
P6	84 B9		D11b	≠ DK
P7	84 A4a		D12	84 A10
P8	84 A1a		D13	84 A12
P9	≠ DK		D14	84 B5
P10	84 A8		D15a	84 B5
P11	84 A1a		D15b	84 B5
P12	84 A7		D16	84 B5
P13	84 A6		D17	84 B5
P14	84 A1		D18a	84 B1
D1	84 B4		D18b	84 A1a
D2	84 B3		D19a	84 A1a
D3	84 B1		D19b	≠ DK
D4	84 B1		D20	84 B2
D5a	84 A18		D21a	84 A13
D5b	84 A16		D21b	84 A13
D5c	84 A17		D21c	84 A14
D6a	84 A19		D21d	84 A14
D6b	*A19 Untersteiner		D21e	≠ DK

D21f	≠ DK	R6	84 A1a
D22	84 A15	R7	84 A10
D23	84 A17	R8	84 B5
D24	84 A18	R9	84 B4
R1a	84 A1a	R10	84 A19
R1b	84 A1a	R11	84 B5
R2	84 A9	R12a	84 B5
R3	84 A4b	R12b	≠ DK
R4	84 B8	R13	*B5 Untersteiner
R5	84 B9		

[35] THRAS.

P1	85 A1	D13a	85 B6
P2	85 A3	D13b	85 B6
P3	85 A10	D14	85 B5
P4	85 A6	D15	*A15 Untersteiner
P5a	85 A7	D16	85 B1
P5b	85 A7	D17	85 B8
P6	85 A8	D18	85 B2
D1	85 A13	D19	85 B4
D2	85 A1	D20	85 A5
D3	85 B3	D21a	85 B6a
D4	85 A9	D21b	≠ DK
D5	85 B7	D21c	*A10 Untersteiner
D6	85 B5	R1	85 A12
D7	85 A2	R2	85 A13
D8	85 A13	R3	85 A3
D9	85 B1	R4	85 B1
D10	85 A12	R5	85 A14
D11	85 A1	R6a	*A12b
D12	85 A11		Untersteiner

R6b	*A12a	R8	≠ DK
	Untersteiner	R9	≠ DK
R7a	*A10 Untersteiner	R10	85 B7a
R7b	*A10 Untersteiner		

[36] HIPPIAS

P1	86 A1	D18	≠ DK
P2	86 A3	D19	86 B17
P3	86 A6	D20	86 B16
P4	80 A9, 86 A7	D21	86 A1
P5	86 A2	D22	86 B6
P6	86 A15	D23	86 B7
D1	86 A1	D24	86 B18
D2	86 A12	D25	86 A10
D3	86 B4	D26	86 B9
D4	86 B1	D27	86 B12
D5	86 A2	D28	86 B8
D6	86 B2	D29	86 B14
D7	86 B3	D30	86 B2
D8	86 A8	D31	86 B15
D9	86 A8	D32	86 B11
D10	86 A9	D33	86 B4
D11	86 A14	D34	86 A11
D12a	86 A11	D35	86 B13
D12b	86 A2	D36	86 B21
D13	86 A5a	R1	86 A2
D14a	86 A11	R2	86 B10
D14b	86 A2	R3	86 B3
D15	86 A12	R4	86 A13
D16	*C2 Untersteiner	R5	86 A5
D17	86 C1	R6	≠ DK

[37] ANTIPH.

P1a	87 A1	D9a	87 B10
P1b	T3 Pendrick	D9b	87 B10
P1c	87 A1	D10	87 B11
P2	87 A2	D11	87 B17
P3	≠ DK	D12a	87 B18
P4	≠ DK	D12b	87 B18
P5	82 A6	D13a	87 B19
P6	T5 Pendrick	D13b	87 B19
P7	87 A8	D14	87 B14
P8	87 A6	D15	87 B20
P9	87 A6	D16	87 B21
P10	87 A6	D17	87 B9
P11	87 B93, T10	D18	87 B22
	Pendrick	D19a	87 B23
P12	≠ DK	D19b	87 B24
P13	≠ DK	D20	87 B24a
P14	≠ DK	D21	87 B25
P15	≠ DK	D22	87 B26
P16	≠ DK	D23	87 B27
P17	≠ DK	D24	87 B28
P18	≠ DK	D25	87 B29
D1a	87 B1	D26a	87 B30
D1b	87 B2	D26b	87 B31
D2	87 B4	D27	87 B32
D3	87 B5	D28	87 B29a
D4	87 B6	D29	87 B33
D5	87 B7	D30	87 B38
D6	87 B8	D31	87 B34
D7	87 B15	D32	87 B39
D8	87 B15	D33	87 B35

CONCORDANCE b (LM > DK et al.)

D34	87 B36	D62	87 B60
D35	87 B37	D63	87 B61
D36a	87 B13	D64	87 B67
D36b	87 B13	D65	87 B67a
D37	87 B12	D66	87 B68
D38	87 B44	D67	87 B69
D39a	87 B43	D68	87 B71
D39b	87 B43	D69	87 B74
D40	87 B3	D70	87 B75
D41a	87 B63	D71	87 B72
D41b	87 B24a	D72	87 B76
D42	87 B48	D73	87 B73
D43	87 B45	D74	87 B77
D44	87 B46	D75a	87 B79
D45	87 B47	D75b	87 A9
D46	87 B70	D76	87 B78
D47a	87 B55	D77a	87 B80
D47b	87 B56	D77b	F80b Pendrick
D48	87 B52	D78	87 B81a
D49	87 B65	D79	87 B40
D50	87 B51	D80	87 B41
D51	87 B50	D81a	87 B42
D52	87 B53	D81b	F42b Pendrick
D53	87 B53a	D82	87 B16
D54	87 B57	D83	87 A3
D55	87 B58	D84	87 A4
D56	87 B59	R1	87 B14, 87 B63
D57	87 B49	R2	≠ DK
D58	87 B66	R3	87 A2
D59	87 B54	R4	≠ DK
D60	87 B62	R5	≠ DK
D61	87 B64	R6	≠ DK

R7	87 B44a	R14	87 B13
R8	87 A2	R15	87 B13
R9	≠ DK	R16a	87 B13
R10	87 B79	R16b	87 B13
R11	87 B81	R16c	F13e Pendrick
R12	87 A7	R17	87 B12
R13	T11a Pendrick		

[38] LYC.

D1	83.2	D5a	83.6
D2	83.1	D5b	83.6
D3	83.3	D6	83.5
D4	83.4		

[39] XENI.

D1	68 B163, 81.	R2	≠ DK
R1	81.	R3	≠ DK

[40] ANON. IAMBL.

89DK

[41] DISS.

90DK

[42] SOPH.

R1	≠ DK	R3	≠ DK
R2	≠ DK	R4	79.1a Untersteiner

188

R5	79.1	R23	≠ DK
R6	84 A2, 86 A11	R24	≠ DK
R7	84 A4	R25	79.2a
R8	≠ DK	R26	79.2a
R9	≠ DK	R27	79.2
R10	≠ DK	R28	≠ DK
R11a	80 A5	R29	79.2
R11b	80 A5	R30	≠ DK
R12	80 A5	R31a	≠ DK
R13	≠ DK	R31b	≠ DK
R14	≠ DK	R32	79.2
R15	≠ DK	R33	≠ DK
R16	≠ DK	R34a	79.3
R17	≠ DK	R34b	≠ DK
R18	≠ DK	R35	≠ DK
R19a	≠ DK	R36a	≠ DK
R19b	≠ DK	R36b	≠ DK
R20	≠ DK	R36c	≠ DK
R21	≠ DK	R36d	≠ DK
R22	≠ DK		

[43] DRAM.

T1	23 B9	T10a	64 C1
T2	23 B12	T10b	≠ DK
T3	21 A15	T10c	Nachtrag II, p. 420
T4	23 B1		
T5	23 B17	T10d	≠ DK
T6	23 B4	T11	1 A12
T7	23 B5	T12	64 A19
T8	23 B2	T13	≠ DK
T9	23 B56	T14	≠ DK

T15	38 A2	T36b	58E.1
T16a	38 A2	T37a	58E.2
T16b	38 A2	T37b	58E.3
T17	≠ DK	T38a	58E.3
T18a	80 A11	T38b	58E.3
T18b	80 A1, 80 A11	T39	≠ DK
T18c	80 A11	T40	64 C4
T19a	80 C2	T41	≠ DK
T19b	≠ DK	T42a	≠ DK
T19c	80 C3	T42b	≠ DK
T20	82 A5a	T43a	59 A30
T21	82 A5a	T43b	59 A20
T22	84 A5	T44	22 A16, 59 A48,
T23	84 A5		64 C2
T24	84 A5	T45a	≠ DK
T25	85 A4	T45b	≠ DK
T26	I A3 G^2	T46	≠ DK
T27	I A5 G^2	T47	≠ DK
T28a	64 C1	T48	59 A20b
T28b	64 C1	T49a	88 B18
T28c	64 C1	T49b	88 B19
T29a	I A10 G^2	T50	≠ DK
T29b	I A10 G^2	T51	≠ DK
T29c	I A10 G^2	T52	≠ DK
T30	I A2 G^2	T53	≠ DK
T31	I A12 G^2	T54	≠ DK
T32	I A1 G^2	T55	≠ DK
T33	T136 Mouraviev	T56	≠ DK
T34	68 C1	T57	≠ DK
T35a	58E.1	T58	≠ DK
T35b	58E.1	T59	≠ DK
T36a	58E.1	T60	≠ DK

CONCORDANCE b (LM > DK et al.)

T61	≠ DK		T74b	≠ DK
T62	≠ DK		T75a	59 A20
T63	88 B25		T75b	59 A1
T64	≠ DK		T76	59 A91
T65	≠ DK		T77	59 A62
T66	90 1.1		T78	59 A112
T67	88 B22		T79a	≠ DK
T68	≠ DK		T79b	≠ DK
T69	≠ DK		T80	59 A33
T70	≠ DK		T81	59 A48
T71	80 B3		T82	≠ DK
T72	21 C1		T83	≠ DK
T73	21 C2		T84	≠ DK
T74a	≠ DK			

INDEX OF NAMES

a
EARLY GREEK PHILOSOPHERS

This index comprises those references to the early Greek philosophers to be found in chapters other than the ones dedicated to them.

ALCMAEON
ATOM. P5
DOX. T6, T15, T18c
PYTH. b T30

ANAXAGORAS
ANAXIMAND. R7, R8, R9
ARCH. P1, P2, P3, P6a, D2,
    D4, D5, D11, D16, D17,
    R1, R3
ATOM. P9, P10, P12a, P16a,
    P17, P23, P38, P42, D46,
    D90, D120b, D200, R10,
    R15, R16, R33, R43, R45,
    R76
DIOG. P1, P2, D17, D46,
    D48, R9
DOX. T13, T15, T16, T17,
    T18, T19, T20, T21, T22
DRAM. T75
EMP. P4, P15, D81, D84a,
    D175, D180, D250a,
    D250c
HER. R44

MEL. P4
PROD. P10, R3
PYTHS. ANON. D1
SOC. P8, D4
XEN. P15, D48

ANAXIMANDER
ANAXAG. D2, R19
ANAXIMEN. P1, D1, D23
ATOM. D114
DIOG. D24, R5
DOX. T17, T18b, T19, T20
EMP. P22
PARM. P6, P16
PYTH. a P14, P15
PYTH. c D16
XEN. P1, P9

ANAXIMENES
ANAXAG. P1, D2, D54
DIOG. P1, D7, D8, R5, R7,
    R18, R19, R20
DOX. T17, T19, T20, T21,
    T22

193

HER. R71
HIPPO D3
PARM. P16
XEN. R26

ANTIPHON
DOX. T18b
HIPPIAS R4
PARM. P4a
SOPH. R25
THRAS. D8
ZEN. P6

ARCHELAUS
ANAXAG. P17, P16, D66d
ATOM. P10
DOX. T17, T19, T20, T21
GORG. R27
SOC. P8, D4, D6a
XEN. P8

ARCHYTAS
EUR. P7, D2
HIPPAS. D6
PHILOL. P5, P7, D10, D12
PYTH. b T28, T30
PYTHS. ANON. D26
PYTHS. R R6c, R6e

DEMOCRITUS
ANAXAG. P3, P4, P10,
    D66d, D95c, D97, R1, R2,
    R12
DOX. T11, T13, T15, T17,
    T18a, T19, T20, T21, T22
DRAM. T34
EMP. D204, D250c, R22,
    R66
HER. P12, R99, R107

MED. T1
MEL. P5
PARM. P3
PHER. R8
PHILOL. P6
PROD. P1
PROT. P5, P6, P7, R22, R29
PYTH. a P31
THAL. P2, R1,
XENI. D1
ZEN. P1, R15

**DIOGENES OF APOLLO-
NIA**
ALCM. D9
ANAXIMEN. R12
DRAM. T40, T82
HER. R43

ECPHANTUS
PYTH. b T30

EMPEDOCLES
ALCM. D2
ANAXAG. P2, D20, D95,
    R15, R16, R33
ANAXIMAND. P10, R7
ATOM. P12b, D30, D126,
    D200, R31, R45, R53
DOX. T2, T4, T6, T8, T15,
    T17, T18b, T18c, T19, T22
GORG. P4, P5, D5
HER. R30, R44, R49, R82
HIPPAS. P3
MED. T1, T7b
MEL. P3
PARM. P3, P13, P14, P15,
    D2, D41, D42, R2a, R3,
    R67

PROT. R28
PYTH. a P10, P33
PYTH. b T30
PYTHS. ANON. D1
XEN. P12, P22, R27, R28
ZEN. R4, R35

EURYTUS
ARCHY. P2b, P3a
ATOM. P5
PYTH. b T29, T30

GORGIAS
ALCM. D2
ANTIPH. P1b, P5
ATOM. P12b
DOX. T6, T7
DRAM. T20, T21
EMP. P16, P24, R5b
PARM. P3a
PROD. P1, P12, D11a, D12
PROT. D19
SOC. P9
SOPH. R7, R35
THRAS. D10, R1

HERACLITUS
DOX. T2, T3, T4, T14, T15,
   T17, T19, T22
DRAM. T5–T8, T33, T74
EMP. D79
HIPPAS. D3, D4
MEL. P5
PARM. P19
PHER. D11, R27
PYTH. c D1b
PYTHS. R R45b
THAL. R1
ZEN. P10

HIPPASUS
ARCHY. D8
DIOG. R5
DOX. T14
EMP. P12
HER. P5, R45
PYTH. a P10
PYTH. b T30

HIPPIAS
ATOM. P12b
GORG. P18
HER. R33
PARM. P3a
PHER. D19
PROD. D12, D22e, D22f
PROT. D19, D37
SOC. D49
SOPH. R6, R7, R11b, R35
THAL. D11b

HIPPO
DIOG. D32a
DOX. T14
DRAM. T15, T16
PYTH. b T30

LEUCIPPUS
DIOG. P2, R9
DOX. T17, T19, T20, T21,
   T22
GORG. D26a

LYCOPHRON
PROT. R26

MELISSUS
ALCM. D2
ATOM. P4

DOX. T6, T7, T11, T17, T22
GORG. D26a, R24a
HER. R40
MED. T6
PARM. P17, D3, R7, R22,
R24, R28, R47
XEN. R7, R10, R12, R14
ZEN. R38

PARMENIDES
ALCM. D2
ANAXIMEN. P1
ARCH. R7b
ATOM. P12b, P26, D32
DOX. T2, T6, T11, T15, T17,
T18a, T19, T20, T21, T22
DRAM. T17
EMP. P2, P10, P13, P14, P15,
D98, D173b, D211, R96
GORG. P4, R24
HER. R28a, R30, R40, R44
MEL. P5, D14, D18, R2, R4,
R5, R7, R8, R10, R20, R22,
R24
PYTH. b T30, T35
XEN. P10, P11, P12, R4, R7,
R10, R12, R14, R17, R27,
R28
ZEN. P4, P5, P6, D3, R2, R5,
R6, R10a, R11, R13, R14,
R25, R32

PHERECYDES
ATOM. R3a, R3b
DOX. T20, T21, T22
HIPPIAS D35
PYTH. a P12, P13, P14, P15,
P29
PYTH. b T25, T27
THAL. R23

PHILOLAUS
ARCHY. P2b, P3a, D6
ATOM. P5, P21
EMP. P8c, P12, R44
EUR. P3, P5, P6
HIPPAS. P3
PYTH. b T29, T30
PYTH. c D1d
PYTHS. R R7, R47, R48,
R49, R50, R51

PRODICUS
ALCM. D2
ATOM. P12b
DOX. T22
DRAM. T22–T24
GORG. P7, D11b
PARM. P3
PROT. P2a, P16, D6, D19
SOC. P9, D49
SOPH. R6, R7, R9, R35
THRAS. D4

PROTAGORAS
ANAXAG. P25b
ATOM. P26, P27, R17, R68b,
R89, R98, R107
DOX. T2, T21
DRAM. T18–T20
GORG. D16
HER. R30
HIPPIAS P4, D17, R5
PROD. P1, P9, D2, D12, D22
SOC. D25, D30, D36, D42,
D49
SOPH. R6, R8, R9, R10,
R11, R12, R28, R35
THRAS. D4
XENI. R2
ZEN. D12

INDEX OF EARLY GREEK PHILOSOPHERS

PYTHAGORAS
ALCM. P1, P3
ANAXAG. D96
ANAXIMAND. R21
ANAXIMEN. R11
ARCH. R7a
ARCHY. P3, P9b, D19
ATOM. P5, P19, P21, P24,
    P45, D1
DOX. T17, T19, T20, T21,
    T22
DRAM. T38
EMP. P8c, P10, P15, D27b,
    R69, R43, R46, R50, R62,
    R86, R104
EUR. P5
HER. D20, D26, R28b
HIPPAS. P2, D2, D6, D8
HIPPO P7
MED. T1
MOR. T38
PARM. D22, D33b, R68,
    R69
PHER. P8, P9, P10, P14,
    P15, P16, R1, R7, R12,
    R13, R14, R17, R18
PHILOL. D14, D27
SOPH. R5
THAL. P5, R27
XEN. D64
ZEN. P1b

SOCRATES (the character in
    the Platonic dialogues is not
    included)
ALCM. P17, P19, R4, R5,
    R6, R7, R24, R31
ANTIPH. P6
ARCH. P1, P2, P3, P4, P5,
    P6a, R2, R3

ARCHY. P9a
ATOM. P10, P11, P22a, P42,
    R100
DOX. T20, T21, T22
DRAM. T26–T33
EMP. P23
GORG. P4, R3
HER. R28
PARM. P4, R53b
PYTHS. R R38
SOPH. R5
THAL. P17b
ZEN. P6, D2, D4

THALES
ALCM. D9
ANAXIMAND. P5, P6, P7
ANAXIMEN. R11
DOX. T14, T17, T19, T20,
    T21, T22
DRAM. T13, T14
HIPPO D2, D3, D20
MOR. T35
PHER. P8, P11, D7, R7,
    R11, R12, R29, R31
PYTH. a P13, P15
SOPH. R2
XEN. R26

THRASYMACHUS
DRAM. T25
GORG. D19a, D52, R17
PROD. D2, D12
PROT. D6, D19
SOC. D14
SOPH. R35

XENIADES
ATOM. P25

197

XENOPHANES
  ATOM. D32
  DOX. T4, T17, T19, T20,
    T21, T22
  DRAM. T2, T3, T72, T73
  EMP. P14
  HER. P4, P5, D20
  MEL. R5, R24b
  PARM. P5, P6, P7, P8, P18,
    D2, R1, R5A, R51
  PYTH. a P5, P27, P32
  THAL. R1
  XENI. R1
  ZEN. R15, R32

ZENO
  ATOM. P2, P3, P12b, P26
  DOX. T7, T17, T19, T20,
    T21, T22
  EMP. P15, R5a
  GORG. D26a
  HER. R50, R51
  MEL. P3, R24a, R26
  PARM. P3, P4, P9, P10, P12,
    P15, P21, R28, R63, R66
  XEN. R10, R14

INDEX OF NAMES

b
OTHER PERSONS

This selective index provides basic identifications, pertinent above all to this edition, for a number of potentially unfamiliar names that are mentioned in the entries, especially those comprised in our sections **P** and **R**. We have added certain authors and historical personalities because of their significance in chronological or other regards. We have also included a certain number of authors who cite the passages we present. The other proper names, be they celebrated or obscure, can easily be identified on the basis of the context or with the help of standard dictionaries and encyclopedias. We have excluded gods, heroes, and other mythological figures.

Achilles Tatius: the author (3rd century AD?) of a work *On the Sphere,* of which one part survives, an introduction to the astronomical poem of Aratus; although the *Suda* identifies this man with the author of a surviving erotic romance, *Leucippe and Clitophon,* most modern scholars distinguish the two.

Aelian (Claudius Aelianus): a Roman citizen who wrote scholarly compilatory works in Greek, end of the 2nd to the beginning of the 3rd century AD; he is included by Philostratus in his *Lives of the Sophists.*

Aelian the Platonist: the author of a commentary on Plato's *Timaeus* that is cited by Porphyry.

Aelius Aristides: a rhetorician and an eminent representative of the Second Sophistic, ca. AD 117–181.

Aenesidemus: a Skeptical philosopher, the renewer of Pyrrhonism, and a contemporary of Cicero; Sextus Empiricus states that, according to Aenesidemus, the Skeptical method is a path leading to the philosophy of Heraclitus.

Aeschines the Socratic: a student and follower of Socrates (4th century BC) and author of Socratic dialogues lost except for fragments; not to be confused with the slightly later Aeschines, an important Athenian orator and opponent of Demosthenes.

Aëtius: the name first assigned by Hermann Diels, on the basis of a single attestation in Theodoret, to the author of a reconstructed doxographic manual that is dated between the end of the 1st century BC and the beginning of the following century; this summary, which has not been transmitted as such but which there are good reasons to postulate, seems to have been used directly or indirectly by various authors, especially Ps.-Plutarch, Stobaeus, and Theodoret, and it is on the basis of them that it is possible to provide a reconstruction. *See* DOX. T17.

Agathemerus: the author of a compendium of geography dating probably to the 3rd century AD.

Aglaophamus: the putative initiator of Pythagoras into the Orphic mysteries.

Akikaros: a legendary Babylonian sage to whom many proverbs are attributed in various ancient cultures.

Alcibiades: a celebrated and extremely controversial Athenian politician and general during the Peloponnesian War.

Alcidamas of Elaea: a Greek sophist and rhetorician of the beginning of the 4th century BC, a disciple of Gorgias, and an adversary of Isocrates.

Alcimus: the name of a Greek rhetorician of the 3rd century BC, of the author of a treatise *Against Amyntas* cited by Diogenes Laertius and containing citations of texts attributed to Epicharmus, and of the author of a history of Sicily; it is unknown whether this is one, two, or three people.

Aleuads: an aristocratic family of Larissa in Thessaly that claimed descent from Heracles via the mythical king Aleuas.

Alexander of Aphrodisias: one of the great commentators on Aristotle, born at the beginning of the 2nd century AD, often cited by Simplicius in his commentary on Aristotle's *Physics*.

Alexander of Miletus (called Polyhistor): a grammarian, author notably of *Successions of the Philosophers*, who lived at Rome in the 1st century BC.

INDEX OF OTHER PERSONS

Alexander Philalethes: a disciple of the doctor Asclepiades of Bithynia (1st century BC).

Alyattes: king of the Lydians (ca. 600–561 BC) who conquered Smyrna and later led campaigns against Miletus.

Ammonius of Alexandria: a Neoplatonic philosopher, born ca. AD 440, and a disciple of Proclus.

Anacharsis of Scythia: a Scythian prince who, according to legend, visited Greece during the Archaic period and distinguished himself there for his wisdom.

Androcydes: a Pythagorean philosopher, to be dated between the 3rd and 1st centuries BC, known especially for his allegorical interpretations of the *akousmata*.

Andron of Ephesus: a historian, dated to the first half of the 4th century BC, who wrote on the Seven Sages, especially Thales, and on Pythagoras.

Antipater of Tarsus: a Stoic philosopher of the 3rd century BC and author of a work on divination.

Antisthenes: a disciple of Socrates (ca. 446–366 BC) and author of discourses and dialogues; he is traditionally considered the founder of Cynicism.

Antisthenes of Rhodes: the author of a *Succession of the Philosophers* that is cited thirteen times by Diogenes Laertius.

Antonius Diogenes: the author of a fictional travel narrative, *The Wonders Beyond Thule*, of uncertain date (2nd century AD ?) but certainly of the Roman era.

Antyllus: the author of a work on Thucydides that Marcellinus used for his biography of this historian.

Apollodorus of Athens: a scholar (born ca. 180 BC), a disciple of the Stoic Diogenes of Babylonia, and a collaborator of Aristarchus in Alexandria; the author *inter alia* of a *Chronicle* or *Chronology* in iambic trimeters, which covered the period from the fall of Troy until his own age.

Apollodorus of Cyzicus: a mathematician, and a disciple of Democritus.

Apollonius: the author of a book on Pythagoras, sometimes identified erroneously with Apollonius of Tyana.

Apollonius Dyscolus: an Alexandrian grammarian, of the 2nd century AD, and the father of Herodian.

Apollonius of Citium: an Alexandrian medical writer, of the 1st century BC; his commentary on the Hippocratic treatise *On Joints* is an important source on early Greek medicine.

EARLY GREEK PHILOSOPHY I

Aratus of Soli: the author of the *Phaenomena*, a celebrated didactic poem about astronomy and meteorological phenomena, of the first half of the 3rd century BC.

Aristarchus of Samos: an astronomer, active in the 3rd century BC, and a disciple of the Peripatetic Strato of Lampsacus; he owes his fame to his formulation of the heliocentric hypothesis.

Aristippus of Cyrene: a disciple of Socrates, often considered to be the founder of the Cyrenaic school (end of the 5th to the beginning of the 4th century BC).

Aristo of Ceos: a Peripatetic philosopher of the second half of the 3rd century BC.

Aristocles of Messina: a Peripatetic philosopher of uncertain date (1st or 2nd century AD).

Aristoxenus of Tarentum: a Peripatetic philosopher and theoretician of music, active toward the middle of the 4th century BC; he is also known for his biographical work, in which he displayed particular interest in Pythagoras and Pythagoreanism.

Artemidorus the dialectician: the author of a book about Protagoras addressed to Chrysippus (3rd century BC).

Aspasia: Pericles' mistress, an influential figure in the intellectual life of Athens in the middle of the 5th century BC.

Assembly of Philosophers, The (*Turba philosophorum*): an alchemical text surviving almost entirely only in a Latin translation from the Arabic original, dating from the 10th century AD; it claims to reproduce the speeches delivered by Presocratic philosophers during an assembly convoked under the direction of Pythagoras.

Athenaeus of Naucratis: the author of *Deipnosophists* (*The Learned Banqueters*), active ca. AD 200; this work is an extensive collection of scholarly discussions noted for its preservation of numerous fragments of earlier Greek poetry.

Athenodorus: (1) the author, otherwise unknown, of a book entitled *Promenades* that is quoted by Diogenes Laertius. (2) the author of a book entitled *On Seriousness and Play,* cited by Athenaeus; he is sometimes identified with Athenodorus of Tarsus (called Calvus), a Stoic philosopher contemporary with Cicero.

Aulus Gellius: Roman scholar of the 2nd century AD, and author of *Attic Nights,* a collection of notes and discussions regarding his reading in a wide variety of subjects.

INDEX OF OTHER PERSONS

Bion of Borysthenes: a Cynic philosopher (ca. 335–245 BC).

Bolus of Mendes: a Neopythagorean philosopher, probably active in Egypt in the 3rd century BC, to whom numerous esoteric and paradoxographic treatises were attributed; he was thought to have been a Democritean, and some of his writings were attributed to Democritus himself.

Cadmus of Miletus: an author, perhaps legendary, associated with the beginnings of Greek prose.

Caelius Aurelianus: a Roman physician and medical writer (4th century AD).

Callimachus of Cyrene: a grammarian and poet, ca. 310–240 BC, active at the court of the Ptolemies in Alexandria; he authored *inter alia* the *Pinakes,* a critical repertory of the whole of Greek literature, gathering biographical and literary information and considering problems of authenticity.

Celsus: (1) a Platonizing author of a polemical treatise directed against the Christians, *The True Discourse,* dating from ca. AD 180; his work survives only in fragments quoted from it by the Christian author Origen in his own polemical treatise *Against Celsus.* (2) a Latin scholar (1st century AD); one book of his encyclopedia, a treatise on medicine, is preserved.

Censorinus: a Latin grammarian whose only surviving work, *The Birthday,* was composed in AD 238.

Charmander: an author of a treatise on comets that is known only from a passage in Seneca concerning Anaxagoras.

Choerilus of Samos: an epic poet, active at the end of the 5th century BC, and the author of a historical poem on the Persian Wars.

Chrysippus: a Stoic philosopher of the 3rd century BC and the most important representative of Stoicism after its founder, Zeno.

Cimon: an Athenian statesman and general of the middle of the 5th century BC.

Claudianus Mamertus: a Christian author who lived in Gaul in the 5th century AD.

Cleanthes: a Stoic philosopher (331–232 BC), student and successor of the founder of Stoicism, Zeno of Citium.

Clearchus of Soli: a disciple of Aristotle, active in the 4th to the 3rd century BC.

Clement of Alexandria: a Christian author, born in the middle of the 2nd century AD, author *inter alia* of *Stromata* (literally, *Tapestries*), which systematically sets in parallel citations from the Bible and statements of Greek philosophy in order to demonstrate the temporal priority of the former.

Cleobulina: a Greek poetess from the middle of the 6th century BC.

Cleon: an important Athenian politician of the 5th century BC, noted especially for his demagogy.

Colotes of Lampsacus: a disciple and companion of Epicurus, born ca. 320 BC, against whom Plutarch wrote a celebrated treatise that discusses *inter alia* the interpretation of several early Greek philosophers.

Columella (Lucius Junius Moderatus Columella): the author of the largest and most systematic surviving Latin agricultural treatise; active in the middle of the 1st century AD.

Corax of Syracuse: traditionally considered as the founder of rhetoric in Sicily in the 5th century BC; perhaps a legendary person (his name means 'Crow').

Cornutus (Lucius Annaeus Cornutus): a Stoic grammarian and philosopher, active in the 1st century AD.

Critias: a celebrated and very controversial Athenian politician during the Peloponnesian War and one of the leaders of the Thirty Tyrants; Plato was a member of his family.

Croesus: the last king of Lydia (ca. 560–546 BC) and son of Alyattes II; his wealth was proverbial; he subjugated the Greek cities of Asia Minor but as a general rule favored the Greeks; the rise of Persia, a potent rival, led him to seek a decisive battle, in which Cyrus defeated the Lydians and captured their capital, Sardis.

Cyril of Alexandria: born 376 AD; bishop of Alexandria from 412 until his death in 444. The chronological notices that appear at the beginning of his book against the emperor Julian abridge the chronography of Eusebius of Caesarea.

Cyrus: the founder of the Persian Empire, which he ruled ca. 559–529 BC; following his victory over Croesus, king of Lydia, he conquered much of Asia Minor, Babylonia, and other regions.

Damascius: a Neoplatonic philosopher, born ca. AD 460, a disciple of Marinus, and a successor of Proclus.

Damastes of Sigeum: a historian and geographer contemporary with Herodotus.

INDEX OF OTHER PERSONS

Damon: a teacher and theoretician of music, born ca. 485 BC, with whom Socrates is reported to have studied; his testimonia and fragments are included in Diels-Kranz.

Darius: king of Persia from 521 until 486 BC and a member (like Cyrus) of the family of the Achaemenids; one of the most important events of his reign was the suppression of the revolt of the Greek cities of Ionia against Persian domination in 499; Athens and the other cities of continental Greece that had been involved in the uprising won the battle of Marathon against the Persian army in 490.

David: a student of Olympiodorus in Alexandria and Greek commentator on Aristotle and Porphyry, probably 6th century AD.

Demetrius of Byzantium: a Peripatetic philosopher of the 1st century BC.

Demetrius of Magnesia: an author of the 1st century BC, known essentially for two works concerning authors and cities of the same name; he is the source of the lists of homonyms in Diogenes Laertius.

Demetrius of Phalerum: a Peripatetic philosopher and Athenian statesman active from the end of the 4th to the beginning of the 3rd century BC; a disciple of Theophrastus, his philosophical works discuss essentially practical morals.

Democrates: an unknown author to whom eighty-six aphorisms are attributed in a Vatican manuscript; thirty-one of these are also transmitted by Stobaeus. It has sometimes been suggested that 'Democrates' might be an error for 'Democritus.'

Diagoras of Melos: a lyric poet and author of dithyrambs, who was charged with impiety at Athens around 415 BC; he incarnates the position of atheism, especially in the doxographic tradition.

Dicaearchus of Messina: a disciple of Aristotle, born ca. 376 BC, and the author of numerous works on various subjects, of which one, *On Lives,* discussed *inter alia* the biographies of philosophers.

Didymus: an important literary scholar of the period of Augustus; according to Clement of Alexandria, the author of a work on the philosophy of Pythagoras.

Didymus the Blind: a Christian commentator and apologist (4th century AD), student of Origen, and professor in Alexandria.

Dinon of Colophon: a historian of the 3rd century BC and the author of *Persica,* a celebrated history of Persia.

Diocles of Magnesia: the author of a *Life of Philosophers,* one of the sources of Diogenes Laertius; the preserved fragments do not permit a precise dating.

Diodorus of Aspendos: a Pythagorean philosopher of the 4th century BC and a typical representative of the akousmatic tradition of Pythagoreans, which later became confused with Cynicism.

Diodorus of Ephesus: a source of Diogenes Laertius, cited in the lives of Anaximander and Empedocles.

Diodorus Siculus (of Sicily): a Greek historian, active in the middle of the 1st century BC, who authored a monumental universal history in forty books (of which fifteen survive) entitled *Historical Library*.

Diogenes of Oenoanda: an Epicurean from Oenoanda in Lycia who lived in the 2nd century AD; he constructed around his villa a wall on which a series of texts by Epicurus and himself were inscribed in order to announce to passersby the good news of this liberating philosophical doctrine.

Diogenes Laertius: the author of *The Lives and Opinions of the Famous Philosophers*, 3rd century AD.

Dionysius of Halicarnassus: a historian, whose *Roman Antiquities* dates from 30 BC, a teacher of rhetoric, and the author of a series of short rhetorical treatises dedicated especially to the Attic orators.

Dionysius of Syracuse: the name of two tyrants of Syracuse; Dionysius II succeeded his father, Dionysius I, in 367 BC, and Plato tried to convert him to philosophy; the story of this unsuccessful attempt is told in the seventh letter attributed to Plato, which is of uncertain authenticity but which supplies precious information.

Dionysius Thrax (Dionysius the Thracian): a Greek grammarian (ca. 170–ca. 90 BC) and the author of a brief but extremely influential surviving treatise on Greek grammar, often commented on by later authors; recent scholarship has questioned the traditional attribution of the text.

Duris of Samos: a Greek historian, a disciple of Theophrastus, and an important source of information about the Seven Sages in Diogenes Laertius.

Ephorus of Cyme: a Greek historian of the 4th century BC and the author of a universal history that began with the sons of Heracles and continued down to his own age.

Epicharmus: a Greek comic poet, originally from Sicily, active between the 6th and 5th centuries BC; in antiquity he was thought to have been the author of philosophical writings.

INDEX OF OTHER PERSONS

Epimenides: a legendary Cretan seer and poet, who was said to have slept for fifty-seven years in a cave and to have awakened to find himself endowed with prophetic powers.

Eratosthenes of Cyrene: a great scholar of the Hellenistic period who lived from ca. 276–195 BC; known especially for having been the founder of mathematical geography (thanks to his measurement of the circumference of the earth) and of scientific chronology (applied to Greek political and literary history), he was also a distinguished philologist.

Eubulides: a Pythagorean philosopher of uncertain date who claimed that a period of 216 years intervened between two reincarnations of Pythagoras; Boethius associates him with Hippasus.

Eubulides of Miletus: a philosopher of the Megarian school and a disciple of Socrates' disciple Euclid of Megara; he was celebrated for his paradoxes.

Eudemus of Rhodes: a Peripatetic philosopher and a direct disciple of Aristotle; his works seem to have been concerned principally with logic and physics, as well as with the history of the sciences.

Eudoxus of Cnidus: an astronomer, mathematician, geographer, philosopher, doctor, and legislator, contemporary with Plato's students.

Euhemerus: a Greek mythographer, active ca. 300 BC, celebrated for his doctrine that the gods were in fact nothing other than human beings who were revered for the benefits they had provided; in antiquity he was considered an atheist.

Eupolis: an Athenian comic poet of the second half of the 5th century BC.

Eusebius of Caesarea: a bishop of Caesarea (now in Israel), born ca. 265, and the author of the first history of the Christian Church; his *Chronicle,* an important source for dating Greek authors, is known essentially from an Armenian translation and from the (enlarged) Latin version by Jerome.

Eustathius: a great Byzantine scholar and ecclesiastic (end of the 12th century).

Evenus (Euenus) of Paros: a teacher of rhetoric, active at the end of the 5th century BC.

Favorinus of Arles: a sophist and philosopher active in Rome between the 1st and 2nd centuries AD, and the author especially of a *Miscellaneous History,* which discussed famous people and places; he is one of the principal sources of Diogenes Laertius.

Gallio (Lucius Junius Gallio Annaeanus): a Roman senator and the brother of Seneca the Younger.

George Syncellus: a Byzantine ecclesiastical functionary and scholar (8th–9th century) and the author of a surviving *Chronicle,* a chronological work in tabular form following Eusebius and other earlier scholars.

Glaucus of Rhegium: the author of a treatise *On the Ancient Poets and Musicians,* active in the 5th century BC.

Harpocration: a Greek lexicographer (2nd century AD).

Hecataeus of Miletus: one of the earliest writers of Greek history and geography in prose, active at the beginning of the 5th century BC.

Hellanicus of Mitylene: a Greek historian from the island of Lesbos, active in the 5th century BC.

Hephaestion of Alexandria: a grammarian and scholar of the 2nd century BC.

Heraclides Lembus: a scholar of the 2nd century BC, known *inter alia* as a compiler of epitomes of the works of Hermippus, Satyrus, and Sotion.

Heraclides Ponticus (of Pontus): a member of the Platonic Academy and the author of a large and diverse corpus of writings; he was influenced by Aristotle too.

Heraclitus: the author of *Homeric Allegories,* usually dated to the 1st century AD; his work is largely Stoic in orientation.

Hermias: a Christian writer, author of a pamphlet entitled *Derision of the Pagan Philosophers.*

Hermias of Alexandria: a Neoplatonic philosopher and the author of a commentary on Plato's *Phaedrus* based on his notes from the lectures of his teacher Syrianus.

Hermippus of Smyrna: a Peripatetic philosopher active in Alexandria during the second half of the 3rd century BC; known principally as a biographer of philosophers, legislators, poets, orators, and historians, he is often cited by Diogenes Laertius.

Hermodamas: a descendant of Creophylus, an epic poet who was considered a rival of Homer; according to Iamblichus, he was the teacher of Pythagoras.

Hermotimus of Clazomenae: a legendary thaumaturge.

Herodian (Aelius Herodianus): a grammarian and the son of Apollonius Dyscolus, active in the second half of the 2nd century AD; he authored works on morphology, accentuation, and grammar.

Herodicus of Selymbria: a celebrated athletic trainer, active at the beginning of the 5th century BC, considered an expert on exercise and diet.

Herophilus of Chalcedon: an Alexandrian doctor and medical writer (ca. 330–260 BC); many important anatomical discoveries are attributed to him, certainly on the basis of dissection of human cadavers (and perhaps as well on that of vivisection of prisoners).

Hesychius: a grammarian of the 6th century AD and the author of an alphabetical lexicon of rare words.

Hierocles of Alexandria: a Neoplatonic philosopher, active at the beginning of the 6th century AD.

Hieron: tyrant of Syracuse from 478 until 467 BC; he increased his city's renown for cultural accomplishments, initiated during the tyranny of his brother Gelon, by welcoming to his court numerous poets, including Pindar and Bacchylides, who celebrated his glory in their epinician odes, as well as Aeschylus, Simonides, and Epicharmus.

Hieronymus of Rhodes: a Peripatetic philosopher of the 3rd century BC and the author of various works, including an anecdotal history of the lives of the philosophers.

Hipparchus of Nicaea: a great mathematician, astronomer, and geographer, active in the second half of the 2nd century BC.

Hippobotus: a historian of philosophy and biographer, active sometime between the middle of the 2nd and the end of the 1st centuries BC; one of the sources of Diogenes Laertius.

Hippocrates of Chios: a celebrated Greek mathematician, active in the middle of the 5th century BC; his name is associated with the Pythagorean school and with the history of the solution of the problem of the duplication of the cube.

(Ps.-?) Hippolytus: many scholars attribute to Hippolytus, the schismatic bishop of Rome (170–235), a treatise entitled *Refutation of All Heresies,* a Christian polemical work of the early 3rd century BC, which is attributed to Origen by the manuscripts of the first book, also called *Philosophoumena,* and containing numerous summaries of the doctrines of the Greek philosophers and a series of fragments of Heraclitus (of which it is in some cases the only source); the authorship is very controversial.

Ion of Chios: a tragic and lyric poet of the 5th century BC of whose works numerous fragments survive; he is also the author of various works in prose, apparently including a philosophical treatise entitled *Triagmoi* (i.e. probably: *Triads*).

Jerome: Saint Jerome (347–420), one of the four most important Fathers of the Latin Church, who translated into Latin in 380 (and continued down to 379) the *Chronicle* of Eusebius of Caesarea, a universal chronology of world history.

John Lydus (John the Lydian): a Byzantine administrative functionary and author of *De mensibus* (*On Months*) on pagan festivals and of works on divination and on the magistracies of the Roman republic, all of which survive; he lived in the 6th century AD.

Junius Otho senior: a Roman orator of the beginning of the 1st century AD.

Libanius: a celebrated Greek rhetorician (314–93) and the author of numerous surviving declamations, rhetorical exercises, public speeches, and 1,600 letters.

Lobon of Argos: the author of a work entitled *On the Poets,* a source of Diogenes Laertius; he is considered untrustworthy.

Lycurgus: the legendary legislator of Sparta.

Lysander: an important Spartan admiral and political figure, largely responsible for the defeat of Athens in the Peloponnesian War; he died 405 BC.

Marcellinus: the name traditionally given to the author of a composite extant biography of the historian Thucydides.

Melanthius: a tragic poet, contemporary with Gorgias.

Melesagoras: the author of a history of Athens, *Atthis.*

Menaechmus: a Greek mathematician of the 4th century BC, known for having discovered the conic sections and solved the problem of the duplication of the cube by using the parabola and the hyperbola.

Menedemus of Pyrrha: a disciple of Plato.

Metrodorus of Chios: a Democritean, perhaps of the beginning of the 4th century BC, known for having maintained an extreme version of Skepticism.

Metrodorus of Lampsacus: (1) a disciple of Anaxagoras, known for his

INDEX OF OTHER PERSONS

allegories of Homer; (2) a disciple and companion of Epicurus (ca. 331–278 BC).

Minucius Felix: an author of the 2nd–3rd century AD, who wrote a philosophical dialogue, *Octavius,* arguing for the compatibility of Christianity (to which he converted at the end of his life) and pagan wisdom.

Mnesiphilus of Phrearrhi: a teacher of rhetoric, from the same deme as Themistocles, who studied with him.

Musaeus: a legendary Attic epic poet, who, like Orpheus, was considered to have been earlier than Homer, and who was associated with the Eleusinian mysteries.

Myson of Chenae: included in the catalog of the Seven Sages by Plato in his *Protagoras,* in place of Periander, who appears in the list of Demetrius of Phalerum.

Neanthes of Cyzicus: an author of historical and paradoxographic works of the end of the 4th century BC; he also studied the biographies of a large number of illustrious people, including certain philosophers, like Pythagoras and his disciples.

Neoptolemus of Paros: a scholar of the Hellenistic period and the author of a work on epigrams.

Nicander of Colophon: a Greek didactic poet of the 2nd century BC.

Nicolaus of Damascus: a court historian and Peripatetic philosopher of the second half of the 1st century BC.

Nicomachus of Gerasa: a mathematician and Neopythagorean philosopher of the 2nd century AD and an important source for the history of ancient Pythagoreanism.

Numenius of Apamea: a philosopher of the second half of the 2nd century AD who combined Neopythagoreanism and Middle Platonism with Oriental, especially Jewish, influences.

Oenopides of Chios: an astronomer and mathematician, contemporary with Anaxagoras.

Olympiodorus of Alexandria: (1) an alchemist, dating probably to the end of the 4th century AD, sometimes identified with (2) a Neoplatonic philosopher, a disciple of Ammonius and commentator on Plato and Aristotle (6th century AD).

Origen of Alexandria: a Christian theologian and the author of a large corpus of writings, active at the beginning of the 3rd century AD.

Orpheus: in Greek tradition, a pre-Homeric poet who was thought to
have lived one generation before the Trojan War; starting in the
middle of the 6th century BC, various theogonic poems, hymns,
and the foundation of a mystery cult were attributed to him.

Ostanes the Mede: a legendary Persian Magus and alchemist.

Pamphile of Epidaurus: a philosopher and historian, she composed a
history of Greece and several epitomes of historical works toward
the middle of the 1st century AD.

Panaetius of Rhodes: a Stoic philosopher (ca. 180–109 BC), who came
from Greece but lived in Rome for a long time.

Periander of Corinth: the second tyrant of Corinth (ca. 655–627 BC),
he improved the city's ports, encouraged the arts and commerce,
and constructed the first transport system across the isthmus.

Pericles: an Athenian statesman (ca. 495–429 BC) and the most pow-
erful Athenian politician during the period between the Persian
Wars and the Peloponnesian War.

Persaeus of Citium: a Stoic philosopher and a compatriot and disciple
of Zeno of Citium, of the middle of the 3rd century BC.

Phemonoê: a legendary Greek poetess, thought to be earlier than
Homer and associated with the Delphic oracle.

Pherecydes of Athens: a historian and mythographer of the beginning
of the 5th century BC.

Philip of Opus: a disciple of Plato and the author of a treatise *On the
Eclipse of the Moon*.

Philo of Alexandria: an important Jewish philosopher and political
leader (1st century AD) and the author of numerous treatises in
Greek, many of them allegorical commentaries, of a Platonic and
Stoic coloring, on parts of the Hebrew Bible; some of his works, lost
in Greek, have survived in Armenian translation.

Philochorus: a local historian of Athens, of the 4th to the 3rd centuries
BC.

Philodemus of Gadara: an Epicurean philosopher of the 1st century
BC; a villa at Herculaneum, destroyed by an eruption of Vesuvius
in 79 AD, contained many papyrus rolls from his library that par-
tially survive and transmit his own and other philosophical works.

Philostratus: the name of various members of several generations of
a family of Greek rhetoricians, of whom the most famous, Lucius

INDEX OF OTHER PERSONS

Flavius Philostratus (ca. AD 170–ca. 247) wrote a treatise entitled *Lives of the Sophists*, which traces the history of the Sophistic movement from its origins down to the 'Second Sophistic,' an intellectual and literary current (2nd–3rd century AD) to which he gives its name and of which he himself is an important exponent.

Phocus of Samos: the presumed author of the *Maritime Astronomy* that was attributed to Thales.

Phocylides of Miletus: a Greek poet of the middle of the 6th century BC, famous for his gnomic couplets.

Photius: a Byzantine scholar and patriarch of Constantinople (ca. 810–ca. 893); his most important surviving work, called *Bibliotheca* (*Library*), is a summary of hundreds of books of classical authors whom he read, many of them now lost.

Polus of Agrigentum: a rhetorician and a disciple of Gorgias, known almost exclusively from Plato's *Gorgias* and *Phaedrus*.

Polycrates of Athens: a rhetorician, contemporary with Isocrates, who counters him in his *Busiris;* he is especially known for his paradoxical encomia and for his *The Indictment of Socrates*.

Polycrates of Samos: tyrant of Samos in the second half of the 6th century BC, who surrounded himself with poets (like Anacreon and Ibycus) and thinkers.

Porphyry: a Neoplatonic philosopher and scholar (234–ca. 305); he wrote commentaries on Plato and Aristotle, historical studies of chronology and religion, philological and other technical treatises, and other works.

Posidonius: a Stoic philosopher (ca. 135–ca. 51 BC) and the author of very influential works on a vast range of subjects, now all lost except for fragments and references.

Proclus: a Neoplatonic philosopher (ca. AD 410–485) and the head of the Platonic Academy in Athens; he authored philosophical treatises, mostly on Platonic theology, commentaries on a number of Platonic dialogues, on Hesiod, and on Euclid, and other works.

Proclus of Naucratis: a rhetorician born at Naucratis, in Egypt, in the 2nd century AD; he emigrated to Rome, where he became the teacher of Philostratus.

Procopius of Gaza: a rhetorician and commentator on the Bible (ca. 465–528).

213

Proxenus of Boeotia: a disciple of Gorgias and a soldier, mentioned several times by Xenophon.

Pythocleides: a famous player of the *aulos* at the time of Pericles; certain sources credit him with the invention of the Mixolydian musical mode; according to a scholium to Plato's *Alcibiades Major,* he was also a Pythagorean philosopher.

Pythodorus of Athens: an Athenian general sent to Sicily in 426/25 BC to replace Laches as the commander of the fleet.

Sabinus: a Hippocratic medical writer, active in the 2nd century AD; he was the teacher of Stratonicus, who was in turn the teacher of Galen.

Satyrus of Callatis: a Peripatetic philosopher, probably of the 3rd century BC, and the author of biographies of famous people.

Scopas: tyrant of Thessaly in the 5th century BC and a patron of the poet Simonides.

Scopelianus: a sophist belonging to the period of the Second Sophistic, born in Clazomenae, active ca. AD 80–115.

Sextus Empiricus: a Skeptical philosopher and medical writer who probably flourished at the end of the 2nd century AD; the most important extant representative of Pyrrhonian Skepticism, he was the author of two surviving works, *Outlines of Pyrrhonism* in three books, and *Against the Mathematicians* (*Adversus Mathematicos*) in eleven books. The latter, which in its present form probably represents the combination of two originally distinct works, is traditionally referred to under the titles *Against the Professors* (Books 1–6), *Against the Logicians* (Books 7–8), *Against the Natural Philosophers* (or *Against the Physicists,* Books 9–10), and *Against the Ethicists* (Book 11).

Simplicius of Cilicia: a Neoplatonic commentator (ca. AD 490–ca. 560), especially on Aristotle's *Categories, On the Heavens,* and *Physics;* his extensive quotations are the major source for a large number of original fragments of the early Greek philosophers, especially Parmenides, Melissus, Empedocles, Anaxagoras, and Diogenes of Apollonia.

Socrates: sometimes called 'the other Socrates,' to distinguish him from another, younger Socrates, who is one of the interlocutors in Plato's *Statesman.*

Soranus of Ephesus: a doctor and medical writer (flourished in the

214

early 2nd century AD), who authored a large number of works on medicine and its history, including a surviving *Gynecology*.

Sosicrates of Rhodes: a Greek historian of the 2nd century BC and the author of *The Successions of the Philosophers,* cited by Diogenes Laertius.

Sotion of Alexandria: a doxographer and grammarian of the 3rd century BC and a source of Diogenes Laertius; his principal work, *The Successions of the Philosophers,* was probably one of the first histories of philosophy to have organized the lives of the philosophers in terms of the schools to which they belonged.

Speusippus: the nephew and successor of Plato as the head of the Platonic Academy from 347–339 BC.

Sphaerus of Borysthenes: a Stoic philosopher (3rd century BC); his writings on many subjects, including Heraclitus, are all lost except for a few fragments.

Stephanus of Byzantium: a Greek grammarian (6th century AD) and the author of *Ethnica,* an important geographical dictionary that survives in an epitome and a few fragments.

Stobaeus (John of Stobi): the (perhaps Christian) author of the *Anthology,* a voluminous collection of quotations organized thematically and intended for pedagogical purposes, probably of the 5th century AD.

Strabo: a Greek geographer (ca. 64 BC–ca. AD 24), the author of *Geographia* in seventeen books, the most important surviving ancient work on the subject.

Suda: the title of a Byzantine lexicon dating to the 10th century AD.

Syrianus: a Neoplatonic philosopher, head of the Platonic Academy in Athens, and rhetorician (4th–5th century AD); he authored surviving commentaries on Aristotle's *Metaphysics* and on various rhetorical treatises.

Theano: according to different texts, either Pythagoras' wife or daughter or disciple, or the wife of Pythagoras' disciple Brontinus; pseudepigraphic texts, especially moral apothegms, were attributed to her.

Themistocleia: a priestess of Delphi, who taught Pythagoras according to a tradition that goes back to Aristoxenus and was probably inspired by the figure of Diotima in Plato's *Symposium*.

Themistocles: an Athenian statesman and general (ca. 524–459 BC) who played a decisive role in the Greek victory during the Second Persian War.

Theodoret: bishop of Cyrrhus (ca. AD 393–457) and the author of *Therapy of the Greek Maladies,* an important source for the reconstitution of the manual of Aëtius; he is the only author who cites Aëtius' name.

Theodorus of Cyrene: (1) a Greek mathematician of the 5th century BC; (2) a philosopher of the Cyrenaic school (ca. 340–250 BC), considered an atheist in antiquity.

Theon of Smyrna: a Greek philosopher and mathematician of the beginning of the 2nd century AD; he authored *On Mathematics Useful for the Understanding of Plato,* an introductory manual to the different branches of the mathematical sciences that is broader in scope than its title suggests and is colored by Pythagoreanism.

Theophrastus: disciple and successor of Aristotle as the head of the Lyceum (ca. 371/0–287/6 BC).

Theopompus of Chios: a Greek historian of the 4th century BC and a disciple of Isocrates.

Thrasyllus of Mendes: a Greek grammarian and literary scholar of the 1st century AD; he edited the works of Democritus and Plato in tetralogies and was also the personal friend and astrologer of the emperor Tiberius.

Timaeus of Taormina: a Greek historian of the middle of the 3rd century BC; his principal work is a history of Sicily from the beginnings until 264 BC.

Timocrates: the older brother of Metrodorus of Lampsacus (2 above); he was a disciple of Epicurus but then violently attacked his doctrine.

Timon of Phlius: a Skeptical philosopher of the 3rd century BC and the author of satires (*Silloi*) in dactylic hexameters that lampooned the dogmatic philosophers.

Tisias: an important figure from the beginnings of the history of rhetoric in Sicily during the 5th century BC, traditionally considered the disciple of Corax.

Tzetzes (John Tzetzes): a Byzantine scholar of the 12th century AD.

Vestinus, Julius: a Latin lexicographer of the second half of the 2nd century AD.

INDEX OF OTHER PERSONS

Xenocrates: a disciple of Plato, elected to the head of the Academy in 339 BC on the death of Speusippus.

Xerxes: the son of Darius and king of Persia from 486–465 BC; he invaded Greece in 480 BC but failed to conquer it.

Zeno of Citium: the founder of Stoicism (335–263 BC).

GLOSSARY

This glossary explains a selection of the most significant Greek and Latin terms that appear in the present edition. It is neither a complete *index verborum*, nor a thematic index, nor an exhaustive systematic index like the one that W. Kranz prepared for Diels-Kranz, which readers can consult in *Fragmente der Vorsokratiker,* volume 3, pp. 5–488. Instead, we have limited ourselves here to clarifying those terms that, for one reason or another, seem to us to require a special explanation: terms that we have been led to translate in different ways in different passages, and for which the translation is often followed by a transcription (e.g. *logos*); terms that Greek differentiates but that are usually rendered by the same word in the translation (e.g. *adêlos/aphanês*); terms that are not necessarily transcribed but that either are particularly important philosophically (e.g. *nomos, phusis*), or recur often (e.g. *agathos*), or are connected to particular aspects of Greek civilization, like religion (e.g. *eusebeia*). Terms not found in this list include the words transcribed in our edition only so as to indicate assonances and alliterations (especially in the chapter on Gorgias), the quasi-synonymous words that Prodicus endeavors to distinguish from one another, and certain words for which the transcription has only a local interest, in particular rare, dialectal, technical, or idiosyncratic terms. As a general rule, the terms presented here belong to the vocabulary of the original fragments; but several terms belonging to the later philosophical tradition and to doxography (e.g. *homoiomereia*) have been added when this seemed useful.

Each term or family of terms is presented first in a transcription, followed by the Greek original and our translations, then usually by a brief explanation (into which sometimes the translations have been integrated); the references are intended to guide the reader to some of the most significant occurrences but do not aim at exhaustiveness.

adêlos (ἄδηλος): invisible. See *dêlos*.

adikia (ἀδικία): injustice. See *dikê*.

aêr (ἀήρ)/*aithêr* (αἰθήρ): air/aether. Greek has a differentiated vocabulary for referring to what we call 'air' and to the processes in
which it is involved. *aêr* refers in principle to a mass that tends to
be humid, dark, and cold, i.e. 'a mist'; hence it can be opposed to
aithêr, a luminous, transparent, and hot medium that can even
become the equivalent of fire (ANAXAG. R15, cf. D9–D11). But
some occurrences of *aêr* are less marked (EMP. D201a.13; MED.
T10; DERV. Col. XVII); and, inversely, *aithêr* can lose its distinctive
characteristics to the point of being able to be substituted for *aêr*
(EMP. D201a.5, 7, 13, 24). The translation 'aether,' which is sometimes unavoidable, never refers to Aristotle's 'fifth element' except
in Aristotle himself and in the tradition deriving from him. Air in
movement can be called *anemos* (ἄνεμος, 'wind') (MED. T10);
pneuma (πνεῦμα, 'breath') (ANAXIMEN. D31, R10; MED. T10,
T28, T29a; DERV. Col. XVIII); *phusa* (φῦσα, 'air flow') (MED.
T10).

agathos (ἀγαθός): good (MOR. T37; PROT. D42). The adjective usually signifies 'excellent,' 'useful,' without necessarily having the
moral connotation that attaches to the term in English, just as *kakos*
(κακός, 'bad,' 'evil') also often has the sense of 'destructive.' For
the expression *kalos kagathos,* see *kalos;* see also *esthlos.*

aidôs (αἰδώς), *aidoios* (αἰδοῖος): *aidôs* is a feeling of respect or reverence that leads to self-restraint and the avoidance of certain kinds
of behavior subject to social reprobation (PROT. D40). It can also
mean 'shame,' and the corresponding adjective can refer to what is
shameful; the substantivized neuter plural can designate the parts
of the body that one feels shameful about, i.e. the genitals (HER.
D16). But the adjective can also refer to what one feels reverence
for, and then signifies 'noble,' 'revered.' It is possible that the author
of the Derveni Papyrus, who also uses the term with reference to
the genitals (DERV. Col. XIII), is playing with this ambiguity in Col.
XVI; but in any case the fragmentary condition of the papyrus
makes it impossible to be certain.

ainigma (αἴνιγμα), *ainizesthai* (αἰνίζεσθαι): riddling, to say in a riddling way. An author who dissimulates what he really means, by
using ordinary language in an unusual way, is expressing himself
indirectly, by 'riddles' (DERV. Col. VII), 'in a riddling way' (Col.

GLOSSARY

IX–X, XIII, XVII). The allegorical interpretation of myths in terms of natural philosophy rests upon this presupposition.

aiôn (αἰών): the vital force that keeps a person alive (MOR. T32c), and hence the length of a human being's lifetime (HER. D76). The meaning 'eternity' is later.

aisa (αἶσα): fate. See *anankê*.

aiskhros (αἰσχρός): ugly, shameful, unseemly. See *kalos*.

aithêr (αἰθήρ): luminous air, aether. See *aêr*.

aitia (αἰτία), *aitios* (αἴτιος), *aitiologia* (αἰτιολογία): The adjective *aitios* designates what causes or is responsible for something; the neuter substantive *to aition*, like the feminine *hê aitia*, indicates the cause of something. *aitiologia*, 'causal explanation,' is specifically linked to Democritus (ATOM. P40). Cf. *prophasis*.

akinêtos (ἀκίνητος): immobile, unmoved. See *kinein*.

akmê (ἀκμή): flowering, full maturity. The term designates originally the cutting edge or point of a sharp object, then, by extension, the culmination or most perfect expression of anything. The corresponding verb, *akmazein* (ἀκμάζειν), is applied to the life of the world in the context of the Atomist doctrine (ATOM. D81). Apollodorus of Athens (2nd–1st centuries BC) based his *Chronicle*, a chronological work in iambic trimeters that was much used by later scholars in antiquity, upon a system of synchronisms linking historical events and the dates of important people; for the latter he used not only their putative dates of birth and death but also their *akmê*, which he conventionally set at forty years. While such dates are at best approximate and must be used with caution, they do give at least some sense of the authors' relative chronology.

akoê (ἀκοή), *akouê* (ἀκούη), *akousmata* (ἀκούσματα), *akousmatikoi* (ἀκουσματικοί): *akoê* or *akouê* can designate either the organ of hearing (DIOG. D42), the act of hearing itself (EMP. D44.10), or the sound that is heard (EMP. D44.11). Among the Pythagoreans, the *akousmata* (literally, 'things heard'; we have translated as 'sayings') are utterances of a certain sort (PYTH. c D15–D25); knowledge of these sayings defines a certain category of adepts, the *akousmatikoi*, 'listeners' (PYTH. b T15–T20), who were probably less fully initiated into the 'mathematical' forms of knowledge than the *mathêmatikoi*, the 'knowers,' were (see also *manthanein; sumbolon*).

akosmia (ἀκοσμία): disorder. See *kosmos*.

akrasia (ἀκρασία), *akratês* (ἀκρατής): the substantive *akrasia* (literally, 'inability to dominate') designates lack of self-control (MOR. T35[4]), intemperance (SOC. D48–D51; DISS. 1[3]); the adjective indicates an intemperate person (DISS. 1[3]).

alêthês (ἀληθής), *alêtheia* (ἀλήθεια): true, truth. Ancient Greek has above all two words to designate what is true, *alêthês* and *etumos* (cf. this word). The adjective *alêthês* is attested already in Homer (e.g. *Iliad* 6.382, *Odyssey* 3.254) and Hesiod (MOR. T17); the substantive *alêtheia* appears in Parmenides (D4.29, D6.4) and, notably, on Orphic tablets dating from the fifth century BC (MOR. T33). These terms derive from the same root as the verb *lanthanein* (λανθάνειν), 'to escape someone's notice,' preceded by the negative prefix *a-*. Thus, to begin with, *alêthês* designates, from the perspective of the object involved, 'what does not escape someone's notice,' or, from the perspective of the observer, 'what records or corresponds to that which is or was the case.' This etymological origin is more or less marked or noticeable in different texts and contexts, the negation implicitly denying the possibility that a given statement might be defective because of problems involving the perception, attention, or intention of a speaker who might have thereby missed, distorted, or dissimulated some aspect of reality. What might have escaped notice can be of very different kinds: the reality of things or events, their number, characteristics, or profound structure. Thus, in different cases, 'true' will be what records or corresponds to what is real or is the case, what is acknowledged, complete, exact, or penetrates beyond the surface of appearances, or some combination of these determinations. In Parmenides and the tradition he inaugurates, the term that is opposed most broadly to *alêtheia* is *doxa* (δόξα, cf. *dokein*), 'opinion,' which in Parmenides is fundamentally fictitious or erroneous (it appears in the plural in the form of "the opinions of mortals") but, already before Plato, can also turn out to be correct (cf. δόκος, *dokos,* in XEN. D49). The antonyms of *alêthês* and *alêtheia* are *pseudês* (ψευδής) and *pseudos* (ψεῦδος), which in different contexts can take on the meanings of 'fictitious/fiction,' 'false/falsehood,' 'erroneous/error,' 'mendacious/lie,' without it being possible in some cases to be certain just which of these meanings is or are being connoted. *Alêtheia* supplies the title to two works, by Protagoras (PROT. D5) and Antiphon (ANTIPH. D1–D40); it is also the title that is traditionally given

GLOSSARY

(though it is not original) to the first part of the goddess' speech in the poem of Parmenides, by opposition to the second part, traditionally entitled *Doxa*. In conformity with a comprehensible semantic development, *alethês*, 'what records or corresponds to that which is real,' will also come to designate the real itself, just like *etumos* (cf. this word).

ameipsikosmiê (ἀμειψικοσμίη): change of a world. See *kosmos*.

ameipsirhusmein (ἀμειψιρυσμεῖν): change of configuration of an atomic aggregate. See *rhusmos*.

analogia (ἀναλογία): a mathematical proportion (ARCHY. D15, D25b; PYTHS. ANON. D17). Cf. *logos* (*ana logon*).

anankê (ἀνάγκη): necessity. Greek does not distinguish systematically between *anankê* and other terms such as *aisa* (αἶσα) (EMP. D77b.2), *heimarmenê* (εἱμαρμένη) (ATOM. D73), *khreôn* (χρεών) (ANAXIMAND. D6; HER. D63), *moira* (μοῖρα) (HER. D122; PARM. D8.42; DERV. Col. XVIII), or *potmos* (πότμος) (EMP. D54), to designate the physical necessity or the moral obligation resulting in certain processes, events, or states of affairs. *aisa* and *moira* (cf. this word) also signify in general an (especially allotted) portion.

anarkhia (ἀναρχία): lack of rule. See *arkhê*, under *arkhein*.

anathumiasis (ἀναθυμίασις): evaporation resulting from the effect of heat upon humidity. The term is characteristic of Heraclitus and even more of the doxographical notices about him, perhaps under Stoic influence (HER. R51), but it is possible that Philolaus used it as well (cf. PHILOL. D18). It went on to become a technical term in Aristotle (who also allowed for a 'dry evaporation') and in the Stoics.

anemos (ἄνεμος): wind. See *aêr*.

anepistêmosunê (ἀνεπιστημοσύνη). See *epistasthai*.

antilegein (ἀντιλέγειν): to speak against, to contradict (PROD. R14). The term and its prefix *anti-*, 'against,' which are found also e.g. in *anteipein* (ἀντειπεῖν, 'to contradict') (PROT. D2), are particularly characteristic of an attitude and practice common to a number of 'sophists,' that of engaging in eristic discussion (cf. *eris*), opposing one argument to another. *antilogia* (ἀντιλογία, 'the art of contradicting') in the plural is the title of a work by Protagoras (PROT. D1); *antilogikos* (ἀντιλογικός) is 'someone who contradicts' (SOPH. R22).

223

EARLY GREEK PHILOSOPHY I

aoratos (ἀόρατος): unseen. See *dêlos*.

aoristos (ἀόριστος): indefinite. See *apeiros*.

apeiros (ἄπειρος), *to apeiron* (τὸ ἄπειρον): that which is without (*a*-) limit (*peras, peirar*) can be unlimited spatially (XEN. D41; MEL. D4) or temporally (MEL. D3), but it can also be without any intrinsic limit at all, i.e. be indefinite. This is the sense in which Anaximander in particular, who uses the term as a substantive, probably takes the term (ANAXIMAND. D6–D11, D13–D14, D16, D17, R1, R3, R6, R8, R10–R13, R19). The term was the object of debates and underwent a process of gradual disambiguation (cf. MEL. R7–R11). The term *aoriston*, 'indefinite,' clearly takes over one of the possible meanings of *apeiron* (PYTHS. R13). Cf. *peras, peirar*.

aphanês (ἀφανής): invisible. See *dêlos*.

aphrodisiazein (ἀφροδισιάζειν): to engage in the works of Aphrodite, the goddess of love, hence to perform sexual intercourse (DERV. Col. XXI). DIOG. D28a, following Hesiod (*Theogony* 191), connects the term with *aphros* (ἀφρός, 'foam'), i.e. of semen.

apokrinein (ἀποκρίνειν), *apokrisis* (ἀπόκρισις): to distinguish, separate. See *krinein*.

aporein (ἀπορεῖν): to be in difficulties or in an aporia, at an impasse (ἀπορία); literally, to be without a *poros* (πόρος), i.e. 'a way out' (ATOM. D19) or 'a resource' (ATOM. D279). The term is particularly applied to the effect of Socrates' argumentative techniques, not only on his interlocutors but also on himself; *euporein* (εὐπορεῖν), inversely, means 'to resolve difficulties with ease' (SOC. D12).

apotupousthai (ἀποτυποῦσθαι): to receive an impression.

araios (ἀραιός), *manos* (μανός): thin, fine, rarefied. The two terms, which seem to be virtually synonymous, are applied to what is present only in small quantity over a large spatial extension and are contrasted with *puknos* (πυκνός, 'dense, compact'); see this word, e.g. in Anaximenes (ANAXIMEN. D3[3], D7, D8), Melissus (MEL. D10), Anaxagoras (ANAXAG. D27, D30), and the Atomists (ATOM. D31).

arariskein (ἀραρίσκειν): to join or fit together (EMP. D75.17, D192.4). Empedocles also uses two other words derived from this verb: *arthron* (ἄρθρον, 'joint') (EMP. D73.253), and *arthmios* (ἄρθμιος, in the plural, deeds 'of union') (EMP. D73.254). The verb *harmozein* (cf. this word) is etymologically related.

224

aretê (ἀρετή): any form of excellence, especially but not exclusively moral excellence or virtue (PROT. D41).

arkhein (ἄρχειν), *arkhesthai* (ἄρχεσθαι), *arkhê* (ἀρχή): *arkhein* and *arkhesthai* mean 'to make a beginning' (DIOG. D2); *arkhê* is a beginning, what comes first (MEL. R21c; ATOM. D79; DIOG. D2; DERV. Col. XV). In cosmological terms, the *arkhê* is that from which one begins when one gives an account of the world, i.e. a principle, which may or may not be thought to have come first temporally; Anaximander may have been the first to use the term in this way (ANAXIMAND. D6–D7, cf. D9–D11). Politically, *arkhê* is what that person has who comes first in a community, i.e. 'rule' (DERV. Col. VIII) or 'a magistracy in a city' (DERV. Col. XIX), and more generally whoever commands or governs; in this latter kind of context, *arkhesthai* can mean 'to be ruled' (GORG. D24[6]) and *anarkhia* is 'lack of rule' (PYTHS. ANON. D54b).

arrhuthmistos (ἀρρύθμιστος): without configuration. See *rhusmos*.

arthmios (ἄρθμιος): of union. See *arariskein*.

arthron (ἄρθρον): joint. See *arariskein*.

asaphês (ἀσαφής): unclear. See *dêlos*.

asômatos (ἀσώματος): incorporeal, bodiless; without form. See *sôma*.

astêr (ἀστήρ), *astron* (ἄστρον): the ancient Greeks, especially in this period, did not always distinguish clearly between different categories of heavenly bodies: the planets—which were later called *planêtes* (πλάνητες, literally, 'wanderers')—, the *astra*, or 'fixed stars' (so called because their trajectory, unlike that of the planets, does not seem to vary), and other phenomena like comets; instead they applied the term *astêr*, 'heavenly body,' to all of them indifferently.

atê (ἄτη): bewilderment or rage that produces or results from destruction, Destruction personified (EMP. D24.3), disaster (MOR. T35[4]1).

athambos (ἄθαμβος), *athambia* (ἀθαμβία): a person who is unastounded, unastoundedness, and the corresponding disposition of steadfastness (ATOM. D230, D322, R75).

atomos (ἄτομος): indivisible (ATOM. D32, R95). Referring to atoms, the adjective is used either in the neuter with an understood *sôma*, 'body,' or in the feminine with an understood *phusis*, 'nature.'

aulos (αὐλός): a reed wind instrument, somewhat similar to an oboe, made of bone or wood and most often played in pairs (ARCHY. P14). Anaximander (D7[4], D23, D26) applies the term to the nozzle, in the form of a tube with a hole, belonging to a bellows (see *prêstêr*).

autarkeia (αὐτάρκεια): self-sufficiency, an important goal for human life in Democritus' ethics (ATOM. D252, D254, D255, cf. D277) and in later Greek thought.

automatos (αὐτόματος): applied to something generated by a spontaneous process (ATOM. R31).

autos (αὐτός): the same. See *to auto*.

axunetos (ἀξύνετος): uncomprehending. Cf. *sunesis*.

barbaros (βάρβαρος): not only, pejoratively, a barbarian in an ethnic sense, but also, and more often, someone who does not speak Greek or does not speak it well. Depending on the context, we translate as either 'barbarian' (ANTIPH. D38b), 'non-Greek' (HIPPIAS D22), or 'people who do not speak good Greek' (DRAM. T20).

bios (βίος)/*zôê* (ζωή): life. *zôê* is life in the sense of existence (EMP. D42.3; ATOM. D285; ANON. IAMBL. (4)[2]), which humans share with *zôa*, animate beings in general and animals in particular. *bios* can also be used in this sense (ANON. IAMBL. (5)[2]), but it can also refer, in contrast with *zôê*, to the particular mode of life characteristic of some or all human beings (EMP. D42.3, cf. perhaps also D73.304). Cf. *diaita*; *zôon*.

daimôn (δαίμων): a divinity (PYTH. a P35; PARM. D14b; EMP. D10.5, D11; ATOM. D238; DERV. Col. III, VI, VIII, IX): either one that can be specified as being a particular named and known god, as is the case for *theos* (θεός), or one that for some reason cannot; in either case *daimôn* suggests more that god's general divine quality than his or her specific individual personality. The *daimôn* can also be an individual's personal protective deity (HER. D111; DERV. Col. III), which watches over him and, if well disposed, provides him with *eudaimonia* (εὐδαιμονία, 'happiness,' literally, 'the condition of having a favorable *daimôn*') (ATOM. D238). Empedocles' *Katharmoi* explains the life of humans by narrating the destiny of *daimones,* which were erroneously assimilated in the post-Platonic tradition to souls (cf. *psukhê*). It is not until Plato's *Symposium* that *daimôn* takes on the sense of a divinity intermediate between the gods properly speaking and humans (PYTHS. R33[32]). In most Christian authors, the term becomes negatively charged and comes to signify 'demons.' Socrates referred to the divine sign that he recognized as peculiar to himself as *to daimonion* (τὸ δαιμόνιον), the substantivized form of a neuter adjective formed from *daimôn*, which makes the term less personalized and more abstract (SOC. P26, cf. P36).

deinos (δεινός): originally, the adjective meant 'terrible' in the sense of 'terrifying,' 'fear-instilling' (PROD. D22d); but in the course of the fifth century BC, it also came to be applied to people whose mastery of some skill (cf. *tekhnê*) permitted them to produce astounding effects, notably in the domain of rhetoric.

dekas (δεκάς): decade, the number ten. Cf. *tetraktus*.

dêlos (δῆλος): manifest, evident, not only to sensory perception (especially sight) but also, and especially, to the understanding. The term is quasi-synonymous with *saphês* (σαφής). The antonym *adêlos* (ἄδηλος, 'invisible') refers not only to what cannot be seen (ANAXAG. D6, R2; MED. T13) but also occasionally to what can be seen but nevertheless is unknown (e.g. GORG. D24[13]). The same ambiguity is found in such other terms, very close in meaning to *adêlos*, as *aphanês* (ἀφανής, 'invisible') (MED. T14) and *asaphês* (ἀσαφής, 'unclear'), though *aphanês* refers somewhat more often to what is invisible and *asaphês* to what is difficult or impossible to understand. By contrast, *phaneros* (φανερός, 'manifest') and *aoratos* (ἀόρατος, 'unseen') are usually applied to what can or cannot be seen rather than to what can or cannot be understood.

dêmiourgos (δημιουργός): a craftsman (GORG. D48a), someone engaged professionally in a productive skill. The word designates etymologically a member of the people (*dêmos*) who makes something (*ergon*); in the city of Larisa, the magistrates who were responsible for assigning citizenship were also called *dêmiourgoi* ('people-makers'), and Gorgias makes a complicated pun in reference to them (GORG. D39). A *dêmiourgikê tekhnê* (δημιουργικὴ τέχνη) is a technical skill that makes a product (PROT. D40, D41).

dêmokratia (δημοκρατία): democracy. See *dêmos*.

dêmos (δῆμος): the populace of a city (SOC. P16); depending upon the context and the speaker's intentions the term can sometimes be pejorative, referring only to the lowest elements of the citizenry, and sometimes positive, referring to the citizenry as a whole. *dêmokratia* is that political constitution in which the power is exercized by this *dêmos* (ATOM. D361).

den (δέν), *mêden* (μηδέν): something, nothing. The pair of terms is particularly characteristic of Democritus (ATOM. D23b, D29, D33, R89); while *mêden* is a normal Greek word for 'nothing,' *den* (which results from depriving *mêden* of its negative prefix *mê-*) does not seem to be attested anywhere outside of Democritus except in a (textually problematic) fragment of the Aeolic lyric poet Alcaeus (ca. 600 BC) and is therefore either a coinage by Democritus or else his elevation of a rare word into a technical term.

diaita (δίαιτα): a mode of life, a regimen; the term is more specific than *bios* (cf. this word) and is more hygienic or medical in orientation (MED. T9).

diakosmos (διάκοσμος): organization of the world. See *kosmos*.

diakrinein (διακρίνειν), *diakrisis* (διάκρισις): to distinguish or separate, distinction or separation. See *krinein*.

dialegein (διαλέγειν), *dialegesthai* (διαλέγεσθαι), *dialexis* (διάλεξις): *dialegein*, in the active voice, means 'to pick out or classify things' (SOC. D18); *dialegesthai*, in the middle voice, means 'to engage in a discussion or conversation' and is a term especially associated with Socrates, indicating his favored mode of dialogical, 'dialectical' argumentation (SOC. D18). A *dialexis* is a public lecture (HIPPIAS D14b).

dianoeisthai (διανοεῖσθαι), *dianoia* (διάνοια): to think, thought. See *noein*.

diaphuein (διαφύειν): to grow apart. See *phusis*.

diathesis (διάθεσις), *diathêkê* (διαθήκη), *diathêgê* (διαθηγή), *diathigê* (διαθιγή): at ATOM. D15, D31, D32, it is not entirely certain whether one should read *diathêkê* (or *diathêgê*), derived from *diatithenai* ('to arrange or dispose') and referring to the disposition of the atoms, or *diathigê*, derived from *diathinganein* ('to touch reciprocally') and indicating the mutual contact of the atoms. *diathêkê* and *diathêgê* are graphically very similar, and *diathêgê* and *diathigê* were pronounced identically in later Greek.

dikê (δίκη), *Dikê* (Δίκη), *dikaiosunê* (δικαιοσύνη): trial, legal judgment, justice. The relations of reciprocity and equity that should obtain among human beings and between humans and gods are a fundamental axiom of Greek moral and political thought (PROT. D40, D41; GORG. D24[16]). In the wake of Hesiod (MOR. T23b, T24), especially Anaximander (ANAXIMAND. D6) and Heraclitus (HER. D89c) elevate justice to the status of a universal principle

GLOSSARY

governing not only actions but also natural processes, and Parmenides goes so far as to place Being under its control (PARM. D8.19, cf. D15a). *adikia* (ἀδικία), 'injustice,' calls for punishment: in Greek, 'to be punished' is *didonai dikên* (διδόναι δίκην), literally, 'to give justice,' which Anaximander (ANAXIMAND. D6) explains by the term *tisis* (τίσις, 'retribution'). During the fifth century BC, certain 'sophists' subjected established concepts of justice to destructive critiques (ANTIPH. D38a and c; THRAS. D17, cf. R7).

dinê (δίνη), *dinos* (δῖνος) or *deinos* (δεῖνος): vortex. The double centrifugal and centripetal effect of the rapid circular movement of a fluid in a vessel or the resulting differential distribution of objects of different weights became a standard model by which various early Greek philosophers conceived especially cosmogonic processes (EMP. D75.4 ; ATOM. D80b, D82, D93, D104); this conception is parodied in Aristophanes' *Clouds* (DRAM. T28b).

diorismos (διορισμός): delimitation (ATOM. D231). Cf. *horos*.

dokein (δοκεῖν), *doxa* (δόξα), *dokimos* (δόκιμος), *endoxa* (ἔνδοξα): the verb *dokein* means that something appears to someone in a particular way (PROT. R9) or that he has a particular opinion about it (HER. D19); depending upon the context and the author's intention, the point may, or may not, be that this appearance or opinion is fallacious or inadequate. A *doxa* is an opinion, more or less justified (PROT. R9a); the term 'doxography,' derived from the neologism 'doxographer' coined by Hermann Diels, is conventionally used to designate an ancient scholarly practice, with philosophical origins going back before Aristotle (DOX. T1–T7, T8–T10), consisting in the collection of authorized opinions, especially those of philosophers. The derived adjectives *dokimos*, 'enjoying a (scil. good) opinion' (HER. D19), and *endoxa*, 'accepted views' (DOX. T8; ATOM. R33), are both positive in connotation.

duas (δυάς): dyad, the number two or the principle of duality, among the Pythagoreans (e.g., PYTHS. ANON. D20b), then in the Platonic tradition.

dunamis (δύναμις): literally, power (MED. T25), hence the property of something, i.e. its ability to achieve a specific effect (ANAXAG. D37a; ATOM. R64).

dusnomia (δυσνομία): lawlessness. Cf. *nomos*.

dustukhia (δυστυχία): misfortune, lack of success. See *tukhê*.

229

EARLY GREEK PHILOSOPHY I

eidenai (εἰδέναι): to know. Cf. *epistasthai; gignôskein; manthanein.*

eidôlon (εἴδωλον): image. An *eidôlon* is originally a phantom or wraith that visually resembles a body but entirely lacks its materiality. The term plays an important role in the Atomists in the context of explaining various kinds of cognition and sensation, especially vision (ATOM. D145, D151–D154).

eidos (εἶδος): originally, the visual form or appearance of something (ATOM. D34b; MED. T2), and in this sense a quasi-synonym of *idea, morphê,* and *skhêma* (cf. these words, the last under *rhusmos*); later, the term can refer to a Platonic Form or to an Aristotelian species.

eikos (εἰκός): plausible, probable. The term denotes the effective quality possessed by a persuasive argument, notably among the 'sophists' (GORG. D24[5], D25[9]), but it has a much broader usage, particularly in the common expression *eikos esti,* 'it is likely that . . .' Cf. *eoikos; peithô,* under *peithein.*

einai (εἶναι), *to on* (τὸ ὄν), *ta onta* (τὰ ὄντα), *eon* (ἐόν), *to mê on* (τὸ μὴ ὄν), *to ontôs on* (τὸ ὄντως ὄν), *ousia* (οὐσία): the verb *einai,* 'to be,' can be used in different ways, especially copulatively, to link a subject with a predicate and thereby to characterize that subject in some way, and existentially, to assert that a thing or a fact exists or is real. Various forms of the participle (*to on, ta onta, eon*) are used to designate that which exists, in particular or in general, and to distinguish this from that which does not exist, *to mê on;* the participle can be strengthened, in Plato and after him, by an adverb derived from the same verb, *to ontôs on,* 'what really exists.' The plural neuter form of the participle, *ta onta,* occurs frequently to indicate things, things that are, beings (but we have tended to avoid the translation 'beings'); cf. *pragma; khrêma.* For the specific problems of translation posed by Parmenides' poem from this point of view, see the Introduction to that chapter. A substantive, *ousia,* formed from the feminine participle, is already used in the fifth century BC to designate a person's wealth or property; starting with Plato and Aristotle, it comes to be used as a technical term in philosophy to designate the substance or essence, answering the Socratic question *ti esti* (τί ἐστιν;), 'what is . . . ?' (SOC. D10b).

eirônikos (εἰρωνικός), *eirôn* (εἴρων): someone who practices irony; originally a negatively connotated term, applied in particular to

GLOSSARY

Socrates on the view that he pretended to know less than he really did (SOC. D14, D17; SOPH. R30, R33).

ekpurôsis (ἐκπύρωσις): the periodically recurring conflagration of the world, according to the doctrine of the Stoics, who, following Aristotle, read Heraclitus as endorsing the same view (HER. R46, R57, R62; cf. D87).

elenkhein (ἐλέγχειν), *elenkhos* (ἔλεγχος): a term orginally marking strong condemnation, *elenkhos* most often signifies 'refutation' (PARM. D8.5; GORG. D24[2]; SOC. D26). The *elenkhos* is particularly characteristic of Socrates' argumentative technique.

elpis (ἐλπίς), *elpizein* (ἐλπίζειν): expectation or hope, to expect or to hope, depending on the context (HER. D37).

emphainein (ἐμφαίνειν), *emphasis* (ἔμφασις): in the context of the explanation of vision, mirrors, and dreams, *emphasis* is an impression (ATOM. D147, D148, D152) but also a reflection (ANAXAG. R23[36]; ATOM. D150).

empsuchos (ἔμψυχος): animate. See *psukhê*.

enarmottein (ἐναρμόττειν): to adapt. See *harmozein*.

ennoeisthai (ἐννοεῖσθαι), *ennoia* (ἔννοια): to think intelligently, concept. See *noein*.

eoikos (ἐοικός): adapted or resembling. The interpretation of the second part of Parmenides' poem depends in part on the sense adopted for this term at PARM. D8.65.

epharmottein (ἐφαρμόττειν): to fit together (PYTHS. ANON. D1). See *harmozein*.

epirhusmiê (ἐπιρυσμίη). See *rhusmos*.

epistasthai (ἐπίστασθαι), *epistêmê* (ἐπιστήμη): in general, the verb *epistasthai* means 'to know,' but it can also take on the meaning of 'to be certain' (HER. D25a); depending on the context, the substantive *epistêmê* is translated as 'knowledge' or 'science'; *anepistêmosunê* (ἀνεπιστημοσύνη) is lack of knowledge (SOC. D33). Cf. *eidenai; gignôskein; manthanein*.

eris (ἔρις): strife, contention. In Homer, *eris* is not only the aggressive and competitive impetus of humans directed against one another but is also divinized as a deity that drives men irresistibly to war and (self-)destruction even against their will. Hesiod in his *Theogony* (225, 226) assigns *Eris* to the baleful progeny of Night, but then in his *Works and Days* (11–19) he recognizes also a positive aspect to strife as the motor for human competition, labor, and prosperity.

Heraclitus elevates *eris* to the status of a cosmological principle, aligned with *polemos* (πόλεμος, 'war'), and responsible for the antagonistic relations existing between all kinds of interconnected entities. Empedocles speaks of 'evil quarrels' (EMP. D73.305, cf. D17.2), and Gorgias refers to war as 'armed conflict' (GORG. D28). A discussion of an eristic type opposes one argument to another in a systematic fashion. Cf. *antilegein; neikos; polemos*.

erôs (ἔρως): sexual desire (ATOM. D265) and desire in general (ATOM. D266); the god Eros also plays an important role in the cosmogonic process in Hesiod (COSM. T11.120), Pherecydes (PHER. D8, R24), and Parmenides (PARM. D16). Cf. *aphrodisiazein*.

esthlos (ἐσθλός): good. *esthlos* sometimes has a stronger moral connotation than *agathos* (cf. this word), with which it is nevertheless often synonymous. The question of the difference between these two words arises during the discussion of a poem of Simonides (MOR. T37) in Plato's *Protagoras* (PROT. D42).

eteê (ἐτεή): reality. Democritus makes a terminological usage of the adverbial dative, 'in reality,' as a technical term that he opposes to *nomôi*, 'by convention' (ATOM. D23b, D24). See *alêthês; etumos; nomos*.

etumos (ἔτυμος): besides *alêthês* (cf. this word), Homer and Hesiod also use another term, *etumos* or *eteos* (ἐτεός), to designate what is true, as an antonym to *pseudês*. Hesiod's Muses declare, "We know how to say many false things (*pseudea*) similar to genuine ones (*etuma*)," before adding that they also know how, when they wish, to "proclaim true things" (*alêthea gêrusasthai*) (MOR. T17). The question whether, in general and in any particular text, *alêthês* and *etumos* are quasi-synonymous, or on the contrary are being intentionally differentiated from one another, and if so how, is controversial, but what is certain is that *etumos* refers positively and directly to the reality of things independently of the cognitive dimension implied by the etymology of *alêthês*. Democritus' recurrent use, next to *alêtheia* (which he also uses), of the adverbial dative *eteêi* (ἐτεῇ) (cf. *eteê*), which shares the same root as *etumos*, suggests that he has in mind the ultimate reality of things, in this case the ultimate constituents of everything that exists (the atoms and the void) (ATOM. D14, D16–D19, D23b, D24, cf. R106), whereas the truth of things, their complete determination (*alêtheia*), remains concealed, as though in a well (ATOM. D24).

GLOSSARY

eudaimonia (εὐδαιμονία): happiness. See *daimôn*.

euestô (εὐεστώ): well-being. The word, a compound of the adverb *eu*, 'well,' and *estô*, a substantive derived from *einai*, 'to be,' is attested occasionally in some other fifth century BC authors, but it becomes a specific technical term in Democritus (ATOM. D229, D231, D232, R78), who in his ethics establishes 'well-being' as an important goal of human life.

eunomia (εὐνομία): respect for the laws (XEN. D61.19; ANON. IAMBL. 6[4]); also considered a divinity, Eunomia, Lawfulness, during the archaic period (MOR. T23b, T25a). See *nomos*.

euporein (εὐπορεῖν). See *aporein*.

eusebeia (εὐσέβεια): an attitude of pious reverence with regard to the established gods and cults, as manifested in participation in the practices of communal worship.

euthumeisthai (εὐθυμεῖσθαι), euthumein (εὐθυμεῖν), euthumia (εὐθυμία): *euthumeisthai*, in the middle voice, means 'to live in contentment' (ATOM. D227); *euthumein*, in the active, 'to provide contentment' (ATOM. D399). *euthumia*, 'contentment,' literally, 'a good disposition (*eu-*) of the heart or spirit (*thumos*),' is an important goal of human life in Democritus' ethics (DOX. T22[14]; ATOM. D226, D229, D230, D231, D382, R99).

eutukhia (εὐτυχία): success, good fortune. See *tukhê*.

gê (γῆ), Gê (Γῆ), Gaia (Γαῖα): the terrestrial mass, and, in theological and mythical texts, a divinity, Earth (COSM. T11; XEN. D41; DERV. Col. XXII). Whereas *gê* suggests the massive solidity of the earth as a solid foundation for all that it bears, its near-synonym *khthôn* (χθών), also translated as 'earth,' denotes rather the visible surface of the earth (EMP. D10.10). In Empedocles' physics, *khthôn* is also the name for the element 'earth' (e.g. EMP. D101.2). The Pythagoreans, who accepted the existence of a central fire, posited the existence, besides the earth, of an invisible 'counter-earth' (also called *antikhthôn*, ἀντίχθων), in order, according to Aristotle's testimony, to obtain ten heavenly bodies (PYTHS. ANON. D1, D36, D37, D40, D42), illustrating the principal role of the decade (see *dekas*).

gignesthai (γίγνεσθαι), genesis (γένεσις): become, birth. The verb *gignesthai* can mean either that something that already exists is transformed into something else or that something that did not exist comes into existence. In some cases, it is virtually synonymous

233

with *einai*, 'to be' (see this word), of which it is however also an antonym elsewhere; this ambiguity is exploited in the discussion regarding the interpretation of a poem of Simonides (MOR. T37) in Plato's *Protagoras* (PROT. D42), cf. also PROD. D22c. The substantive *genesis* is usually derived from the second sense of the verb and denotes a birth or generation (cf. e.g. PARM. D8.26; EMP. R35).

gignôskein (γιγνώσκειν): to know, recognize, understand (HER. D25a). From the verb derives the substantive *gnômê* (γνώμη). Like *doxa* (cf. this word, under *dokein*), *gnômê* indicates a personal view or opinion, but tends in comparison to be more authoritative, more reliable, less merely personal, even though it often has an intentional dimension. We have translated it as 'knowledge' (ATOM. D20), 'thought' (HER. D44; ATOM. D226; GORG. D24[19]), 'judgment' (HER. D74; GORG. D28; ANTIPH. D1), and 'conception' (PARM. D8.66). *gnôstikos* (γνωστικός) is someone who knows (EMP. R82). Cf. *doxa*, under *dokein; eidenai; epistasthai; manthanein*.

glôssa (γλῶσσα): the word designates a rare or dialect term (ATOM. D2[XI.1], R2a).

gnômê (γνώμη): thought, judgment, conception, knowledge. See *gignôskein*.

gnômôn (γνώμων): derived from *gignôskein* (see this word), *gnômôn* denotes someone that knows or something that provides exact knowledge, for example a carpenter's square or the pointer of a sundial. Anaximander was said to have invented the *gnômôn* and to have placed it on sundials in Lacedaemon (ANAXIMAND. R14). In geometry, to begin with, the term *gnômôn* designated the figure which, when added to a square, increases its size without altering its form. In Pythagoreanism, it was used first in the context of the study of even and odd numbers (cf. PYTHS. ANON. D12a). By combining and generalizing these usages, one can define the *gnômôn* as a geometrical or numerical form that preserves the form or species (even/odd) of the geometrical or arithmetical object to which it is added: "everything that, when it is added to a number or a figure, makes the whole similar to that to which it has been added" (Heron of Alexandria, def. 58).

harmozein (ἁρμόζειν), *harmonia* (ἁρμονία): the verb and substantive refer to all kinds of things fitting together or being fitted together and hence being in accord with one another (HER. D50, D62, R32; PHILOL. D2, D5, D15; DERV. Col. XXI); the prefix *sun-*, 'with,' in *sunarmozein* (συναρμόζειν) reinforces the idea of union already present in the simple form of the verb (PHILOL. D3; ARCHY. D25a; EMP. D61.4). The verb *arariskein* (see this word) is related etymologically to *harmozein*. In musical contexts, the mutual according of the tones of an instrument leads to its receiving the specific designation of 'harmony' (HER. D23, D62; ARCHY. D25A; PYTHS. ANON. D25). Within the framework of Theophrastus' explanation of the mechanism of sensation in Empedocles, the compound *enarmottein* (ἐναρμόττειν) indicates the adaptation to a *poros*, 'a passage' (see this word) (EMP. D211, D218, D222, R25; cf. also in a different context D148).

hêdonê (ἡδονή): derived from the verb *handanein* (ἁνδάνειν, 'to please'), the term *hêdonê* indicates originally the object of a sensual pleasure of any sort or that pleasure itself (e.g. PROD. D6a); it can come to be specified as the object of one pleasure considered as being typical, namely a flavor (ANAXAG. D13; DIOG. D10, D42[43]). It refers most often to pleasures that we would designate as corporeal, but this connotation is not automatic in Greek. It is possible that the use of the quasi-synonym *terpsis* (τέρψις) in Democritus was intended to remove this ambiguity. In any case we render *terpsis* by 'satisfaction' and *terpesthai* (τέρπεσθαι) by 'to derive satisfaction' (ATOM. D241, D243, D245, D284, cf. also PROD. D6).

heimarmenê (εἱμαρμένη): destiny. See *anankê.*

heuriskein (εὑρίσκειν), *heuretês* (εὑρετής): the verb can mean either to discover something that already existed but was not known or to invent something that did not exist previously. The ancient Greeks endeavored to identify the *prôtos heuretês*, 'the first inventor or first discoverer,' of all kinds of cultural and technical artifacts and institutions, thereby creating traditions that are most often mythical or fictitious (see e.g. THAL. R13–R19, R25, R26–R31; ANAXIMAND. R14–R17; PYTH. c D9–D14; PROT. P6a; DRAM. T57), and sometimes in competition with one another (cf. PARM. D22; PYTH. c D14).

hieros (ἱερός): sacred, as belonging to a divinity (EMP. D93.4). Epilepsy was termed *hiera nosos* (ἱερὰ νόσος, 'sacred disease'), as being incapable of explanation or treatment by human means and hence was thought to derive from a divine domain (MED. T5, T18). Applied to a human poet, the term suggests a quasi-divine quality (ATOM. D217).

historiê (ἱστορίη): investigation of any sort, not only what we call historical (HER. D26). *historia peri phuseôs*, 'investigation about nature,' is the expression that Plato puts in the mouth of Socrates (SOC. D7) in order to characterize the writings of those people that Aristotle would go on to call the *phusikoi* (see *phusikos*); the context suggests that this was an expression that had not yet entered ordinary language.

hodos (ὁδός): originally and literally, a road or way along which one moves through space in order to reach a goal (e.g. HER. D51, D52, D98, R54; PARM. D4.2, 5); then, by an easy metaphorical generalization, the method that one should follow through a temporal series of phases in any kind of practical or theoretical activity in order to arrive at a certain desired result (PARM. D6.2, D8.2, 3, 6, 23). *keleuthos* (κέλευθος), which designates a road in the concrete sense (EMP. D10.8, D75.15), can also be taken metaphorically (XEN. D64; PARM. D6.4), just like *atrapos* (ἀτραπός) (EMP. D46.2). Prodicus' tale of the choice of Heracles makes an allegorical usage of two roads in order to express metaphorically two different ways of life (PROD. D21, e.g. [21], [23], [27]).

holos (ὅλος), *oulos* (οὖλος), *ta hola* (τὰ ὅλα): all, entirely (e.g. XEN. D17; PARM. D8.9). *ta hola* (singular *holon*), like its synonym *ta panta* (cf. *pan*), designates the whole, the universe (PYTHS. R33[33]).

homoiomereia (ὁμοιομέρεια), *homoiomerês* (ὁμοιομερής): homoeomery, homoeomer. In Aristotle, these terms are applied to homogeneous substances, i.e. ones of which each part is of the same nature as the whole, e.g. blood. Aristotle (cf. ANAXAG. D18, D20), and following him the whole doxographic tradition (cf. ANAXAG. D2, D3), use these terms to describe Anaxagoras' theory of the infinite divisibility of the material elements; they certainly do not go back to Anaxagoras himself.

homoios (ὅμοιος): the term, which means, strictly speaking, 'similar' (ANAXAG. D3) can be understood according to the context in the sense of 'equal' (THAL. R28) or 'the same' (ZEN. D6). Thus in certain passages it can become quasi-synonymous with *isos* or *to*

GLOSSARY

auto (cf. these words), and the substantive *homoiotês* (ὁμοιότης) signifies 'equality' in ANAXIMAND. D30. For an attempt at disambiguation, cf. PROD. D22a.

horizein (ὁρίζειν): to delimit. See *horos*.

horos (ὅρος), *horizein* (ὁρίζειν): limit, term, definition (PROT. R28); to delimit, define (DERV. Col. XIV). Aristotle attributes the first attempts at definition to the Pythagoreans (PYTHS. R15) and emphasizes Socrates' efforts to achieve definitions in ethical matters (SOC. D10, cf. D9).

hosios (ὅσιος): sanctioned by legal and religious norms (EMP. D44.7).

hubris (ὕβρις): behavior consisting of arrogant, outrageous violence (HER. D112; HIPPIAS D19); or a disposition of arrogance, even when it is not expressed in violent action (MOR. T25a, T26b, T31); or a specific outrage committed against a person's dignity (ATOM. D391)

hupothesis (ὑπόθεσις): the verb *hupotithenai* (ὑποτιθέναι) means to place one thing under another in order to support it. The derived substantive *hupothesis* is used to designate a variety of logical foundations, and in different contexts is translated as 'hypothesis' (ZEN. D4), 'thesis' (ZEN. R2), 'postulate' (MED. T7, T20), or 'argument' (THRAS. D5).

idea (ἰδέα): form, e.g. that of atoms (ATOM. D34a), a quasi-synonym of *eidos, morphê,* and *skhêma* (cf. these words, the last under *rhusmos*); or species, e.g. of seeds, in Anaxagoras (ANAXAG. D13).

isonomia (ἰσονομία): equality from a political point of view, literally, equality before the law. Alcmaeon seems to have used the term metaphorically to define the conditions of good health (ALCM. D30). See *nomos.*

isos (ἴσος): equal. See *homoios.*

kairos (καιρός): this term originally designated the circumstances, of whatever sort, that had to be respected if an action were to have success; gradually the meaning evolved to specify these circumstances as temporal, i.e. the opportune moment in which an action had to be performed in order to be successful. In different contexts the word is translated differently: 'the right moment' (PYTHS. ANON. D40), 'opportune moment' (GORG. D11–D12), 'appropri-

ate time' (MED. T3), 'right occasion' (DISS. 2[19]), 'particular
circumstance' (MED. T21), 'proper measure' (ATOM. D248), 'sea-
son' (PYTHS. ANON. D40).

kakos (κακός), *kakia* (κακία): bad, evil, with the connotation of destructive; defect or vice (GORG. D53), by opposition to *aretê* (see
this word). See *agathos*.

kalos (καλός): beautiful, fine, seemly. *kalos* is often applied not to ex-
ternal appearance but to behavior that is approved socially or to
those people who behave accordingly; the same applies, *mutatis
mutandis*, to its contrary, *aiskhros*, 'ugly, unseemly' (DISS. 2). *agathos* is sometimes added to *kalos*, particularly in the formulaic expression καλὸς κἀγαθός, *kalos kagathos* (e.g. PROT. P15; PROD.
R4; SOPH. R6), to emphasize the moral dimension of the term and
to indicate a quality of (often aristocratic) moral perfection, as
manifested especially in battle but also in all forms of social interac-
tion.

katharmos (καθαρμός): purification, originally from religious pollu-
tion, often as a preparation for initiation to the mystery religions
(later it is applied also to purification from legal guilt and from
medical illness); in the plural, 'purificatory rites' (cf. EMP. R65).
The various connotations of the term are all present in the (doubtless original) title of one of the poems of Empedocles (cf. EMP.
D1–D40), or, according to a different hypothesis, of one of its parts.

kenos (κενός), *to kenon* (τὸ κενόν): empty, the void. Originally, the
term is applied to a physical object that happens temporarily not to
contain a particular entity that might have been expected to be
present (e.g. a house and its inhabitant). In the physical theories of
certain early Greek philosophers, it is generalized as emptiness of
any possible body whatsoever, 'the void' or 'vacuum.' The existence
of a void is denied by Melissus (MEL. D10), Empedocles (D49,
D50), and Anaxagoras (D59, D60), but the Atomists posit it as a
second principle next to the atoms (e.g. D14, D23b, D24). The
Latin equivalents are *vacuus* and *vacuitas* (ATOM. R113).

khrêma (χρῆμα): thing. Derived from the verb *khrêsthai* (χρῆσθαι),
to make use of a thing, the term indicates something that is made
use of and signifies, especially in the plural, 'goods,' 'money,'
'wealth'; but often it simply means 'thing'. In certain cases one
might wonder, as has sometimes been suggested in the case of a
fragment of Protagoras (PROT. D9, R14a), whether the word might

GLOSSARY

perhaps conserve the connotation of 'something useful,' just as *pragma,* itself often translated as 'thing,' can have the connotation of 'something done' or 'achieved.' Cf. *einai; pragma.*

khreôn (χρεών): obligation, necessity. See *anankê.*

khronos (χρόνος): time in general or a period or moment of time. *Khronos* also appears as a personified power in archaic poetry and tragedy (MOR. T10–T13; DRAM. T49, T63) and is an allegorical interpretation of Cronus, the father of Zeus (PHER. D11, D12, R20).

khthôn (χθών): earth. See *gê.*

kinein (κινεῖν): to move. *kinein,* in the active, signifies 'to set in motion'; *kineisthai,* in the middle-passive, 'to be set in motion,' 'to move.' In early Greek philosophy the verb usually denotes only locomotion through space or rotation in place; in this period its use to indicate, as in Aristotle and later philosophy, change or transformation from one condition to another without spatial movement, is rarer, but possible.

kosmos (κόσμος): originally an ornament or adornment (GORG. D24[1]), then by extension the world inasmuch as it is ordered and arranged. Even in its most neutral sense of 'world,' when it is a quasi-synonym of *pan* or *holon* (cf. these words, the latter under *holos*), the term *kosmos* preserves a connotation of 'arrangement,' indeed of 'beautiful arrangement,' in conformity with its original meaning (cf. PYTH. c D13). It is impossible to translate it always by the same term; we have rendered it as 'world' (DOX. T17; EMP. D98, R79), 'ordered world' (ATOM. D221), 'organized world' (ATOM. R43), 'world order' (HER. D85; ATOM. R112; SOC. D3), 'beautiful organized whole' (PYTH. c D13), 'ordered arrangement' (EMP. D77.5), 'order' (HER. D60). The prefix *dia-* in *diakosmos* (PARM. D8.65) puts the accent on the distribution that is presupposed by the arrangement of the world (cf. also *diakosmêsis,* διακόσμησις, HER. R82). From the term *kosmos* derives the adjective *kosmios,* applied to a person who is orderly, i.e. 'obedient' (ATOM. D366), and the antonym *akosmia,* 'disorder,' applied both to the world as a whole and to particular objects (EMP. D98; GORG. D24[1]). In Democritus (ATOM. D83b), the process of transformation of one cosmic arrangement into another one is called *ameipsikosmiê* (ἀμειψικοσμίη).

krinein (κρίνειν), *krisis* (κρίσις): the root meaning of the verb *krinein*

239

is to distinguish or separate, hence to decide (PARM. D8.20). Especially Empedocles, Anaxagoras, and Democritus use compound forms with a prepositional prefix, such as *apokrinein* (ἀποκρίνειν) (EMP. D54.4; ANAXAG. D10, D12, D13, D14, D23, D25, D27, D28, D29b, D31; ATOM. D82), *diakrinein* (διακρίνειν) (ANAXAG. D15, D16, D27, D29.b), *proskrinein* (προσκρίνειν) (ANAXAG. D28), and *sunkrinein* (συγκρίνειν) (ANAXAG. D13), and the substantives derived from these (ANAXAG. D2), in order to denote various processes of separation and dissociation (*apo-*, *dia-*) or of reunion and aggregation (*sun-*, *pros-*) of the components of a composite body.

leukos (λευκός): usually white, perhaps bright or brilliant in EMP. D77a.3.

logios (λόγιος): wise man. See *logos*.

logismos (λογισμός), *logistika* (λογιστικά): calculation, the art of calculation, argumentation. See *logos*.

logos (λόγος): the verb *legein* (λέγειν) means originally to pick up or out certain items from a plurality and to gather them for oneself; but its most common usage in Greek is to indicate the act of speaking meaningfully. The derived substantive *logos* is one of the most common terms in Greek philosophy, and it is impossible to translate it always with the same word in English. Referring to language, it denotes a single instance of meaningful linguistic expression, or language as a whole as a well organized system of signification; it can also denote that factor which above all permits and produces meaningful utterance, i.e. the rational faculty in humans or other animate beings, or the rational structure of the universe as a whole, or a specific instance of rationality, i.e. an argument or account; it can also denote a rational relation, i.e. a ratio or proportion, for example between numbers or sounds. In different contexts we have rendered the term by different English equivalents, sometimes within a few lines of the same text (see e.g. GORG. D24[13]): 'account' (HER. D1, D2, D8, D43, D46, D86, D98, D99, R3, R88; GORG. D25[28]), 'discourse' (PYTHS. R54; PARM. R39; GORG. D24[11]), 'speech' (GORG. D4, D24[2], [9], [14], D25[6], [7], D26a[21], D26b[83]), 'argument' (PARM. D8.5; PROT. D39; GORG. D24[5], [9], [13], [15]), 'word' (GORG. D28), 'reason' (HER. R73; PHILOL. D28; ARCHY. D10; PYTHS. R33[30];

GLOSSARY

PARM. R40, R44; EMP R88; ATOM. D202[9], R108 [139]; GORG. D26b[77]), 'rational discourse' (SOC. D38), 'ratio' (ARCHY. D25b), 'relation' (GORG. D24[14]), 'sense' (GORG. D25[37]), 'theory' (ANAXAG. D23). *analogia* (ἀναλογία) means 'relation' or 'proportion,' and *ana logon* (ἀνὰ λόγον) means 'proportionally' (ARCHY. D10, D25b). A man who is *logios* (λόγιος) is one who is much versed in *logoi*, i.e. 'a wise man' (ATOM. D210). From the related verb *logizein* (λογίζειν) are derived *logismos* (λογισμός) and *logistika* (λογιστικά), which denote, in mathematics, 'calculation' (ARCHY. D4; DRAM. T9) or 'the art of calculation' (ARCHY. D5), and, more generally, 'argumentation' (GORG. D24[2]).

lupê (λύπη): pain, grief. The substantive and the related verb *lupein* (λυπεῖν) denote not only physical, bodily pain, but also various kinds of mental distress or emotional suffering.

Magoi (Μάγοι): originally, the term 'Magi' denotes a Persian tribe, then the members of this tribe who were particularly noted as religious experts and interpreters of dreams. In Heraclitus (HER. D18) and the Derveni Papyrus (DERV. Col. VI), the word refers to (Greek?) experts in religious cults; in Heraclitus it may already have the derogatory connotations found in later authors but apparently absent from the Derveni Papyrus.

manos (μανός): thin, rarefied. See *araios*.

manthanein (μανθάνειν), *mathêsis* (μάθησις), *mathêmata* (μαθήματα), *mathêmatikoi* (μαθηματικοί): *manthanein*, in contrast to *eidenai*, *epistasthai*, and *gignôskein* (cf. these words), emphasizes that aspect of knowing that depends upon a person's acquisition of knowledge by a process of learning, whether the source is other people or experience (e.g. HER. D31). *mathêmata* are thus, literally, 'things learned,' and *ta mathêmata* can designate the branches of knowledge in general or the mathematical disciplines in particular (PYTHS. ANON. D1). Among the Pythagoreans, the term *mathêmata* also denotes sayings of a certain sort (cf. PYTH. c D15–D25); knowledge of these sayings defines a certain category of adepts, the *mathêmatikoi*, 'knowers' (PYTH. b T15–T20; HIPPAS. P2), who were probably more fully initiated into the 'mathematical' forms of knowledge than the *akousmatikoi*, the 'listeners,' were (see also *akoê*; *sumbolon*).

martus (μάρτυς), *marturein* (μαρτυρεῖν): witness, to bear witness. A *martus* is originally a person who provides testimony on one side or the other in a legal proceeding (GORG. D25[7], [9], [22]–[23]); its application to wider epistemological issues (HER. D32, D33; GORG. D25[15], cf. D28) is typical for the tendency of many early Greek thinkers to apply the terminology and forms of the concrete social experience with which they and their readers were familiar to the new domains of philosophical inquiry.

mêkhanê (μηχανή): a means, in the sense of a device or artificial contrivance (ATOM. D268, D363). The term was applied in particular to the crane used in the theater to bring gods down onto the scene and to involve them in the human action. In Aristophanes' *Clouds* (DRAM. T10), Socrates is introduced swinging in a basket and studying the heavenly bodies, by means of a *mêkhanê*. The use of this device in some tragedies in order to resolve at a single stroke a complicated human predicament, apparently unresolvable in any other way, led to criticism, within the domain of philosophical thought, of what is still called the *deus ex machina*, i.e. an unsatisfactory and artificial solution of a complex difficulty (ANAXAG. R10)

metanoein (μετανοεῖν): to think too late. See *noein*.

metarhusmoun (μεταρυσμοῦν): to modify the configuration (ATOM. D403). See *rhusmos*.

metempsukhôsis (μετεμψύχωσις): the passage of a soul (*psukhê*, cf. this word) after death into another body, not necessarily human; this process can also be called *metensômatôsis* (μετενσωμάτωσις, EMP. R41), the soul's passage from one body to another (EMP. R41). This is an important part of Pythagorean doctrine (PYTH. a P37–P39; PYTH. c D4–D5; PYTHS. ANON. D52) and is attributed to Pherecydes by later authors who make him the teacher of Pythagoras (PHER. R14–R16). The notion plays an important role in the reception of Empedocles.

meteôros (μετέωρος): up high, suspended in the air. The substantivized neuter plural of the adjective, *ta meteôra*, covers all the atmospheric and celestial phenomena that constitute an obligatory object of investigation for the natural philosophers (*phusikoi;* see *phusikos*); Aristophanes uses the term in his parodies of natural philosophers (DRAM. T10.228, T23.690).

metron (μέτρον): measure, whether in the sense of moderation (MOR. T35[1].1, [4].18), of a determinate measure (HER. D85,

D89c), or of a measuring instrument (PROT. D9). *summetros* (σύμμετρος) denotes something that, because it possesses the right measure, can fit itself to something else, and hence can mean 'adapted.' In different contexts, *summetria* (συμμετρία) is adaptation (ANAXAG. R23[35]; EMP. D210, D212, D248), proportion (PYTHS. ANON. D54b; ATOM. D226), commensurability (PARM. D52, D57), or equilibrium (ATOM. D231).

moira (μοῖρα), *Moira* (Μοῖρα): portion, Destiny. In contrast to other words for necessity or fate (see *anankê*), *moira* stresses somewhat more the idea that a particular destiny is the portion (*meros*, μέρος) that is allotted to a person for his share (HER. D122; DERV. Col. XVIII).

monas (μονάς): term for one, unit, or unity in the Pythagoreans (PHILOL. D10; ARCHY. D6; cf. also ATOM. R20a).

morphê (μορφή): shape, form (PARM. D8.58; EMP. D29.1, D77a.2; ATOM. D26a), a quasi-synonym of *eidos, idea,* and *skhêma* (cf. these words, the last under *rhusmos*).

mustês (μύστης): an initiate into a Greek mystery religion (μυστήρια), a secret religious society with its own rites and doctrines, often involving survival of the soul in some form after death (HER. D18; DERV. Col. VI).

muthos (μῦθος): in early Greek, *muthos* denotes any authoritative utterance, especially a narrative (PROT. D39; cf. the verb *muthologein*, μυθολογεῖν, HIPPIAS D14a), and can also signify 'word' (so, perhaps, in PARM. D8.6). Thus it does not necessarily cover what we call a 'myth,' and originally it does not have the pejorative connotation that it will often take on after Plato.

neikos (νεῖκος): quarrel, strife. Heraclitus already elevated social discord (*eris*), which Hesiod had thematized, into a universal principle. The term *neikos*, which is near in meaning but to which no positive value can easily be assigned (*neikos* is always destructive, it cannot imply emulation, as *eris* can), is closely associated with the doctrine of Empedocles, who makes *Neikos* one of the two fundamental cosmological principles, next to *Philia* or *Philotês: Neikos* is responsible for the disaggregation of the wholes that *Philia* brings together. Cf. *eris; philein; polemos.*

noein (νοεῖν), *nous* (νοῦς), *noos* (νόος), *noêsis* (νόησις), *noêma* (νόημα), *noêtos* (νοητός): the verb *noein* denotes in the most gen-

243

eral terms an act of apprehension, one that often belongs to the intelligence, whether this is human or not, but that is not necessarily, or even most often, of a discursive nature; comprehension and intuition are often connotated, sometimes specifically aimed at (EMP. D44.12); analogously, *nous*, like *noêsis*, can sometimes even represent, in their broadest sense, any faculty of act of discernment or discrimination whatsoever (cf. PYTHS. R33[30]). The substantive *nous* (or *noos*) also indicates the organ or function responsible for such an act; *noêsis* and *noêma* designate, respectively, the act of apprehending and the correlative product, i.e. 'thought'; the adjective *noêtos*, in the Platonic tradition, is most often the object of *nous*, 'the intelligible,' but it can also designate in certain late texts that which is endowed with intelligence (cf. DIOG. D45). *nous* plays a central role in Anaxagoras (ANAXAG. D26–D28, D29), who himself received the nickname *Nous* (ANAXAG. P42–43); Diogenes of Apollonia employs the term *noêsis* in order to emphasize not so much the faculty as rather its operation (DIOG. D9, D10; cf. R7). The polysemy of these terms makes it impossible to translate them univocally. We have tended to avoid translating *nous* by 'intellect,' which is colored by Aristotelian connotations, except in some late texts (PYTHS. R46b, R55b), and have preferred to render this term instead by 'mind' (see, besides the passages from Anaxagoras already cited, MOR. T26a; XEN. D18; PARM. R31; EMP. D42.8, D73.252; ARCH. D2[1], [6], D9–D11; DIOG. D44[44]; DERV. Col. XIV–XVI, XXVI; DRAM. T42a, T63.18), especially, but not only, when the object of thought is called *noêma;* but we have used 'mind' for other terms too, such as *phrên* (see *phronein*) and *prapides* (see this word). For the *noêsis* of Diogenes, which is not limited to the intellectual domain but includes the senses as well, we have used the term 'mental activity' (DIOG. D5a, D9, D10; cf. R7). The compounds *ennoeisthai* (ἐννοεῖσθαι, 'to think intelligently,' DIOG. D5b), and *ennoia* (ἔννοια, 'concept,' ATOM. R76), are also found. The prefix *dia-* ('through'), in the verb *dianoeisthai* (διανοεῖσθαι, 'think,' GORG. D26a[19]) and the substantive *dianoia* (διάνοια, 'thought,' ATOM. D226; DIOG. D44[44]) indicate a discursive dimension that is absent from *noein* and *nous*. *metanoein* (μετανοεῖν) and *pronoein* (προνοεῖν) are, respectively, 'to think afterward' and 'to think beforehand' (GORG. D25[34]). The Latin equivalent of *nous* is *mens* (THAL. R42; ARCH. D5).

GLOSSARY

nomos (νόμος), *nomizein* (νομίζειν), *nomisti* (νομιστί), *nomothetêma* (νομοθέτημα), *nomimon* (νόμιμον): the substantive *nomos*, like the substantivized adjective *to nomimon*, designates the recognized social custom (sometimes formalized as a law) that is characteristic of a defined society of people, most often in contrast with the custom of another society or societies; during the fifth century BC, *nomos* was often opposed to *phusis*, 'nature,' as that which was arbitrary or only locally valid as opposed to that which was free of the constraints of a particular society or universally valid (cf. e.g. HIPPIAS D17; MED. T9[11]). In different contexts we render this term and related ones as 'law' (MOR. T27a; GORG. D24[16], D28; DRAM. T53–T55), 'convention' (ATOM. D23a–D24; HIPPIAS D17), 'institution' (MED. T2), 'custom' (MED. T9[11]), 'legal institutions' (ANTIPH. D38a), the compound *nomothetêma* as 'institution' (MED.T2), and the adverb *nomisti* as 'conventionally' (ATOM. D23b). The verb *nomizein* means originally 'to recognize or practice a *nomos*,' then by extension 'to recognize the validity of a thought or proposition,' 'to believe that something is the case.' The two levels of meaning coexist in the expression *nomizein theous*, 'to demonstrate by one's public behavior that one acknowledges the gods of the city' or 'to believe in the existence of the traditional gods' (SOC. P36). *dusnomia* (δυσνομία) designates a political condition in which social norms are no longer valid (MOR. T25a). Alcmaeon (ALCM. D30) seems to have applied the term *isonomia* (ἰσονομία, 'equality,' literally, 'equality before the law'), to the equilibrium of different opposed powers. Cf. *phusis; themis.*

on (ὄν), *to on* (τὸ ὄν): being, that which is. See *einai.*

onoma (ὄνομα): name (both proper and common), and, more generally, word. There is a rich tradition of justifications of names by means of 'etymological' explanations. These are most often fanciful from the point of view of modern linguistics, but they were thought to reveal the true nature of a thing by means of the analysis of the name that designated it (see e.g. DERV. Col. XIV, XVIII, XIX, XXI, XXII). Cf. *orthotês onomatôn, orthoepeia.*

orthotês onomatôn (ὀρθότης ὀνομάτων), *orthoepeia* (ὀρθοέπεια): correctness of words or of language. The term is applied to the analysis of linguistic usage and the attempt to define the correct way to use words, a matter of concern for Democritus (ATOM. D2[XI.1]) and various 'sophists' (PROT. D21, D22; PROD. D5; HIPPIAS D15), and one that Aristophanes makes fun of (DRAM. T19c).

ouranos (οὐρανός): sky, heavens, world. Most often *ouranos* designates the whole of the celestial vault visible above the world, in which the heavenly bodies are seen to move; but it can also refer to a definite portion of the sky (PARM. D12.5) or else to the totality of the world (XEN. R12; MEL. R9c). Hesiod personifies *Ouranos* as a primordial cosmogonic deity, associated with *Gê*, 'Earth' (COSM. T11). Cf. *gê*.

pan (πᾶν), *ta panta* (τὰ πάντα): all, the whole, everything. As a term indicating the totality of all the things that are, i.e. the universe, *ta panta* can be synonymous with *ta hola* and designate the universe; cf. *holos*.

panspermia (πανσπερμία): this term appears in the summaries of Democritus' doctrine (ATOM. D46, D59, D132, R15) and is difficult to translate. It suggests that the totality (*pan-*) of things comes from the totality of the seeds (*-spermia*), i.e. of the atoms. We have rendered it as 'universal seminal reserve,' adding explicitly the notion of 'reserve.'

parapêgma (παράπηγμα): an astronomical observation table, such as Democritus is reported to have composed (ATOM. D2[VIII.3]).

paskhein (πάσχειν), *pathos* (πάθος): the verb *paskhein* denotes either, neutrally, the fact that something, whatever it might be, happens to someone or something, or, specifically, that what happens is a cause of suffering; it is translated as 'experience' or 'suffer.' The substantive *pathos* connected with it is most often rendered as 'affection' (ARCHY. D25a; PYTHS. ANON. D54f; PYTHS. R36[41]), but in some contexts it takes on the meaning of 'attribute' (PYTHS. ANON. D1).

pêgnusthai (πήγνυσθαι): to solidify. See *sunistanai*.

peithein (πείθειν), *pistis* (πίστις), *peithô* (πειθώ), *pistôma* (πίστωμα), *pistos* (πιστός), *eupeithês* (εὐπειθής): this series of terms regards the practitioners and results of persuasive discourse. The verb *peithein*, 'persuade,' denotes the effect that a persuasive discourse can have of securing the audience's assent to the speaker's aims; the range of connotations can reach from the one extreme of convincing them, *peithô*, by means of rational arguments alone to the other extreme of sweeping them away by appeals to their emotions or

GLOSSARY

indeed by the exercise of violence. In Parmenides, persuasion is the inseparable companion of the truth of philosophical reason (PARM. D6.4). By contrast, the 'sophists' explored ways of achieving persuasion in public and private discourses for which the truth of the matter (whatever that was) was often not a central, or even a pertinent, consideration, though it could also sometimes be so (GORG. D24[8]–[15], D48, D51; ANTIPH. D38a). At the same time, Greek tragedy and comedy explored the dangers and limits of persuasion (MOR. T20–T21; DRAM. T64–T67). *eupeithês* in Parmenides designates the truth that succeeds easily (*eu-*, literally, 'well') in convincing (PARM. D4.29). *pistis* can be the effect produced by persuasion, 'belief' or 'conviction' (PARM. D4.30, D8.33; EMP. D61.1; cf. ATOM. R108[136]), but also 'trust'; *pistos* is what is worthy of trust (PARM. D8.55) and *pistôma* the proof that one supplies and that is supposed to inspire confidence (EMP. D47.2)

peras (πέρας), *peirar* (πεῖραρ): limit.

periekhein (περιέχειν): to envelope, surround, encompass. *to periekhon* (τὸ περιέχον), what surrounds, the surrounding mass, is what surrounds the earth, i.e. the sky, the limits of the sky (ANAXAG. D10, D28; ATOM. D89), but also what we would call the atmosphere (ANAXIMEN. D31).

peritropê (περιτροπή): self-refutation, literally, reversal (ATOM. R107; PROT. R22).

phaneros (φανερός): clear. See *dêlos*.

phantasia (φαντασία): a mental representation (XEN. R10; ATOM. D64, D154, R107; PROT. R12, R22; XENI. R2, R3).

philein (φιλεῖν), *philos* (φίλος), *philia* (φιλία), *philotês* (φιλότης): the verb *philein* originally indicates that something belongs to oneself or that one occupies oneself with it or loves it as if it did; *philos* is one's own or what one loves as one's own, and *philia* is the sentiment one feels in such cases, more 'friendship' or 'deep affection' than 'erotic love.' Following but transforming Hesiod's conception of *Erôs* (cf. this word), Empedocles elevates *Philia* or *Philotês* (EMP. D65, D73.251) to the status of a cosmic principle, opposing it to *Neikos* (cf. this word).

philosophos (φιλόσοφος): philosopher. The verb *philosophein* (φιλοσοφεῖν) appears in Herodotus with regard to Solon (one of the Seven Sages) in the sense of 'to love knowledge and to be curious about things' (cf. SOPH. R24). The adjective *philosophos* and

247

the substantive *philosophia* (φιλοσοφία) are attested earlier than Plato (GORG. D24[13]; MED. T7b), but the history of this family of terms has certainly been massively shaped by Plato and Platonism. An ancient tradition attributes to Pythagoras the invention of the term (PYTHS. R29), but it is likely that this is an honorific attribution on the part of the Platonic Academy (cf. PYTHS. R28). It is unlikely that any of the early Greek 'philosophers' called himself a 'philosopher.' The term appears in HER. D40, but if that word does indeed belong to Heraclitus, its meaning there is close to the one found in Herodotus, and it may belong instead to the author who cites the fragment, Clement of Alexandria; it also appears in the alleged title of a work attributed to Zeno by the *Suda* (ZEN. R35), in a maxim attributed to Gorgias (GORG. P22) but of which the exact wording is unlikely to go back to him, and in PROD. D7, which is however a passage taken from Plato's *Euthydemus*. It is likely that the term came into circulation by the mediation of Socrates and his circle; the appropriate meaning to attribute to it remained an object of debate, notably in Isocrates. Cf. *sophos*.

phônê (φωνή): This term, like its near-synonym *phthongos* (φθόγγος), can denote any kind of sound in general but is usually specified to indicate the sound that an animate being makes, especially that produced by an articulate human voice (ANAXAG. D75). The related verb *phônein* (φωνεῖν) means 'to utter' (DERV. Col. X). By contrast, *psophos* (ψόφος) is originally 'the noise made by one thing hitting another' and continues to denote mere 'noise,' 'inarticulate sound' (ANAXAG. D74). Cf. *sumphônia*.

phronein (φρονεῖν), *phrên* (φρήν), *phronêsis* (φρόνησις), *phrontis* (φροντίς): the verb *phronein* is the most general term in Greek for conscious mental activity or thought; in contrast to *noein* (cf. this word), which designates various forms of apprehension, notably intellectual cognition, *phronein* tends rather to denote the practical (and sometimes the emotional) dimension of thinking—the difference is clearest in some of the nouns that are derived from the two verbs, with *phronêsis* denoting 'practical judgment' or 'prudence,' *nous* 'intelligence' or 'intellect.' The organ associated in Homer with this mental activity is the *phrên* (φρήν), more often in the plural *phrenes* (φρένες), located originally, like the *prapides* (cf. this word) in the midriff, the seat of the emotions; *phrontis* (φροντίς) is thought applied to the care of or for an object, or more

GLOSSARY

generally a thought or the faculty of thinking. Given the variety of nuances of the words of this family, it is not possible to translate them all with the same English term. We have used such renderings, for *phronein*, as 'to think' (EMP. D244a) or 'thinking' (DIOG. D44[44]), and, in the passive, 'to be an object of thought' (GORG. D26a[17]) or 'to be thought of' (GORG. D26b[77]), but also 'to apprehend' (PARM. D51.3) or 'prudent thinking' (ATOM. D293a); for *phrên* or *phrenes*, 'mind' (MOR. T39a; EMP. D6.3, D9.3, D73.245, D93.4; ATOM. D23), 'organ' [scil. of the mind] (XEN. D18), 'intelligence' (PYTHS. R33[30]; SOPH. R16), and once, for lack of a better translation, 'spirits' (MOR. T32a); 'thought' is used to translate *phrontis* (EMP. D93.5) and sometimes *phronêsis* (HER. D2; EMP. D244b; GORG. D26b[77]), while 'mind' is used for *phronêma* (GORG. D24[17]). But *phronêsis* is more usually 'wisdom' (ANAXAG. R12) or 'prudence' (ATOM. D274, D293a, D306), or in certain contexts 'intelligence' (SOC. D36) or 'knowledge' (SOC. D38).

phusa (φῦσα): air flow. See *aêr*.

phusikos (φυσικός), *hoi phusikoi* (οἱ φυσικοί): literally, 'the naturalist(s),' the man or men who were occupied with the explanation of nature, i.e. of the totality of natural phenomena. This is the term by which Aristotle designates the first orientation of philosophical research, according to the narrative he provides in *Metaphysics* A3. Given that the word 'naturalist' has a different meaning in English, and in the absence of any other suitable term, we have systematically translated φυσικός by 'natural philosopher,' thereby introducing into the expression the word 'philosopher,' which, to be sure, is neither expressed nor even implied by it, but which nonetheless does not betray its meaning. The *phusikos* is someone who, according to an expression attested for the first time in Plato, dedicates himself to the *historia peri phuseôs* (ἱστορία περὶ φύσεως, 'the investigation of nature'); see *historiê*.

phusiologos (φυσιολόγος): natural philosopher. The term *phusiologos* is a synonym of *phusikos* and comes likewise from Aristotle. Although much less frequent, it is also more explicit, the suffix *-logos* indicating the explanatory dimension of the research on nature (cf. *aitiologia*, under *aitia*). *Phusiologia* (φυσιολογία), which therefore designates 'natural philosophy' (ANAXAG. P43; ARCH. P3), can also be the title of a treatise on nature (ARCH. D1).

phusis (φύσις): ever since its first (and sole) usage in Homer (*Od.* 10.303), to indicate a plant and its properties, *phusis* designates indissociably both the nature of a thing and the fact that it grows, and then, by extension, is born. The nature involved is first of all the nature of a single thing, *a* nature (HER. D1, D35, D114b; PARM. D12.1, 5, D51.3); but then, by a further extension, the term is broadened to designate the totality of nature and comes to be applied to nature in general, and thus to everything that is born (EMP. R35; MED. T9[11]; HIPPIAS D17; DRAM. T53–T55) and that thus also becomes (cf. *gignesthai*). The generic title *On Nature* doubtless only began to be applied generally during the course of the last third of the fifth century BC, to characterize a number of works that had come to be felt to belong to the *historia tês phuseôs* (ἱστορία τῆς φύσεως, 'the investigation of nature,' cf. ALCM. D1, D2). But at least with regard to the more ancient writings, like those of Heraclitus or Parmenides, that title is certainly not original (cf. PARM. R46, R47). The verbal forms *phun(ai)* (φῦν) and *phuesthai* (φύεσθαι) signify, respectively, 'to be born' (PARM. D8.15) and 'to grow' (EMP. D77b.8); the compounds *sumphuein* (συμφύειν) and *sumphuesthai* (συμφύεσθαι, 'to grow together') (EMP. D77b.7) are used in the context of the explanation of the way in which things are constituted, cf. *sunistanai;* and *diaphuein* (διαφύειν) means 'to become separated' (EMP. D77b.9).

pneuma (πνεῦμα): breath. See *aêr.*

polemos (πόλεμος): war. The term is used frequently to denote armed combat among groups of human beings (e.g. ATOM. D357; THRAS. D16; ANON. IAMBL. (7)[6], [10]). Heraclitus elevates *polemos* to the status of a cosmological principle, aligned with *eris* (ἔρις, 'strife'), and responsible for the opposing relations between all kinds of interconnected entities; in calling *polemos* "the father of all and the king of all" (HER. D64), Heraclitus attributes to war the honorific epithets traditionally reserved for the highest Olympian divinity, Zeus. Cf. *eris; neikos.*

poros (πόρος): the term denotes concretely a passage through which a material element can move; in this sense, *poros* is a principle used for explaining sensation or physiological functions such as respiration (PARM. D57; EMP. D201a, D210, D211, D218, D233, D248; GORG. D45b); more broadly, it can be a path (EMP. D75.1) or a resource (DRAM. T57.477, cf. T58.360). The two meanings are

GLOSSARY

combined in the negative formations *aporia* and *aporein*, cf. the latter word.

potmos (πότμος): fate. See *anankê*.

pragma (πρᾶγμα): thing. The noun is derived from the verb *prassein*, 'to do' or 'to effect,' with a suffix (*-ma*) suggesting the result of an action, 'a doing' or 'effecting' (*praxis*). Thus a *pragma* is originally 'something done' or 'effected'; but most often it has lost this connotation and taken on instead the neutral sense of 'thing.' Aristotle substitutes *pragma* for *khrêma* (see this word) when he discusses a fragment of Protagoras (PROT. R15). The term is used to designate the reality of something (what a thing really is), by opposition to what is said about it (DISS. 1.[11]), and also the referent (DISS. 3.[13]). In the plural, *ta pragmata* can mean 'legal matters,' 'trials' (ANON. IAMBL. 7[3]). Cf. *einai*; *khrêma*.

prapides (πραπίδες): in Homer, this term, like *phrên* (cf. *phronein*) denotes a bodily organ, the midriff or diaphragm, and also the cognitive and affective faculties, which were thought to be located there. In later authors it can designate both the organs of thought (EMP. D8, D38.2, 4, D257.1) and the thought itself (DRAM. T52). See also *phronein*.

prêstêr (πρηστήρ): a violent, tempestuous atmospheric phenomenon whose precise nature is difficult to determine; we render it as 'lightning storm' (HER. D86, D96; ANAXAG. D53b). Anaximander (D23, D26) applies the term to a bellows, which creates a flare or jet of flame when air is blown through its nozzle (see *aulos*) onto a fire.

pronoein (προνοεῖν): to think beforehand. See *noein*.

prophasis (πρόφασις): cause. In the Hippocratic corpus, the term is used as a synonym for *aitia* (MED. T18a); it also appears with the meaning 'pretext' in an aphorism attributed to Democritus (ATOM. D330).

proskrinein (προσκρίνειν): to join something to something else. See *krinein*.

pseudês (ψευδής), *pseudos* (ψεῦδος): false, falsehood, lie, error. See *alêthês*.

psophos (ψόφος): sound. See *phônê*.

psukhê (ψυχή): the term originally designates the breath, the principle of life, and hence life itself; 'life' is often the most appropriate translation (e.g. ANAXAG. D13; DIOG. D9). But sometimes one

251

must recur to the rendering 'soul' (e.g. DIOG. D10), despite the burden imposed on this word by its later history since Plato. Several fragments of Heraclitus, in particular, illustrate the transformation of *psukhê* from a principle of life in general into a principle directing the specific mode of life of each human being (HER. D33, D98–D104, D116, D121). Like *psukhê*, the Latin term *spiritus* can designate either 'breath' or 'soul' (THAL. R42).

puknos (πυκνός): dense, compact (PARM. D8.64). See *araios*.

rhusmos (ῥυσμός): configuration, a dialectal form of *rhuthmos* (ῥυθμός) that is used by Democritus (ATOM. D31, D32). Aristotle, by interpreting the term as meaning *skhêma*, 'form,' suppresses the dynamic value that is inherent in it and is perhaps also present in the term *arrhuthmistos* (ἀρρύθμιστος), translated as 'that does not possess configuration' (ANTIPH. D8), and that can also be seen in the psychological use of the verb *rhusmeisthai* (ῥυσμεῖσθαι) to describe the process of the formation of a person's character (ATOM. D297). Democritus uses the compound *ameipsirhusmein* (ἀμειψιρυσμεῖν) for the change of configuration of an atomic aggregate (ATOM. D38). *epirhusmiê* (ἐπιρυσμίη), translated as 'rhythmic afflux,' is the flow of atoms that penetrates the organs of apprehension (ATOM. D18).

saphês (σαφής): clear. See *dêlos*.

sêma (σῆμα), *sêmeion* (σημεῖον): a sign, piece of evidence (PARM. D8.7, D12; MEL. D11; DIOG. D9). Like *tekmêrion* (τεκμήριον), the term designates something well known or visible that is invoked as evidence in support of an affirmation, and hence can often be rendered as 'proof.'

Silloi (Σίλλοι): *Mockeries*. The term refers originally to someone who squints; Timon of Phlius (4th–3rd centuries BC) used this title for his collection of satirical poems written in dactylic hexameters (cf. THAL. R4; XEN. R15–R16; etc.) and it was also applied by later authors to the poems of Xenophanes (XEN. D2–D5).

skênos (σκῆνος): body. See *sôma*.

sôma (σῶμα): body, or bodily shape (MEL. D8); hence *asômatos* (ἀσώματος) can mean not only 'incorporeal, bodiless,' but also 'without shape' (MEL. R21c, d). In certain contexts, the term can

GLOSSARY

mean 'reality' (DISS. 2[1]). To designate the body of a human being, Democritus uses the term *skênos* (σκῆνος), which originally
means 'tent' (ATOM. D176, D236): it is the shelter of the soul (see
psukhê).

sophos (σοφός), *sophia* (σοφία), *sophistês* (σοφιστής), *sophisma*
(σόφισμα), *sophisteia* (σοφιστεία), *sophizesthai* (σοφίζεσθαι),
sophistikê (σοφιστική): *sophos* and related words can be translated
in a great variety of ways, each one emphasizing one of the possible
aspects of 'skill' or 'cleverness,' certainly both the most fundamental and the most general meaning of the term *sophia*. Except when
it is used ironically, *sophos* always has a positive value—the *sophos*
is 'wise' (PROT. P10; SOPH. R26; DOX. T6; ANAXAG. P24;
DIOG. D1; GORG. R24a; SOPH. R2, R3), 'a sage' (HIPPIAS D4;
SOPH. R5), 'clever' (PROT. D38, D40), 'expert' (HIPPIAS D15;
SOPH. R14; DOX. T8; EMP. R6); analogously, *sophia* can denote
not only 'skill,' but also 'cleverness' (PROT. D38, D40; SOPH.
R25), 'expertise' (PROD. P9; HIPPIAS D15), and 'wisdom' (EMP.
D44.8; PROT. R9a; GORG. P11; PROD. P11, D17, R1a; THRAS.
P6; ANTIPH. D57; SOPH. R4, R34a). *sophistês* was originally an
equivalent of *sophos;* but those people who know a lot can be sus-
pected of knowing too much, and already before Plato the term
sophistês often has a pejorative connotation (DRAM. T10.d, T22),
which it often retains later (SOC. P38, D3; SOPH. R26, R34a), even
if in some cases *sophistês* can be an equivalent of *sophos* (DOX. T6;
ANAXAG. P24; GORG. R24a) and in others it is hard to decide
(DIOG. D1; MED. T7b). So too, *sophisma* can designate positively
a 'technical resource' (MED. T3), an 'established medical routine'
(MED. T21), or an 'invention' (DRAM. T56, T57). It is the negative
perspective that, at least during the classical period, comes to be
attached to the meaning of the term *sophistikê* (*scil. tekhnê*), 'sophistic art,' as is amply illustrated in the chapter SOPH. (e.g. R11,
R34a); *sophisteia* (σοφιστεία) is an equivalent used less often
(GORG. P17). Cf. *philosophos*.

sôphronein (σωφρονεῖν), *sôphrosunê* (σωφροσύνη): *sôphronein*
means 'to think with moderation' (HER. D30). The term probably
derives from the coalescence between a root meaning 'safe and
sound' (*sws*) and *phronein* (see this word), and this etymology
remains perceptible in the usage of this central term in Greek moral

reflection. The substantive *sôphrosunê*, which is derived from it, is also found very frequently; it is traditionally translated as 'temperance' (PROT. D41).

stoikheion (στοιχεῖον): element. Originally, the term denotes the letters of the alphabet, but in the language of classical philosophy it comes to signify 'element,' in the sense of primordial constituent in general. The passage from the original meaning to the technical one is clearly illustrated by the doctrine of the Atomists, in which the atoms are compared to letters, of which different combinations produce different words (ATOM. D29). But the term does not otherwise form part of the vocabulary of the early Greek philosophers.

sumbolon (σύμβολον): symbol. The term denotes originally a token of recognition consisting in one half of some object that has been broken into two pieces, which are taken by each of two people, who can then demonstrate their identity because the parts that they possess fit together; it then becomes generalized to denote any token of identity, and beyond that a symbol in general. Among the Pythagoreans the word designates a set of sayings and precepts (the *sumbola*) that not only distinguish the members of their group from other people (in this sense they are tokens of identity) but that also quite naturally call for a 'symbolic' interpretation (PYTH. c D15–D25). See also *akoê; manthanein*.

summetros (σύμμετρος), *summetria* (συμμετρία): adapted, adaptation. See *metron*.

sumpêgnusthai (συμπήγνυσθαι): to solidify. See *sunistanai*.

sumphônia (συμφωνία): accord. See *phônê;* cf. *harmozein*.

sumphuein (συμφύειν), *sumphuesthai* (συμφύεσθαι): to grow together. See *phusis*.

sunarmozein (συναρμόζειν): to fit together. See *harmozein*.

sunesis (σύνεσις): understanding. Alcmaeon uses *sunienai* (συνιέναι), the verb connected with this term, to distinguish human intelligence from animal sensation (ALCM. D11). *axunetos* (ἀξύνετος), in Heraclitus, is applied to someone who does not understand (HER. D1, D4). See also *noein*.

sunistanai (συνιστάναι), *sunistasthai* (συνίστασθαι): to put together, to be put together, to become constituted. The verb is used frequently to designate the way in which things are formed by the assemblage (*sun-*) of different elements, constituents, or parts (e.g.

254

GLOSSARY

PHILOL. D5; PARM. D10.4; EMP. D75.6; DIOG. D3; DERV. Col. IX). The idea that the assemblage can produce a solid entity, whose components are firmly united with one another, can be expressed by a verb meaning 'congeal' or 'solidify,' like *pêgnusthai* (EMP. D52, D147b, D241, cf. D200, D213) or *sumpêgnusthai* (ANAXAG. D31). The *sustêma* (σύστημα) resulting from such an assemblage is then a 'stable ensemble' (ATOM. D80b).

sunkrinein (συγκρίνειν), *sunkrisis* (σύγκρισις): to distinguish, separate. See *krinein*.

tekhnê (τέχνη): art, technique. The term designates any kind of productive skill that creates useful objects according to rules that can be taught. It includes but is not limited to artisanal craftsmanship and can thus be applied to metallurgy, calculation, or the art of politics, *tekhnê politikê* (PROT. D40; DRAM. T57.477, 497, 506). With regard to the art of rhetoric (*tekhnê rhêtorikê*), *tekhnê*, used without further specification, can designate a manual of rhetoric and serve as the title of a work of this sort (GORG. D1, D6). The Latin equivalent, also in this latter sense, is *ars* (GORG. D5).

tekmêrion (τεκμήριον), *tekmairesthai* (τεκμαίρεσθαι): a sign, evidence, proof (ZEN. R2), to conjecture on the basis of signs (ALCM. D4), to conjecture (DRAM. T79). See *sêmeion*, under *sêma*.

terpesthai (τέρπεσθαι), *terpsis* (τέρψις): to derive satisfaction, satisfaction. See *hêdonê*.

tetraktus (τετρακτύς): the name given by the Pythagoreans to the number ten, which they revered and considered perfect (PYTH. c D10; PYTHS. ANON. D16–D17). The *tektratus* is the result of the addition of the first four (*tetra-*) numbers (1 + 2 + 3 + 4 = 10) and was thought to be endowed with special properties.

themis (θέμις): the traditional order of things, the norm (MOR. T23b; PARM. D4.28), and thus what it is licit to do or to say (EMP. D44.4, D54.5). The term connotes what is necessary and, often, universal, and can be opposed to *nomos* when this latter designates an institution, especially a local one, and hence something arbitrary. Cf. *nomos*.

theôrein (θεωρεῖν), *theôria* (θεωρία): to observe, observation. These terms refer originally to the official observation, on the part of a delegated foreigner or embassy, at a religious ceremony. They scarcely if ever appear in the original fragments of the early Greek

philosophers (ATOM. D226 may be the only exception; cf. also
perhaps ATOM. D335, D353). It is only later that, applied to the
observation and knowledge of the world (cf. PYTHS. ANON. D1),
they become emblematic of the 'theoretical' attitude in Aristotle
and are applied retroactively to characterize the views and activities
of those earlier philosophers themselves (THAL. R11; ANAXAG.
P35, P36, P37, P40).

theos (θεός): god. See *daimôn.*

thesis (θέσις): the act by which someone 'posits' or 'places' something
(the noun derives from *tithenai,* τιθέναι, 'to place'), with some
degree of connotation of 'arbitrariness' (ATOM. D205), in the domain of laws or of language; hence, probably, the 'meaning imposed' (DERV. Col. VII). *thesei* (θέσει), 'by convention,' and *nomôi*
are often interchangeable; cf. *nomos.*

thumos (θυμός): the term denotes the intense emotional impulse that
also gives a vital energy to humans. In Homer it is sometimes
located in the diaphragm or midriff (*phrên;* see *phronein* and
prapides), and Empedocles still uses it to refer to the heart (EMP.
D30.2); it can also signify 'the vital spirit' (PYTHS. R33[30]). But
usually it is best understood as an intensely focused emotional state,
and we translate it as 'ardor' (HER. D116; ATOM. D296). In later
Greek, it usually denotes 'anger' (DRAM. T82), and Aristotle seems
(mistakenly) to have interpreted the term's meaning in Heraclitus
in this way (cf. note on HER. D116).

timê (τιμή): the concrete honor due or given to a social position, a
value, a hero, a god, or the like (e.g. EMP. D15; GORG. D24[1],
[4], D25[1], [16]). Empedocles applies the term metaphorically to
the two forces that govern the becoming of the world, *Neikos*
and *Philia,* in order to designate their prerogatives (EMP. D39.3,
D44.6, D60.8, D73.259, D73.272, D77a.12, D94.2).

to auto (τὸ αὐτό): the same. *autos* (αὐτός) is a pronoun designating
persons or things (e.g. PARM. D8.63; MEL. D8; EMP. D73.265).
It very often has an emphasizing, intensifying function; after Plato
and Aristotle it comes to be applied to abstract ideas and to mean
'in and of itself.' In all periods, combined with the definite article,
it means 'the same' and indicates the exact identity of one person
or thing with someone or something else. The term is used frequently by Heraclitus to indicate the identity of apparent opposites
(HER. D16, D51, D57, D65, D85, D109, and cf. MED. T9[4]–[5])

and by Parmenides with regard to various aspects of his doctrine of being (PARM. D6.8, D7.8–9, D8.34–35, 39, 62–63, D51.2); the author of the *Pairs of Arguments* devotes the first five chapters of his treatise to examining whether various apparently opposed terms, such as 'good' and 'bad,' or 'seemly' and 'unseemly,' are in fact the same as or different from one another (DISS. 1–5). Cf. *homoios; isos.*

tropê (τροπή): turning, hence the particular position of an atom (ATOM. D31); also applied to the time, or to the place in the heavens, at which the sun reverses its trajectory after having attained its highest or lowest point, the solstice (ATOM. D104). Heraclitus applies the word to the transitions by which fire is turned into other things (HER. D86).

tropos (τρόπος): a particular 'turn' of someone's personality, hence 'character' (ATOM. D304).

tukhê (τύχη): chance (ATOM. R31), and, personified, Fortune (GORG. D24[6]). *eutukhês* (εὐτυχής) and *dustukhês* (δυστυχής) denote someone who enjoys, respectively, 'good fortune' or 'success' (*eutukhia*, εὐτυχία) and 'bad fortune' or 'lack of success' (*dustukhia*, δυστυχία, and the related verbs) (ATOM. D278, D406; GORG. D24[7], [9], [15], [19], D28).

zôon (ζῷον): animated being, animal (ANAXAG. D13). Given that plants are animated, the term *zôon* can refer either to animals alone or to plants as well (ALC. D11; ANAXAG. D93, D95). Cf. *bios/zôê.*

257